Look Back
With Mixed Feelings

By DODIE SMITH

Novels

I Capture the Castle
The New Moon with the Old
The Town in Bloom
It Ends with Revelations
A Tale of Two Families
The Girl from the Candle-lit Bath

For children

The Hundred and One Dalmatians
The Starlight Barking
The Midnight Kittens

Plays

Autumn Crocus
Service
Touch Wood
Call it a Day
Bonnet over the Windmill
Dear Octopus
Lovers and Friends
Letter from Paris
I Capture the Castle
These People: Those Books
Amateur Means Lover

Autobiography

Volume I   Look Back with Love
Volume II   Look Back with Mixed Feelings

Look Back
With Mixed Feelings

Volume Two of
AN AUTOBIOGRAPHY

by

DODIE SMITH

W. H. ALLEN · LONDON
A Howard & Wyndham Company
1978

Printed and bound in Great Britain by
The Garden City Press Limited,
Letchworth, Hertfordshire SG6 1JS
for the Publishers, W. H. Allen & Co. Ltd,
44 Hill Street, London W1X 8LB

ISBN 0 491 0 2073 2

TO

My husband whom, in spite
of the *increased* critical help
he gave me with Volume Two,
I still don't really dislike.

CONTENTS

ILLUSTRATIONS

Gwen Ffrangcon-Davies as Betty in *The New Morality*.
Nadine March.
Madge Compton.
Starting for the Three Arts Club Fancy Dress Ball.
Lord Leverhulme.
Ambrose Heal.
Heal's in Tottenham Court Road.
'And already I was twenty-five'.

I

To London, 1910

If I were writing a novel instead of an autobiography I might feel that my early years, in Manchester, were a sufficient prelude to the heroine's grown-up life, and it might have been no bad thing had this been the case with me. I had lived so much with grown-up people who treated me as an equal, my happiness at school had made me self-assured and I was, at fourteen, quite well equipped to cope with adult responsibilities—always provided someone would have cleared up those plaguy facts of life for me. But the next four years were in some ways retrogressive, in spite of the fact that I acquired an excellent education. And by the time I was eighteen, and let loose in the world on my own, I was introspective, self-conscious and far less self-confident, though I doubt if I realised this at the time.

However, no prophetic miseries troubled me when I arrived in London, in the autumn of 1910, to welcome my mother back from the Belgian honeymoon of her second marriage, that marriage which had transplanted us both from Manchester. Indeed, though I was sorry to leave the uncles and aunts with whom I had been brought up, I was greatly looking forward to my new life, especially as I saw living in London as a stepping-stone to going on the stage, which I had wanted to do since the age of seven. And, though I thought my stepfather a trifle too hearty, I got on with him fairly well and he had always been kind to me.

With me came our Lancashire maid, Charlotte, to whom I felt a trifle patronising because she had never been to London before, as I frequently had. From the first, she declined to be impressed; it was, she said, just like any other town, if a bit larger. She complained that the shops were dear, the meat poor and the tradesmen forgetful, and it irked her to have to haul deliveries up to the kitchen and hurl imprecations down a speaking tube. Neither she nor I thought much of the furnished flat, chosen by my stepfather's mother, and were staggered that Londoners were willing to sleep in bedrooms looking into dark wells; however, the two front rooms faced Battersea Park and we knew we only had the flat for three months.

After a few days, my pleasure at being with my mother again was dimmed because I realised that she wasn't happy. She didn't deny this, simply said there was nothing she could talk about; and later, having seen that I was worrying, she assured me things were better. I didn't believe her and it was soon obvious, without any delving beneath the surface, that her second marriage was unhappy.

It was to grow progressively more so. It seemed unbelievable that a man who had waited seven years for a woman, and ousted another suitor, could have treated my mother as my stepfather did. But I see now that he was simply behaving in character and the trouble was that my mother, knowing him mainly through his many, but brief, visits to Manchester, and our occasional ones to London, had little conception of what that character was—or what his normal behaviour was. He drank far too much, gambled beyond his means, was most unreliable and had an explosively bad temper. That jollity which I had sometimes found slightly overpowering was now turned on only when my mother had to entertain his many friends. She played up to it so loyally that they must have thought we were an ideally happy household.

However, things weren't too bad that first autumn, though there were no more theatres, treats or presents and he was already becoming critical of me. He particularly disliked my habit of arguing and, as he had seen this in full spate with my Manchester family and seemingly admired it, I resented his change of attitude. He soon invented an oft-repeated phrase, 'Well, there we have it, as usual. Sixteen dictating to thirty-six.' I was fourteen and he was considerably more than thirty-six, but he had to have it his way.

I tried to avoid friction for my mother's sake and we were

free of him all day. (He was a representative of a famous firm of electrical engineers.) I was not to go to school until after Christmas but had plenty to occupy me. There was an election and I have always dearly loved elections. I remained staunchly Conservative, though a little shaken after hearing the Socialist, John Burns, speak in Battersea Park. (The only other Conservative in the family was my Uncle Arthur, who, while admitting that Tariff Reform would ruin his business, had said, 'But I'm thinking of the good of the country.' Uncle Harold and Uncle Eddie, both Liberals, had then told him he was not only a fool, but a damned fool.) I developed a great admiration for F. E. Smith, the well-known KC, which led, after the election, to an interest in the law. For years I followed all his cases (in those days newspapers devoted many columns to important law cases), planned his cross-examinations for him and was delighted when he brought out points I had thought of. He did, of course, bring out others, but I really became quite good and, had there then been women barristers, my determination to go on the stage might have wavered.

When not occupied by newspapers, I was busy reading fifty or so Nelson's red sevenpenny novels which my stepfather had acquired on his many train journeys to and from Manchester. Never had I had such an orgy of early Edwardian novels. I took Mrs Humphrey Ward very seriously but there were Anthony Hopes, Miss Macnaughtons, Agnes and Egerton Castles and many others for light relief. I have often thought I would like to collect Nelson's Sevenpennys, but much of their charm lay in their brilliant red, which will have faded now. And their contents may have faded too.

Under the influence of the Castles, I started a play about a highwayman, the dialogue mainly consisting of 'Egad, Madame' and 'Lud, child'. I also began a soul-searching journal which had a very short life. I recall one phrase from it: 'I must guard against the fatal facility with which I fall in love.'

We went back to Manchester for Christmas. Never had I liked my uncles better and they were obviously overjoyed to see me, as was Peter the dog, now being overfed by their housekeeper. We could only stay a few days, because of my stepfather's business, and were soon back in that depressing Battersea flat. But by now we had found a new flat and I enjoyed helping to choose the furniture for it—until I discovered how worried my mother was. My stepfather had disclosed that she would have to pay for everything herself, which meant selling out most of her few securities.

In January I went to St Paul's Girls' School for my entrance examination and was impressed by the fine modern building, at Brook Green, Hammersmith. The ground-floor classrooms opened off the Great Hall, which had a gallery off which the upper classrooms opened. As well as their outer windows, all rooms would be full. I felt I should be entering a new and across it, into other classrooms. I noticed this after I had finished my paper and imagined the bustling life of school when all the rooms would be full. I felt I should be entering a new and exciting world and greatly looked forward to it.

My only feeling of nervousness on my first day was in case I failed to arrive in time, for as we were still living in Battersea Park, the journey was complicated and I was not used to going about alone. However, I got there only slightly flustered and joined the flock of entering girls in their hideous hard straw hats. From the moment they were inside the school a monastic silence fell and I discovered that one was not allowed to speak in the cloakroom or passages. I later learned that one was not allowed to speak except in the classrooms or in the Great Hall. If, any-where else, one asked a girl the way to any part of the school she usually took no notice. If unusually courteous, she would beckon silently until she could get at least a foot inside the Hall before answering.

The mistress in charge of the cloakroom allotted me a locker, but omitted to tell me that I should be fined sixpence every time I forgot to bring the key. The hard hat played havoc with my hair—then worn with side-combs in a style copied from Zena and Phyllis Dare—and I went in search of a looking-glass. There was not one in the whole school. This may have acted as an antidote to vanity, but it was also an antidote to tidiness and many girls looked neither neat nor pleasing.

Eventually I arrived in one of the downstairs classrooms,

along with three other new girls. The rest of the form were enjoying a chat before prayers and took not the slightest notice of us. They proved stone deaf to questions, except for one girl who favoured me with a withering glance, and said 'You're new, aren't you?' and then turned away. I found myself comparing this to my reception at my Whalley Range High School, Manchester, where the beautifully-mannered girls had acted like hostesses. Then the form mistress came in and we trooped in to prayers. These were read by Miss Wenham, the second mistress, a gentle, Madonna-faced lady substituting for the High Mistress, who was to be away for some months owing to ill-health. The magnificent organ rang out and the whole business was far more impressive than our simple prayers at Whalley Range High School, where little Miss Allen, at the piano, would accept requests for favourite pieces from her repertoire for our march in and out. I retain the impression that the sun always shone for prayers at Whalley Range High School, and never for prayers at St Paul's.

My first few weeks at that undoubtedly magnificent school were unadulterated agony. The rudeness of the girls in my form was staggering and when I told one of them so she said, 'But we *never* speak to new girls.' They would not direct us, so we were frequently lost; they would not tell us the names of the mistresses. I was driven to ask one mistress her name because it was a double-barrelled one and I could not pick it up. She said no girl had ever asked her before and I must ask one of the girls. I said, 'But they don't answer questions from new girls.' She then told me her name and was particularly pleasant to me from then on.

Every moment of our days was filled and yet we new girls had to fit in being examined by the school doctor and being measured and fitted for gym dresses, playground shoes, etc.—with the result that we were always late for classes and never seemed to get in at the beginning of any subject. Another handicap was that it seemed impossible to find out the rules of the school; there was no printed list and no one would tell us what they were—we only found out each time we broke one. The discipline was superb and yet it was maintained without any punishments. If girls behaved badly during a class they were told to 'take a report'. They then took it to their form mistress who looked grave and entered it in a book and there the matter ended. And yet the girls had a horror of getting reports. There was a story that, if you got too many, you were sent for by the High Mistress; and, if you still went on getting them, you were quietly expelled. But I never heard of any girl getting as far as the High Mistress, let alone being expelled. And the habit of getting reports seemed to wither away entirely as girls became seniors.

The one class in which my own form behaved outrageously was Singing, which was taken by Gustav Holst, then an ugly, likeable man in his middle thirties, already well-known as a composer. Later I found him a brilliant teacher whose accompaniments could make folk songs entrancing, but that first term he was teaching us two insipid modern part-songs—which may have accounted for the class's lack of interest. The girls talked and giggled, making no effort to sing properly. Poor Holst (usually referred to as 'Gussie') would begin by looking helpless and murmuring, 'No other class behaves like this one does' and then work up into a temper. His hair would become more and more ruffled, his pale face would flush with anger and he would start showering reports around. On one occasion he told the whole form to report itself, which it did with great joy. Our form mistress, faced with entering the name of every girl in her book, murmured, 'Yes, well, I'll just have a word with Mr von Holst. The 'von' was still in use, though I believe his family had been English for generations.

Holst was universally liked so I never understood why he incurred such ruffianly treatment from my own class, nor why we reformed seemingly overnight. I only know that after my first term he was always able to teach us with enthusiasm and good humour. But apart from his own music and a little Palestrina (neither of which came my way until my third year in the school), I cannot recall that he chose such interesting and unusual songs as Miss Allen taught us at Whalley Range. Most of the time he concentrated on the more conventional folk songs, only made interesting by his accompaniments.

While we were still living at Battersea Park I had to lunch at school, and on my first day the waitress whispered to me, 'Are you special, miss?' I felt sure my mother would have ordered me the best lunch available, so I said Yes and a plate of food was put in front of me which looked different from what the girls near me were having. The girl sitting next to me remarked, 'Funny, you don't *look* Jewish' and I then discovered that the 'Special' lunch was for Jewesses. I did not like to tell the waitress of my mistake in case it seemed as if I was spurning Kosher food. Perhaps as a reward for this, some of my best friends in the school (when I eventually made any) were Jewish.

The zero hour of my days came after luncheon when—unless it poured with merciful rain—we were forced to go into the playground for an hour and a half. The idea, of course, was that we should play games and, though I had no intention of risking my front teeth at hockey, I had no objection to a little gentle basketball and put my name down for it. But no one would explain the rules, so I made an even worse hash of it than I might have done otherwise, and the next time I turned up the games mistress said there was no room for me. Apart from games there was nothing to do but walk round and round, bitterly cold, for coats were never worn in the playground. I was usually alone as my fellow new girls, being more normal than I was, were often playing games, and I imagined I was looked at scornfully. I was torn between smiling ingratiatingly and wanting to punch the scorners.

After the cold hell of the playground we spent an hour on Preparation, which was by comparison heaven, especially as it meant the long school day was nearly over. Also I was able to get through most of my homework and I should not have to work much in the evening. On my way home I always bought two brown scones which Charlotte toasted for my tea. I had it by the fire while my mother listened to the general awfulness of St Paul's Girls' School. Her instinct was to go straight to it and complain of everybody and everything, but I dissuaded her.

One thought buoyed me up during those early weeks: I was to go to the first night of Fred Terry's new play, *The Popinjay*. My stepfather graciously undertook to book the seats after I undertook to pay for them out of my Christmas present money. We got the front row of the Upper Circle from which I could watch people arriving in the Stalls. My stepfather seemed more like his old gay self until, after he had pointed out a woman with flaming red hair as being Ellen Terry, I assured him her hair was now white. Then sixteen was dictating to thirty-six again.

The Popinjay was an adaptation of Daudet's novel, *Rois en Exil* and, though much sentimentalised, was nothing like Fred Terry's usual, romantic plays. Still, I thought it wonderful. Possibly I should have been equally enchanted if Fred Terry had recited the Railway Guide.

It was found necessary to take a taxi home and my stepfather, while rebuffing my offer to pay for it, said this proved how ruinous theatres were and I must not go to another for at least six months. I accepted this with surprising tameness, partly because my mother asked me to, and partly because life at school was so worrying that I could think of little else. Blanche Guthrie, my mother's second cousin and our only London relation, said she would take me to a theatre whenever I liked, but I only let her do so once; I seemed to have been suffering from a curious flattening of spirit.

Soon after *The Popinjay* we moved into the new flat in Riverview Gardens, Barnes, which my mother and I greatly liked, though 'Auntie' Blanche said it was the wrong side of the Thames. If so, it was only just the wrong side, for the gardens led down to the tow-path and the drawing-room had a fine view of graceful Hammersmith Bridge. Every room was light and there were three balconies; there was one attached to the kitchen which enabled Charlotte to give up the speaking tube and to shout down at the tradesmen. Ours was a top flat in a three-storey building. My mother had chosen white wallpapers, plain green carpets and light, delicately patterned curtains; I realise now that her taste was quite ten years ahead of the period. My stepfather's was quite twenty years behind and he hankered for draped mantel-borders and plush. My mother said she could not exist in the same flat with mantel-borders, let alone plush, but she did let him have an atrocious red silk lampshade over the dining-room table. He would look at it with pride while my mother eyed it with dislike, during our argumentative meals.

My own small green and white room had a view of the Thames, Fred Terry over the bed and, later, a flock of Rossetti reproductions. There was also a very large photograph of my father, taken by my photographer grandfather and made to look like a tinted drawing. My mother had asked me to give this a home. I often gazed at his soulful eyes and pale blue tie, but with no sense that he had ever existed.

The new flat was only fifteen minutes walk from school so I was able to lunch with my mother, but I had to hurry back for that deadly session in the playground. I soon worked out a technique for shortening this. From the moment I had signed the book to show I was back by two-thirty, I would walk at a snail's pace and take a very long time to open my locker and change into playground shoes. I would then wash and, if there was no one about, I would spend a good five minutes leaning on my elbows in hot water. I would then go back and sit on the floor by my locker until someone else came into my part of the cloakroom. Next, I went to the games notice board and read and re-read all notices about games I never played. There then remained the lavatories where I would sit, pulling the plug every three minutes or so. I never thought of reading, probably because I had never been allowed to read in the lavatory at home, so eventually sheer boredom drove me out to the cold playground.

After I had been at St Paul's well over a month one of the haughtiest members of the form approached me with an astonishingly pleasant smile. She said, 'I've noticed you have an unusual accent. It's Scottish, isn't it? My mother's Scottish.' Delighted with this friendliness I told her that if I had an accent it was Lancashire. Her smile faded and she left me flat. I gathered that in London a Scottish accent might be distinguished, but a Lancashire accent was just plain common.

It was partly this incident which made me wonder if the girls did think me common and I told my mother this might be due to my dresses, which she made beautifully in soft woollens of pleasant colours. Most of the girls wore heavy navy serge, ugly but, I imagined, correct schoolgirl wear. So my mother, though with misgivings, got a dressmaker to make a rigidly conventional navy dress with a chokingly high neck. I discarded my bright hair ribbons and scragged my hair back with plain slides. But my well-bred, ill-mannered form-mates were no nicer to me, so I soon reverted to pretty dresses and skittish hair ribbons. I hadn't really enjoyed looking like a midget wardress.

Actually, my first step towards popularity was made through extreme unconventionality. One day, for Literature home-work, we had to memorise Browning's 'Incident of the French Camp' and the next week we were asked to stand up and recite it. Never had we been asked to recite before and I was deter-mined to do Browning proud. Girl after girl recited with com-plete lack of expression. Then my turn came. I used different voices for the narrator, Napoleon, and the wounded soldier. I used a wealth of gesture, assumed Napoleon's attitude and what I imagined to be his facial expression. The end of the poem approached. I gave a quick glance to see how much room I had. Yes, I could do it. I flung my head back and delivered the last lines:

> 'I'm killed, Sire!' And, his Chief beside,
> Smiling, the boy fell dead.

And then *I* fell dead, with a resounding crash, between the rows of desks.

The girls must have been too staggered to giggle. The Liter-ature mistress said that was very nice indeed, but she thought it might be as well if no one else fell dead as there was so very little room. I suddenly felt I had made an utter fool of myself. But after the lesson a number of girls crowded round wanting to know how I had done that fall without hurting myself. As I had no idea how 'stage falls' were done, my method was simply to relax and pitch myself on the floor. I obliged with several demonstrations and soon the classroom resounded with crashes as girls tried to imitate me. I trust some of the snooty little beasts hurt themselves.

Shortly before the end of term Holst played the organ at morning prayers in honour of the return of Miss Frances Gray, the High Mistress. A short, sturdy woman in late middle-age, with strong features, a grey-white skin and white hair which suggested a barrister's wig, walked the full length of the Great Hall and mounted the platform, moving with such stateliness that she seemed liable to fall over backwards. Always having had a prejudice against unusually dignified women I disliked her on sight, but I realised she read prayers superbly. She also made a speech and it was either in that one, or one made a few days later, that she said it had been brought to her notice that girls had developed a habit of feeling faint during prayers, and going out. She desired that, in future, such girls would merely put their heads down between their knees and not cause any disturbance.

I had never seen a girl leave prayers, but from that day on many of them took to putting their heads between their knees or even, disobediently, staggering out. I began to fear that I, too, might be stricken. On the last day of term, examination marks were read out after prayers, form by form; a long job as we had so many examinations. Actually, we were graded, not marked, and the grade 'A-Distinguished' meant over 90 per cent and had to be warmly applauded by the whole school. The first subject came along, my form was reached, girl after girl was mentioned and then, in solitary splendour, came my name with 'A-Distinguished'. Applause followed: I basked. And with the next subject, the same thing happened, and with the following subject, too. By now I was no longer basking. My astonishment had caused the dreaded faintness to come upon me—though what I really felt was sick. I feared putting my head between my knees would be a highly risky proceeding liable to cause a disturbance which Miss Gray had not bargained for. So I went swiftly out, hearing myself gain another 'A-Distinguished' as the door swung to behind me.

I sped to the lavatories, was quite unable to be sick, but went on feeling sick and weak in the legs. Eventually I went to my classroom where the form had just returned from Assembly, and asked my form mistress if I could go home. One might have expected her to feel pleased with me, after my staggeringly good marks, but she merely looked nonplussed and said I would have to get Miss Gray's permission. I had never spoken one word to Miss Gray and an interview with her was considered a shattering business even by pupils in rude health, but I went along and knocked on her door. Sometimes a girl would stand so long outside that door without the courage to knock that a passing mistress would stop, rally her, and knock for her.

Miss Gray's superb voice instructed me to come in and thus I had my first interview with our impressive High Mistress. At close quarters her dignity was really overpowering and I was not feeling too sick to resent it. On hearing my name she at once remembered it and was very gracious about my examination marks, but she instantly became unsympathetic when I said I felt 'faint'. Had I told her I felt sick perhaps she would have been more understanding; as things were she obviously suspected me of schoolgirl nerves. She said I must get my form mistress's permission before leaving and when I said my form mistress had referred me to her, she said I must go and see the gym mistress. It took me twenty minutes to find the gym mistress and she, after telling me to see Miss Gray and my form mistress and being thwarted, told me I must lie down in the Red Cross room, where she would join me. It had an admirable sofa but no facilities for a girl who was feeling sick; but by now I was feeling more furious than sick and when she arrived to see how I was she found me writing her a farewell note. I was then allowed to depart, some twenty minutes before the school was due to break up for the Easter holidays.

I went home and told my mother about my morning, sitting with her on the big window-seat in her pretty drawing-room, looking towards the Thames. It was a sunless day, the willow trees on the tow-path were still bare and for once I found the view cheerless. My mother wondered why I wasn't excited about my unexpected success in examinations; I suppose I was still feeling ill. During my three years at St Paul's I quite often felt just a little sick, just a little headachey and just a little sore-throated. Perhaps these small ailments were imaginary (though my bad colds were real enough) and I daresay Miss Gray was right to discourage girls from indulging in faintness. But, in my case, I blamed her for putting the idea into my head.

It must have been in those Easter holidays that I got to know some of the girls who strolled round the riverside gardens of the flats; two of them called and invited me to join their troop of Girl Guides. Friendless, I would have joined almost anything so I bought a lethal pole and a fierce khaki hat, and went out to drill. I learned the points of the compass, how to tie a number of knots and how to clean my teeth with a frayed twig; and I got on well with everyone until we went for our first route march. Then our leader said we must walk in the road, amidst traffic, even when we came to Hammersmith Bridge. This struck me as far too dangerous so I mounted the pavement, walking along beside the troop. Our leader told me I was undermining her discipline and disobeying Miss Baden Powell's orders, and we argued fiercely for the full length of the bridge, while motor buses hooted angrily behind her and her flock. After that, we went for no more route marches, but we gave a concert to provide more equipment (tents and water bottles appeared to be called for). I hogged the evening, singing, acting in a play, giving three recitations and playing Grieg's 'Norwegian Wedding Day.' As the hall was lent to us (we were considered a deserving charity), we cleared five pounds which, having by now tired of being Girl Guides, we divided between us.

It was one of the Girl Guides who finally cleared up the facts of life for me—appropriately, seeing that the Guides shared the Scouts' motto of 'Be Prepared'. We sometimes pretended to be ladies at the Court of Charles II, calling each other by their names, though we had to leave Nell Gwyn out because everyone wanted to be her; I chose to be Frances Stuart. It was, I think, Lady Castlemaine who enlightened me. She had noticed that during the telling of disreputable stories, of which the Girl Guides had a very fine collection, my expression remained blank —as well it might, seeing that I rarely understood a word of them—and she felt something should be done about this. So at her flat one Saturday afternoon, during a thunderstorm, she took the matter in hand.

It must have been over five years since little Maudie Prim, during a Scripture lesson at Mrs North's, my first school, had handed me a note on which was a diagram intended to explain not where babies came from, which I already knew, but how they got there. The diagram having defeated me, she later explained more fully and added the interesting information that babies were born quite flat and had to be blown up by means of a red rubber pipe. Sometime later, I mentioned this to the greatest friend of my childhood, Mary Slater, who was four years older than I was. She told me it was completely untrue and I understood her to be referring not merely to the blowing-up business, but to Maudie's views on sexual intercourse. Believing Mary, one might say I not so much threw the baby out with the bath water, as threw out its means of getting into the bath. And in this state of ignorance I had surprisingly remained.

Now, at fifteen, I learned that all Maudie Prim's information had been correct—except the bit about blowing up the flat babies with a rubber pipe, which had rather appealed to me. Nothing else did. Was that really *all*?

'Aren't you shocked?' enquired Lady Castlemaine (or was it the Duchess of Portsmouth?)

I said No, just bored and disappointed.

'But can you imagine *that* happening to you?'

I said I supposed so, seeing it had been happening since the beginning of time. Lady Castlemaine (or was it, after all, Moll Davis?) said she thought I had an insensitive nature; she, herself, had been deeply shocked, but perhaps her nature was too sensitive. Judging by her later adventures, it must have toughened up.

When the thunderstorm was over, I went home and sat on the drawing-room window seat staring at the sullen river. It was amazing how many puzzles I could now solve. My sensitive friend's information had been extensive and Mrs Warren's profession was now an open book to me, as were other mysteries, historic as well as literary. But how fantastically *unlikely* the facts of life were, and it was depressing to find they didn't attract me any more now than when Maudie Prim had revealed all at the bottom of Mrs North's cellar steps.

My mother and stepfather were out to dinner so Charlotte brought me mine on a tray. There was a particularly good white soup which cheered me up and, while making a hearty meal, I decided the facts of life might not be so bad. I didn't believe

I had an insensitive nature but had I, perhaps, a sensual one? I went and looked at myself in the glass and decided my mouth was a bit sensual. I didn't mind at all.

Ever since I had come to London I had frequently leaned out of my bedroom window at night and taken a good sniff of air because it was the same air that Fred Terry was breathing. (I discontinued the practice when he went on tour.) Tonight I sniffed without much enthusiasm for I found I could not think of him as my partner in the facts of life. He was more than thirty years older than I was *and* married. The young men who strolled in the riverside gardens were unthinkable. (There was much competition for them, from which I remained aloof, possibly because they remained aloof from me.) I ended by going to bed with Charles II. The fact that he was married didn't count.

II

St Paul's Girls' School

When the new term started I found I had been moved up into the higher division of my form, so I was in a sense a new girl again. But my new classmates were civil and one of them was particularly interested in the theatre, so I had someone to walk round the playground with. My trouble now was that the class was far ahead of me and I could never catch up.

Early in the term Miss Gray took us for several lessons on Shakespeare during which *Julius Caesar* was read aloud. Each girl read one speech, no matter what its length was, and by counting up I quickly saw that all I was going to get was 'Beware the Ides of March'. This was disappointing, still it was an important line and I said it very powerfully. Miss Gray stopped the reading, told me I had the kind of voice that interested her, but it was entirely wrongly produced. She then proceeded to lecture me on the misuse of my throat, my inability to use my lips, my deplorable breathing and the false theatricalism with which I had said the line. I asked her to hear me read a longer speech, but she said that one line had shown her all she needed to know. Sometime later she told me her recent absence from the school had been because she had found herself losing her voice and had needed to take a complete course in voice production which amounted to re-learning how to speak and she had instantly detected some of her own faults in the way I spoke that one line. Much as I resented her criticism at the time, I now realise that everything she said to me was true.

As the summer came, and with it the Coronation of George V, I felt there was a glamorous excitement in the atmosphere of London. I reflected ironically that, had we still been living in Manchester, my mother and I would almost certainly have come to stay with Auntie Blanche and seen the procession, whereas now the best that came our way was a bus drive to see the decorations. Still, this was something, though it was not so much the decorations that fascinated me as London itself. It was looking its blithest, with gay window-boxes, bright sun-blinds and newly-painted spick-and-span houses.

Life was reasonably cheerful in the white riverside flat where my mother, though far from happy, entertained my stepfather's friends charmingly. There had been forty people to watch the Boat Race, there were dinner parties and bridge parties every weekend. I never played bridge, nor had any desire to, but I liked the company, especially as Auntie Blanche almost always came. She shared the interest my mother and I took in Woman's Suffrage. My stepfather once said that my mother's belief in it was ruining his business, having heard one of his friends say to her teasingly, 'And how's the little Suffragette?' My mother said she found her belief in votes for women a useful social asset as men seemed to prefer telling her how wrong she was, to telling the anti-suffragettes how right they were.

Actually, she called herself a Suffra*gist*, a word used by non-militants, but I think that, but for my stepfather, she would have been game to break a few windows. I certainly would, but the only demonstration we ever made was when we walked in the Great Procession. Shepherded by Auntie Blanche we went one summer afternoon to a narrow street in Westminster where we decked ourselves in purple, green and white ribbons, learned to sing 'The March of the Women', specially composed by Ethel Smyth, and after a very long wait at last marched off.

I secured an outside place and proudly carried a small banner on a pole, but when we reached Trafalgar Square my mother decided the crowd was making menacing noises, so she grabbed my banner and prepared to defend me with it. The worst that happened was that an elderly man said, 'Hey, little 'un wants the vote,' and insisted on shaking hands with me, while my mother stood ready to hit him on the slightest provocation. We marched through gay London all the way to the Albert Hall and I have always regretted that we had not been able to get seats for the mass meeting being held there. (But I did later hear

Mrs Pankhurst speak and was happy to find that, though deeply impressive, she was a quiet little woman and not falling over backwards with dignity.)

By the time I got home, to enjoy a celebratory dinner of cold salmon, I was feeling almost an historic character, with just a tinge of martyrdom. (Well, it *had* been a long, hot walk.) Even my stepfather, after reading the evening papers, had to admit that the march had been superbly organised and extremely dignified. In spite of his antagonism to Votes for Women, he was, I think, a little proud that we should be associated with something well spoken of in the papers.

(Two years later, his attitude to Woman's Suffrage involved him in an embarrassing confusion of mind when a woman flung herself in front of the King's horse at the Derby. At first he cursed her as being a creature of lowest mentality and coarsest fibre—and considering the injury to the horse and to the jockey, I was rather on his side. He then discovered she was a distant relation of his, after which she became a woman of superb courage and unimpeachable breeding.)

In my summer holidays my mother went with my stepfather on a round of visits and I went to Manchester, reluctant to be parted from her, but relieved to be away from an atmosphere which was seldom less than strained. I sent her a postcard every day, never missing, and for years to come was to have nightmares that I had forgotten that postcard.

I loved being with my uncles who did everything they could to keep me amused. I was taken on motoring holidays to Scotland and to the Lake District and, finally, for a seaside holiday at Criccieth where Auntie Bertha and Uncle Bertie joined their golfing friends, some of whom had young families. I got on well with everyone. By now London had become (and was to remain) the town of towns for me, but I still felt that, even apart from my own family, the people of Lancashire were my people.

On my return to London my mother, though delighted to have me with her again, complained that I looked fat, untidy and, in her opinion, none too clean. No doubt a month's separation had caused her to see me with clearer eyes. She said I must take more interest in my appearance. (I had been rather pleased with it, having had a mild success with the *jeunesse dorée* of Auntie Bertha's golfing friends.) It might help if I had some new clothes. So I was given a 'Paddy' hat, a vaguely conical shape of red felt, and a shantung dress to be worn with a red belt and red coral beads. Nothing was done about my weight, which was nine stone (and me under five feet tall) because my mother said *she* had been nine stone at my age and had dropped to seven stone in no time at all—which was exactly what happened to me. No one suggested dieting and I had never even heard slimming discussed; though there were advertisements for something called Antipon, showing pictures of enormous ladies magically reduced to sylphs, though the sylphs still retained enormous busts and behinds.

Back at school I found I had rejoined the lower division of my form, which made life much easier as I could maintain high marks. Also the girls seemed quite pleased to see me and I soon made friends, never failing to tell them how disgusting their previous behaviour had been. Though I still had no great love for St Paul's, I had by now realised how brilliant the teaching was. Literature was particularly well taught by a moth-like lady who made one long to read every book she described. I at last began to read solidly, going through Jane Austen and the Brontës, and then falling in love with Thackeray; a neighbour had a handsome complete set, which I read from beginning to end. I then turned to Dumas, which must have been quite a change. I can still read Dumas but not, alas, Thackeray.

In the spring of 1912 my mother, tired of trying to propitiate my stepfather, entirely lifted the restraints on theatre-going. (During 1911 it had needed a great effort to see a special performance of *The Merry Wives of Windsor*, with Ellen Terry as Mistress Page. Enchanted by her, I sent her my new autograph album, asking her to start it, which she did—after six months—writing on the first page, 'Wishing you your heart's desire'.) One of the plays of the new theatre-going régime was *Hindle Wakes*, to which my mother and I went with Auntie Blanche, I feeling proudly possessive of Stanley Houghton, our family friend. It was only a few years since I had acted with

him in Manchester amateur theatricals. Now he was the famous
author of this much discussed play.

I soon realised that *Hindle Wakes* was linked with the information about sex which I had acquired from my fellow Girl
Guides the previous year—and even without that I should have
known it was a grave social error to have a baby without being
married. My mother seemed embarrassed throughout the evening; I think for some time she had felt she ought to clear up
the facts of life for me, but could never bring herself to do it.

Quite recently we had shared a peculiar conversation about
hospital nurses. She had warned me that they might, at any
time, come to me in the street, tell me she had been taken ill,
and offer to drive me to her in a car. 'And you must on no
account get into that car,' she said impressively, 'for they would
drug you and you would wake up in the Argentine and never
be able to come back.'

I asked why not and she said, 'Because you'd be ruined and
nobody would have anything to do with you—well, *I* would, of
course, but you'd have to be kept out of sight.' Questioned further,
she became evasive and merely repeated her warning about hospital nurses. It astounds me that I let her off so lightly, but I
daresay I was as embarrassed as she was. And İ was still embarrassed. Not until a year after we saw *Hindle Wakes* together
did I help her out by giving her Rossetti's poem about a pros-
titute, 'Jenny', to read and asking her if she did not think it
beautiful. When she had finished it she looked at me with wide
open eyes and said it was a wonderful poem and, though she
was surprised I could understand it, she was very glad I did.
We discussed the subject no further.

Once the ban on theatres was lifted we went whenever my
stepfather was out for the evening. One of his more trivial faults
was his habit of failing to turn up for dinner. Many, many times
we waited and waited, while Charlotte's admirable dinner spoiled
and my mother got more and more anxious in case he'd had
some accident. He would return after midnight, having had
too much to drink and merely say that some important business
had turned up.

At last my mother told him that if he hadn't come back by

seven-thirty (six o'clock was his normal time to return) we would accept that he wasn't coming, and feel free to go out. As the deadline approached on such evenings, Charlotte would make sandwiches (doing what she could to salvage the dinner) and at seven-thirty precisely I would force a sandwich on my still wavering mother and then drag her out of the flat. By the time we got to the theatre, the Pit queue would have gone in, so we seldom got good seats, unless we chose a show that was failing. Just sometimes, however, my stepfather warned us he would be out and then we did things in style, having a meal in some restaurant and then getting good places in the Pit queue. My mother paid for the meal out of the housekeeping and I paid for the seats—my uncles kept me well supplied with pocket money. These evenings were known as our jaunts and were my greatest joy, but I sometimes feared my mother's enjoyment was assumed, to please me.

She was still so pretty and young-looking but every day she got thinner and often, in spite of her determined gaiety, there was a desperate look in her eyes. I see now that, as well as being constantly worried, she must have been lonely when I was at school for she had no real friends in London except Auntie Blanche and even that friendship my stepfather eventually broke up. One pleasure she never tired of was window-gazing at the West End shops; but I found shopping boring and would seldom go with her. The shop she liked best was Bourne and Hollingsworth where there were pretty things at reasonable prices. I never pass that shop without feeling grateful to it for pleasing her, and guilty because I was too selfish to accompany her.

No doubt I was selfish in many ways. Certainly I went off to Manchester again for my summer holidays without a thought to her loneliness. True, she needed to spend a short holiday with my stepfather, but I could have come back weeks earlier than I did. I enjoyed myself avidly. That was the summer that Ragtime hit the seaside towns of England and I hummed 'Alexander's Ragtime Band' from morning till night.

Soon after I got back to London I went to see the Granville Barker production of *The Winter's Tale*. My mother and Auntie

Blanche found it too modern but, to me, it was magical. Yet I also loved the absolute realism of Tree's productions at His Majesty's and still remember them with pleasure. Giant cycloramas, starry skies, gardens, exquisite interiors—Tree's *School for Scandal* spoilt me for every other performance of the play I ever saw—and all scene changes done with unbelievable swiftness and smoothness. I am told Tree's productions would now look ludicrously old-fashioned, but I sometimes think modern audiences would get quite drunk with pleasure while watching them.

When, as usual, we went home for Christmas, 1912 (I still called Manchester home), Uncle Harold had a surprise for me: Stanley Houghton joined us for Christmas dinner. He remained quiet, and almost shy, seemingly unchanged by success in the theatre. He told me he would help me to get on the stage and I believe he meant it. When we were about to sit down for dinner it was found that we should be thirteen at table. My uncles were completely unsuperstitious but my mother and my aunts weren't, and it was suggested that my Auntie Nan's children should be put at a separate table. But the idea was laughed off, particularly by Stanley Houghton—who, I noticed, very determinedly sat down last.

It had been agreed I should start training for the stage in the autumn so I was now in my last year at school. Perversely, I was greatly enjoying it. I contributed to a typewritten magazine started by some intellectual Jewish girls and I had become popular with a rather more rakish set through bad behaviour too mild to be described—one could get a reputation for being a daredevil by so much as dropping a desk lid. Also, as a senior I could now attend some debating societies, go on various outings and spend my spare time in the library, into which juniors were not admitted. I liked best to sit on top of a ladder, reading books from high shelves and often glancing down at the quiet room flooded with late afternoon sunlight—at last I remember sunlight at St Paul's. Perched there, I had the feeling of being both part of the school and also aloof from it.

Next door to the library was the mistresses' room and it amused me to wonder what their private lives were like. They fell into three types: the modern, would-be smart type (we were apt to giggle each time one of these had a new dress); the willowy ladies who wore hand-embroidered Liberty materials; and the old-fashioned women who wore high-necked shirt blouses to which were clipped their fountain pens and the container into which the fine chain attached to their pince-nez zizzed back. Their hair was invariably dragged into a hard bun. I preferred the old-fashioned ones, though my much admired Literature mistress was definitely modern.

She was now taking us through the Romantic poets, also later nineteenth-century ones; and I had at last acquired a taste for poetry. There was a shop in Westbourne Grove where one could buy complete, leather-bound editions of non-copyright poets for one shilling and eleven pence. I had a collection of these and woke up at six every morning to read them. I read every line of Shelley, including the Juvenilia, greatly preferring him to Keats; vast quantities of Browning, greatly preferring him to Tennyson; much Coleridge, little Wordsworth, less Scott; and, simply because he was entirely omitted at school, most of Byron. I had a romantic admiration for Byron's personality and was fascinated by the brilliant versification of *Don Juan*; but, try as I might, I could not like his serious poems.

Shelley was my god, indeed I did sometimes pray to him, as well as writing sonnets to him. Later he had to share his throne with Dante Gabriel Rossetti; I couldn't get him for one-and-eleven so I kept the school library copy out for the whole of the spring term. I not only read every line of his, but also memorised many of them, sitting up in bed in the bright spring mornings, with the reproductions of his long-necked ladies all around me.

Poetry reading had to end at seven so that I could get time for my piano practising before I went to school. I recited while in my bath and once composed a sonnet to Shelley while cleaning my teeth. When dressed, I hurried down the long passage to the chilly drawing-room, gazed for a moment at the gleaming Thames and then got down to scales—which must have been nice for sleeping neighbours. I was beautifully taught at St Paul's and now played rather well, but nothing could ever be done about my inability to memorise music.

I was being prepared for Confirmation that spring, largely because I liked the idea of being confirmed in St Paul's Cathedral. Still, I took the matter seriously, intending to give religion its chance, and I was impressed by Miss Gray's preparation classes. She was followed by a clergyman whose name and imposing rank I am glad to have forgotten. Two points he particularly stressed were the sinfulness of saying one's prayers in bed and the utter wrongness of the modern disbelief in a personal Devil. We were assured that there was a real Devil and I got the impression that he was complete as regards to horns, hooves and tail. Then I learned that unbaptised babies were in some danger of Hellfire, news which caused me to have a private chat with our imposing cleric, in which I told him I wasn't going to be confirmed if it entailed believing any such thing. He finally said it was a case for God's mercy and that, though he couldn't promise heaven for unbaptised babies, he thought it 'doubtful' if they would go to hell. So I decided to go through with Confirmation—perhaps influenced by the fact that my mother had just finished my dress.

It was a beautiful dress of white muslin; my mother had ignored fashionable skimpiness and it had full sleeves and a very full skirt. One of our Art mistresses, who went to the Cathedral with us to arrange our veils, was particularly enchanted by it and took particular trouble with my veil. Owing to my shortness it was I who led the line of girls into the Cathedral and my mother reported later that I was smiling radiantly and stepping out as if leading a beauty chorus. This surprised me as I was feeling overawed by the size of St Paul's and was fully prepared for something wonderful to happen when the Bishop put his hand on my head. Nothing did, although I waited until he gave my head a gentle push.

I was so disillusioned that, in the private bus which took us back to school, I became facetious and was rebuked for making the other girls laugh. But, once home, I recovered my serious mood and when my mother came in she found I had parted my hair down the middle (which I thought Madonna-like), unearthed a silver cross from her jewel box to hang round my neck, and was reading *Paradise Lost* which seemed the holiest book in the house as my bible was at school. I had won a superbly bound Milton as a school prize.

The following Sunday my mother came with me to Holy Communion, a brave gesture as church services were apt to make her feel faint and this did not, in her case, mean that she felt vaguely sick, but was frequently a prelude to unconsciousness. She bore up fairly well until it was time to go up to the altar, when she swayed, sat down hastily and shook her head, so I went alone. What with worrying about her and feeling squeamish about drinking out of the same cup as other Hammersmith communicants, my first communion was not an elevating experience. I was thankful to get back to my mother and take her out into the open air, where she instantly recovered. We then went for a walk along the towpath. The sun shone, the Thames glittered. I said that God was more likely to be out of doors than in any church. My mother said she had thought so all her life, but never dared to say so.

Soon after this I began writing a Ruritanian novel about an actress who became a King's mistress. I loved the word 'mistress', but also found it embarrassing so I always wrote it in minute handwriting, thus giving it the importance of italics and a curious air of indecency. I usually wrote on Saturday evenings when there was a bridge party in the drawing-room and I could get the dining-room to myself. I was officially doing my Literature homework and my stepfather said I could perfectly well do it in the drawing-room and stop wasting electricity, the truth being that he liked to pick up my quite ordinary school essays ('not longer than three pages, no sentence longer than three lines, no sentence to end with a preposition, quote freely') and make such remarks as 'I really must see about getting this clever child's work published' to the bridge players. This infuriated me—also I certainly couldn't write novels about mistresses except in strict privacy, so I offered to pay for the electricity, or provide myself with a candle. This caused a serious row, but I went on working in the dining-room.

The Ruritanian novel—*Roseleaves, or a Summer in Slavania* —was soon discarded in favour of a short story called *Temperament* which I intended for the *English Review*, regularly brought home by my stepfather. Some important friend had praised it to him, but I don't remember his reading it, or anything like it; his most admired author was Kipling. *Temperament* was about a girl living with a married man in the heart of London (none of my early heroines had their marriage lines). She was proposed to by a kind and well-to-do man and sat alone in her sinful flat imagining life with him in a highly respectable suburb; but after standing on her balcony and listening to the whirr of London traffic on a summer evening, she decided to stick to sin.

I usually ended my Saturday evenings by standing on our dining-room balcony where, if one couldn't quite feel close to the whirring heart of London, it was reasonably romantic with the street lamps shining and the sound of piano-playing floating on the summer air; 'In the Shadows' was the piece most favoured by the residents of Riverview Gardens that year. I would think about my enthralling future. The Academy of Dramatic Art ahead of me in the autumn! Stanley Houghton had been to dinner at the flat and again promised to help me. We had got to know that fine old actor, Alfred Bishop, who, after hearing me recite, had said he really thought I should be allowed to try the stage 'provided you are prepared to starve'. I had been promised, through Auntie Blanche, an introduction to Nigel Playfair . . . I was almost on the stage already.

And then, during the last weeks of the summer term, I found myself unwilling to leave my once so-much-disliked school. Now the sun shone in every classroom, irrespective of its aspect. The playground seemed a green and gold pleasance instead of a bleak wilderness. I mooned about thinking, 'This is the end of my childhood' and numerous friends hung round me begging me not to leave. Far more impressive, Miss Gray sent for me and asked me to stay.

I had never really liked our stately High Mistress and had had several small skirmishes with her, culminating in one, a year or more earlier, in which she said my frequent colds were holding my work back and she thought I might have fewer of them if I wore longer dresses. I replied, I hope not too pertly, that as my mother chose my clothes it would be best to write to her which, indeed, Miss Gray did, but instead of mentioning my dresses she suggested I might try hardening myself by going in the swimming-bath every day instead of the usual twice a week, and carry on right through the winter. This was an unheard of privilege. Though as bad at swimming as at all school sports, I loved it, and practised diving with great determination, undeterred by gruesome stories of girls who dived flat and had to have the buttons of their bathing dresses dug out of their stomachs with penknives. Sometimes on winter afternoons I would be quite alone in those beautiful baths, lazily floating beneath the gradually darkening glass roof. I loved every minute of it, but it didn't cure my colds.

Gratitude for the bathing privilege, and Miss Gray's extreme graciousness now, pretty well overcame me at last. She said she had detected 'a spark of the real thing' in an essay I had recently written for the William Watson competition, in which I came third. The subject was Shelley's 'Poetry redeems from decay the visitations of the divinity in man'. If I would stay on she could almost promise me a scholarship for a University, where I could work towards becoming a lecturer on literature, thus making use of my desire to act without going on the stage. And—a final lure—if I would stay on, she would let me skip the sixth form and go into the French Seventh, as she thought that concentrating on the French language would help me to speak more with the lips and less from the throat.

I had no intention of giving up going on the stage, but I did fancy being in the French Seventh which, with the exception of the Olympian Eighth where most of the girls were grown-up, was the most enviable in the school. There were seldom more than eight girls in it, they were taught by a French woman, did all their lessons in French and discarded such dreary subjects as mathematics. I said I would talk to my mother.

She was surprised but she was also willing; for I think she always hoped something would distract me from the stage. She had no prejudice against it but, I guessed, feared I would not succeed. It astonishes me to remember that I saw myself as unflatteringly as she must have seen me; I realised that I lacked both height and beauty, yet never doubted I was going to be a great actress. All my life my mind seems to have been a meeting place of modesty and conceit.

Once it was decided I should stay on, I was able to enjoy the end of the term to the full and a halcyon mood remained with me for my summer holidays in Manchester. I was now trying to look like the typical 'flapper' of the period. I had a red tam o'shanter, a white Lily Elsie V-necked blouse worn open as low as I dared, and a white skirt in the new corselet style, beltless and fitting tightly right up to the bust—my uncles said it reminded them of a horse-blanket. I probably looked like a sturdy tree trunk, whereas the typical flapper was willowy and long-legged.

A visit to Auntie Bertha and Uncle Bertie was enlivened by burglars. On our return from a motoring holiday, Auntie Bertha looked into the dining-room and found it stripped of all Uncle Bertie's silver golf trophies. She called back into the hall with calm philosophy, 'Bertie, they've been.'

I usually stayed about a month with the family, but I was enjoying myself so much this year that I asked my mother if I could stay a little longer. Feeling sure I could, I was planning another motoring holiday with my uncles, when I received a telegram from her saying she missed me and was ill. She was the most unselfish of women; never before had she made any claim on me. Now I was conscious-stricken for, though I had never failed to send the daily postcard, I had been thinking of her very little. I hurried back to London.

It was her custom to meet my train, wearing a new dress, and the sight of her never failed to make me wonder how I had got on a whole month without her. This time my first memory of her is when we were back at the flat and sitting on the drawing-room window seat. She was looking wan, in spite of a little gallant rouge, and very, very sad. She only admitted to feeling vaguely ill, but there was nothing vague about her unhappiness. For the first time she fully poured out the miseries of her marriage, which were far worse than anything I have recorded here, stopping herself from time to time to say, 'I oughtn't to burden you with all this.' I gathered she had never talked like this to anyone, not even her sisters, always trying to keep up a façade of something approaching happiness. I encouraged her to say all she would, and gradually I felt a weight of misery descend on me, which was like a physical pressure on my heart and ribs. It was the coldest of summer days, the white room was pretty but cheerless, the steely river beautiful but saddening and the high, pale, sunless sky utterly aloof.

I said I would make money on the stage and she could come and live with me, but I knew she still felt young enough to want a normal married life of her own, not just a mother role in my life. But she said it was a relief to be able to talk to me as if I were a grown-up woman and I think she was a little comforted.

A few days later, a visit to a specialist revealed that she must have an instant operation. She was suffering from that most cruel ailment which, like so many people, I still cannot bear to name.

The next weeks were a nightmare from which a few incidents have photographed themselves on my memory. I recall sitting with her in a nursing home in Lisson Grove, staring out of the window at the gold cross on top of some church; watching her sitting up in bed playing a little instrument called an auto-harp, which she had insisted on bringing with her saying she might as well get in practice for heaven; buying yellow roses for her in a gas-lit greengrocer's shop in near-by Crawford Street.

My mother made a fairly good recovery and was home again before I went back to St Paul's. Auntie Bertha and Uncle Bertie came to stay in London and take her on daily motor rides and we were all determined to believe she would now get completely better. I was so relieved the operation was over that I was in reasonably good spirits.

Although I now appreciated St Paul's as a school, and had become happy there, I had continued to find it sadly lacking in charm. There were never any flowers to be seen, I don't recall any pictures, and entertainments were rare, also dull. Some of the recreations of my Manchester schooldays—spring bulb shows, Mayday festivals, tableaux, school plays—would have done wonders for frigid, if beautiful, St Paul's, which was in real need of a Miss Allen of Whalley Range High School. And during my last term it acquired one, though her influence, unfortunately, did not extend beyond the happy members of the French Seventh.

The official form mistress was away on a year's leave and her place was taken by a Mademoiselle Fouquet, a plain woman possessed of such magnetic vitality that it made one wonder if looks were of the slightest importance. She could hardly be said to teach at all as we understood teaching; she merely talked to us, read to us, encouraged us to recite the French classics and, from the first, treated us as if we were the most charming and intelligent young women, each of us possessed of great individuality. No word of English ever passed her lips and none was supposed to pass ours, and the strange thing was that though, when the term began, I was utterly at sea, within a few weeks I could understand everything quite easily—though I never, alas, got as far as speaking French fluently.

I learned that French history taught by a Frenchwoman is quite different from French history taught by an Englishwoman; that the French Revolution was an excellent thing and never to be confused with the Reign of Terror. I discovered I was better at reciting Molière than reciting Shakespeare—Mademoiselle Fouquet seemed to think my Molière trembled on the verge of genius, though she found my Racine a trifle over-emotional. And I was delighted to learn that it was an insult to a French lady's honour to call her a *vache*. My next-door neighbour and I instantly called each other *vaches* and fought a duel with rulers, while Mademoiselle Fouquet tried to look disapproving, but was hampered by laughter.

But the most important thing I learned from that likeable, vivacious woman was something she never put into words: the fact that all knowledge should add to the fullness of life and not just be a collection of facts shut up in compartments of the brain.

Several mornings a week Mademoiselle Fouquet would lead us down to the handsome new Music School, request us to group ourselves round her at a piano, and then teach us French Folk songs and seventeenth-century Bergerette songs. I think my most charming memory of St Paul's is of that group of girls, who seemed to grow better looking as the term proceeded, standing round that plain, middle-aged, captivating Frenchwoman, singing 'Jeune Fillettes'.

I would willingly have exchanged my three years at the school for one full year in the French Seventh, but I soon saw I should have to leave at Christmas. As I was still determined to go on the stage my mother, always with a great fear hanging over her, wanted to see me make a start and I felt she was right. Mademoiselle Fouquet was much distressed; the French Seventh, in the summer term, supplied one of our few entertainments, and she had planned to present me to an astonished school as Rostand's *L'aiglon.* Miss Gray was less distressed than angry. When I went to say goodbye to her she told me that, had she known I would leave so soon, she would never have let me go into the French Seventh (thus presenting me with the term I valued most). However, she relented a little when I hinted at my circumstances and finally said she was glad I had stayed for a full three years so could be allowed to keep my school hymn-book, which she then signed.

It seems to me now that she again and again took trouble over me and, rebuffed by that too formidable façade, I was extremely unresponsive. Not that I didn't feel grateful; indeed, I was grateful to the school as a whole, for the education I received there, for Holst's music, the impetus to read poetry, the admirable drawing lessons, the fine buildings, the library and, eventually, some good friends. But far too much stress was placed on games, the discipline was too rigid, and ugliness amounted almost to a cult. I cannot feel that it is advisable to discourage vanity so heavily that some girls tied up their hair with string.

I did not work up emotion about my last day at school, but I recall feeling some when, in my chilly riverside bedroom, I took off my hard straw hat for the last time. It was a brute of a hat, hideous and uncomfortable, and when it became old and dirty I refused to spend my mother's money on an equally hideous replacement. It was therefore, by now, in a very bad state indeed and, as I looked at it with the sudden interest induced by being about to discard it for ever, I was staggered that I could have walked about London in it. I now jumped on its crown and dropped it into the wastepaper basket. It was still there when I went to bed, looking utterly derelict. I suddenly felt sorry for it.

III

The Academy of Dramatic Art

My mother was well enough to go to Manchester for Christmas, but she found the long Christmas dinner tiring; and none of us were very gay for, as well as anxiety about her, we had with us the memory of our thirteenth at table the previous year. Stanley Houghton had died in November.

I have often wondered how good a playwright he would have become had he lived longer; very good, I think, for his work had originality, courage and humour. Apart from my affection for him, his death was a blow to my ambitions for he would certainly have done his best to help me get started on the stage.

On New Year's Eve there was another full family party and Nan flung the old year out of the window very dramatically, saying it had been a bad year for us all (she had some rapidly increasing troubles of her own, connected with her marriage) and that 1914 was going to be a better year for everyone—a statement which could hardly be said to prove prophetic.

My mother was to stay with my uncles for several weeks, but I went back to London early in the New Year to attend the entrance examination at the Academy of Dramatic Art. It was always spoken of as 'the Academy', having not yet acquired its 'Royal' and become known as RADA, a name I never could take to. It remains the Academy for me, plus a nostalgic memory of the name by which I first heard it called, which was 'Tree's School'.

Back in the flat I gave serious thought to what I should wear for the entrance examination. In spite of her illness, my mother had managed to keep an eye on my clothes, but I had thrown everything out of gear by suddenly insisting on going into long dresses. Some of my dresses could be lengthened, but not much could be done about my schoolgirlish coats so I looked very odd indeed. I had one becoming hat, completely covered in white gull's feathers, but I became self-conscious about this after a drunk man on a Manchester tram pointed an accusing finger at me and said, 'That's Robinson Crusoe's hat.'

I decided I must have a new hat for the entrance examination and I would make it myself. This seems surprising as my entire sewing experience was limited to a never-finished bed-jacket beg⁻n at Whalley Range High School. I bought some black velvet which I cobbled into a kind of mob-cap, which I trimmed with swansdown and a bunch of pink roses. I doubt if there was any other hat remotely like it in the world. From it my two long, heavy plaits streaked down each side of my face. I wore a short, grey, imitation-astrakhan coat; a long, tight black satin dress that had once been my mother's; and a pair of Auntie Bertha's shoes which were two sizes too large for me and could only be kept on by a curious sliding walk. But when I set out for Gower Street I was quite satisfied with my appearance.

Once settled in the waiting room at the Academy I became less so, for there were about thirty girls there, and most of them were beautifully dressed in clothes quite unlike mine. My mother, while keeping on bowing terms with fashion, was too original to follow it completely, and these handsome young women, with their well-cut, up-to-date clothes plus their Marcel waved hair and lipsticked mouths quite over-awed me. Remembering my early days at St Paul's I feared they might not wish to speak to me. But they were all smiling and friendly and one particularly beautiful girl, tall and fair, crossed the room to sit beside me and discuss our nervousness.

My turn came at last and I went into the office of the Administrator, Kenneth Barnes. (I had already met him when Auntie Blanche brought me to a preliminary interview, before Christmas, and had liked him very much.) He had several Academy teachers with him, but I took in little except his encouraging smile, before I launched into a speech from *The Taming of the Shrew.*

This was hardly a wise choice as it represented Katharina's

most sulky period and I felt it called for a baleful voice and a highly unbecoming scowl. However, I followed it with a gay extract from *The School for Scandal* in which I played both Sir Peter and Lady Teazle, changing voices with lightning speed to the confusion of all listeners. My high spot was when I went into paroxysms of girlish laughter, not indicated by Sheridan but well to the fore in Phyllis Neilson-Terry's performance in Tree's production. I began with a low, bubbling noise and worked up to something near hysterics. I much regretted the judges stopped me before I got to this laugh.

After I returned to the waiting-room there was a pause of about five minutes before anyone else was called for. There had been no such pause after the return of other entrants and I wondered what could be happening. I had heard that, on very rare occasions, the judges awarded a scholarship at the entrance examination and it occurred to me that I might have bowled them over to this extent. Some months later Kenneth Barnes told me they had been discussing whether it was advisable to let me come to the Academy at all.

Fortunately I was far too self-confident to suspect anything like this and I went out to have coffee with several newly-made friends in the highest spirits. And a day or so later a letter came to say I had passed the examination.

The new term was not due to start for some weeks and during that time my mother came back from Manchester. The day she arrived soot fell down the dining-room chimney. I saw the look in her eyes when she heard of this and knew she had a superstitious belief that a fall of soot presaged death. She must have known plenty of soot-falls which had no adverse effect, except on carpets; still, it was a cruelly unfortunate happening just then, for the next day she learned she must have another operation. Again the nightmare atmosphere descended, but both she and I insisted that it was a smaller operation this time and, once it was over, she would recover completely. We discussed the advisability of my giving up the Academy, but both of us were against that. I think we felt (I certainly did) it would amount to an admission that her illness was fatal and we were just waiting for the end, whereas I was still determined to believe she would get better. But I cannot acquit myself of selfishness. Much as I loved her, I was now avid to start my training, all the more so since I had been inside the Academy. Perhaps I should have made her believe I *wanted* to be with her more than anything else. Eventually, her doctor decided the matter by telling me I would do neither her nor myself any good by staying at home brooding and, if nursing proved necessary, it would have to be done by someone older and more experienced than I was.

She was safely through the operation, but still in the nursing home when the term began. As I was only allowed to see her once a day, I had arranged that this should be in the late afternoons, but I called in for news of her on my way to the Academy that first morning. I had asked her to put something belonging to her in the window near her bed to wish me luck and when I looked up I saw a nurse holding the auto-harp and waving. The report about her had been good, so I hurried along Marylebone Road in high spirits.

The Academy was then in two old and rather ramshackle Gower Street houses. There was a canteen in the basement, cloakrooms in a rabbit-warren of little attics, numerous large bare classrooms and, on the first floor, a small theatre. This had been made by knocking down the dividing wall between the two houses and replacing it with a curtain. The stage was raised in the drawing-room of one house, the auditorium was in the drawing-room of the other; and beyond this another wall had been knocked down so that a little back room could serve as what was known as the Royal Box, for the Administrator and distinguished guests. The news that someone important was in the box would travel all over the Academy like wildfire. This queer little makeshift theatre had an atmosphere at once highly professional and extremely intimate; and the acoustics were so peculiar that it was said if you could be heard in the box you could be heard in the largest of theatres.

Up in the little attic cloakroom I met my tall, fair friend of the entrance examination, whose name was Dorothy Webb. Together we went downstairs, studied a notice board, and were glad to find we were in the same division—there were so many new students there had to be three divisions with about twelve girls and three men in each. I later discovered that all the best-looking and best-dressed girls were in my division and can only imagine I was put there to bring the average down.

Dorothy and I went to a class in the theatre—called 'the stage room'—where Miss Gertrude Burnett proceeded to cast St John Hankin's *The Cassilis Engagement* with astonishing rapidity. She was a small, trim white-haired woman usually clad in the plainest of suits and with a school-mistress-like personality—which made it all the more amusing when she got down to showing you how to act, say, a tipsy soldier. Her speciality was technique, how to walk, talk, sit, move and place one's voice; I was to learn much from her. She did her initial casting with great fairness. With most teachers it was the custom for different students to play leading parts in each act of a play, but only Miss Burnett used a system of duplicate casts competing for parts; which meant one had the chance to rehearse good parts even if one didn't finally win them. She would also let us volunteer to understudy parts, give the understudies one chance to rehearse in front of her and, if they happened to be better than either of the original castings, they could win the parts. She was a strict disciplinarian and would take a part away from any wretched student who forgot to bring a pencil.

After Miss Burnett's class we lunched in the dark basement, where the walls were lined with photographs of earlier students; it was depressing to note how few of them had ever got anywhere. A buxom woman known as Hennie sold sandwiches, Bourbon biscuits, and an occasional plutocratic chop. She was kind to new students and willing to point out those few members of the Final Division who had achieved the glory of walk-ons in London theatres. Our division clung together, distinctly awed, bursting with friendliness to each other, and inclined to look critically at the two other new divisions.

In the afternoon we went to Miss Elsie Chester who was to produce us in a much-cut version of *Hamlet*. Miss Chester was the antithesis of Miss Burnett, being stout, untidy and excitable, apt to storm and even swear during emotional moments. She had a strange, shapeless hat which she was alleged to turn back to front at half-term. Her expression was tragic and there had, indeed, been tragedy in her life for her stage career had been cut short by the loss of a leg. She had a beautiful voice, and a ravaged charm which I never succumbed to; I was too resentful of her unfairness in casting.

After a glance at the whole division she asked the tall, fair Dorothy Webb to read the part of Hamlet, and finding that Dorothy had a good voice and could imitate inflections, let her keep it throughout the play to the keen resentment of the whole class and Dorothy's embarrassment. The King was given to the best looking man; Ophelia was divided between four fair, pretty girls; the Queen between four dark, handsome ones; Horatio and Laertes doled out to the next-best-looking students. Finally, there was no one without a part except myself and a plain, fat girl who was even shorter than I was. Miss Chester said to her, 'We must have a girl with a deep voice for the ghost. You look as if you've got one.' The girl had a high, bright voice but Miss Chester ordered it down to the depths and down it had to go. She then said she supposed I would have to be Polonius, obviously wishing I didn't have to be anything.

Miss Chester did not expect students to bring pencils and, on the whole, she preferred them not to bring books of the play. She liked them to say every line after her and if they dashed ahead and read three or four lines on their own she would irritably take them back. This made most of us feel so demented we found ourselves imitating her without any idea of what the lines meant. It was not only inflections we had to copy, but also meaningless pauses. Gestures, too, were meaningless. For my line, 'Neither a borrower nor a lender be', I had to indicate a borrower on the ceiling and a lender beneath the floor—which suggested to me that borrowers went to heaven and lenders, most unfairly, went to hell. Going through the play day after day merely imitating, and never getting the chance to try other parts, was a miserable business.

But despite her preposterous method of teaching, the artificiality of her intonations and the general chaos of her rehearsals, the final productions by Elsie Chester were almost the best at the Academy. When the performance was due she would bring from her home certain screens, draperies, bits of furniture and really dress the stage. She used the lighting equipment to its best advantage. And whenever I saw a production of hers, I found myself forgetting I was watching fellow students and simply enjoying the play. People were effective in her shows who seemed wooden when handled by other teachers. Perhaps the truth was she had more sense of theatre than is possessed by many far more skilled teachers. But her Svengali-like methods of obtaining performances had no lasting value and neither then, nor when in later terms I worked with her, did I learn anything at all—nor was I given one good part.

As well as acting classes we had lessons in dancing, fencing, gesture, voice production and elocution. Dancing was taught by Louis Hervey d'Egville who played a violin and imparted an air of the eighteenth century to his classes. I had hoped that wearing block-toed ballet shoes would enable me to dance on my points quite easily; I was wrong. Fencing attracted me, but my efforts never earned a word of approval. Still, when we held a small tournament I proceeded to win by the simple plan of trying to, without bothering about the correct method. This was considered very low indeed and I gathered a fencer should die in good style, rather than live by the exercise of anything so ungallant as common sense.

I loved the gesture classes, which were taken by Mrs O'Neil, a wild-eyed lady who complained that we were all cold and English when we ought to have been warm and Italian, and continually implored us to 'Keep it loose and flowing, dear.' I received no praise until one happy day Mrs O'Neil looked at me intently and said, 'You have Italian blood, dear. I can tell.' She then beckoned me to sit on the floor, beside her chair, swept my hair back from my forehead and regarded me tenderly, then took my hand and held it throughout the lesson, showing no inclination to relinquish it even when the class ended. The next class trooped in to find me still firmly held and only the thought of Miss Burnett's class ahead of me, and her treatment of latecomers, gave me the courage to release myself.

At my next class with Mrs O'Neil I expected warm praise after my first exercise. (It was staggering across the room in a fainting condition, beating upon the door, slithering down it, and finally collapsing in a deep swoon.) Mrs O'Neil looked at me without a spark of recognition and said, 'Hopeless, dear— just a cold little English girl.'

I keenly regret that never, during my entire stage career, did I get the chance to make use of anything taught me in those gesture classes. We learned back falls, front falls, side falls and spiral falls. We died of poison, shooting, stabbing and strangulation. The last was more popular with the strangler than with the stran-gulee, for the victim was seized by the throat, forced to her knees, had her head shaken violently from side to side and was finally flung the full length of the classroom. There was one rule that applied to all our agonising deaths: always we had to finish up on our backs with our arms flung wide and our feet neatly crossed. No huddled, untidy corpses were allowed.

It is easy to make fun of Mrs O'Neil, but everyone liked her classes and she really was a valuable teacher. She taught us to relax, lose self-consciousness and, above all, to act with our emotions, not our nerves. That is, she *tried* to teach the last; I doubt if it can be fully learned without great experience of acting, but she did at least get the idea into our heads. And most young players would do well to remember Mrs O'Neil's dictum: 'Keep it loose and flowing, dear.'

I loathed voice production because it meant doing positively acrobatic things with one's tongue, lips, throat and ribs and my struggles were received by Miss Burnett's sister, Mrs Mackern, with a brusque, 'Not a bit like it, dear.' But I enjoyed the elocution lessons, taken by a veteran of His Majesty's Theatre, A. E. George, a small man with a tremendous voice. After a few lessons I asked him to help me cure my Lancashire accent. He said I had none and was one of the few members of the class who spoke reasonably pure English. He told me that most upper-class Londoners spoke affectedly, and he greatly disliked 'crorse' for 'cross' and 'noe' for 'no'. I longed to relay his opinion to some of my snobbish ex-classmates at St Paul's.

Soon my mother was back from the nursing home and eager to hear me my parts in the evenings. She said she could not imagine anything lovelier than being young and going to the

Academy, and she was wistfully anxious to hear all that happened to me. She would obviously have welcomed the news that I was creating havoc among the young men and, on hearing this was not the case, she offered a suggestion for attracting them. I had always thought the expression 'making eyes' was just a comic phrase, but my mother thought otherwise and proceeded to flicker her eyes in a way she had found infallible when she was a girl. I could well believe it for the effect was enchanting, though deeply pathetic because of her frailty. (Many years later I noticed that Marie Tempest occasionally used her eyes in this pretty, kittenish way, both on and off the stage.)

I decided I would try a little eye-making myself and soon had a good opportunity. Several classes were assembled in a half-circle to listen to some lecture and, almost opposite to me, was a young man from another division who had occasionally been quite polite to me. I put in what I took to be very good work indeed and was delighted with my success when he joined me in the canteen and was most attentive, pressing me to have a second cup of cocoa. When we were alone he told me I ought to take care of myself as I was obviously in a very nervous state. 'I was watching you during the lecture,' he said, 'and your eyes were never still for a minute. I wouldn't be surprised if you were on the verge of St Vitus's Dance.'

But if I was proving no Delilah to the men, I was getting on wonderfully well with the girls and never have I met a more pleasant set of young women. My special friends, as well as the tall, fair Dorothy, were two charming and wealthy Americans, Emily and Julia, who were at the Academy simply to amuse themselves. They decided I was being unfairly treated about parts and were convinced it was because my hair was still down and I was looked on as a child. So up went my hair, in plaits worn over the ears (a style highly becoming to Gladys Cooper). Emily and Julia then banned Auntie's Bertha's shoes and set about getting rid of my corsets, which had been chosen by Auntie Blanche and were said by Emily to be Victorian. She and Julia wanted to buy me a new pair but, as I would not let them, they advised me to get on without any, which I did very satisfactorily being now only seven stone and a reasonably good shape. (Auntie Blanche, who had got over her feud with my stepfather in order to spend much time with my mother, warned me I should 'spread', but I never did.) I took to using lipstick and powder and once I was out of the flat every morning I undid the buttons of my 'split' Tango skirt right up to the knee most dashingly. But I didn't get any better parts.

Miss Burnett's final casting left me with nothing I liked at all. Emily and Julia were indignant, insisting I acted better than nearly all the girls in the division and, to be honest, I did. I was, in fact, one of the few girls capable of acting at all. I could, at least, throw myself into a part, laugh, cry, assume an accent, whereas most of my companions were beautiful wooden dears who read their lines in a gentle monotone. And yet Miss Burnett and even Miss Chester were probably justified in their casting, for the beautiful and wooden, rightly cast as to appearance and carefully taught, were better than I should have been in parts I wasn't physically right for; and though I could act, I acted badly. But I saw none of this at the time and was pretty bitter when I found myself with little more than some character bits—and Polonius.

My most unhappy time was when we rehearsed to compete for the scholarships which were awarded every term to one man and one girl out of all the new students. We did scenes from *Cousin Kate* and I played a maid with five lines. I was assured a student had recently won honourable mention in that part, but I knew I hadn't a comic personality and could make no impression with so little to say. (I learned later that the student in question had been Kathleen Harrison, a character actress of genius. I wish I could have known then that, twenty years after, when the Academy put up some photographs of its most successful students, Kathleen and I would be side by side—but my success, unlike hers, was never as an actress.)

By now my life at home was difficult as my stepfather had an accident to his leg, was bedridden for weeks and had to have my room; I moved in with my mother. His parents tried to make me give up the Academy and nurse him but, as my mother had already told me not even to go into his room, I refused and threatened to write to my Manchester uncles. This had an instant effect and other arrangements were made, a daily nurse at first and then Charlotte took over. There is a strange blank in my memory about my stepfather at this time, perhaps due to the fact that I had for many months ignored him. He had behaved no better since my mother's illness and my regret at losing my own room vanished when I found out how thankful she was to have me with her instead of him. By now the strain of getting up every day was too much for her and a specially high single bed was bought and put in the big bay window so she could see the street, watch the people coming and going, and get, at the end of the road, a glimpse of the curve of the Thames.

Just before my end-of-term performances began I learned that her illness had recurred and I decided I could not stay on at the Academy for another term, even if she wished me to. So I now said I just wanted to be with her. We still did not admit she could not get better for, though there could be no more operations, she was to have treatments and we told each other these could be most effective, and again made plans for our life after her recovery.

My last weeks at the Academy were a mixture of misery about her, regrets that I was leaving, and excitement about the performances. We made-up in the little attic cloakrooms; I had been made-up for amateur theatricals in Manchester, but few of my friends had ever put on grease-paint before. Then we clattered down the many stairs and huddled in the wings of the tiny theatre to listen to last minute admonitions and whisper entirely unfounded rumours that some famous actor was in the Royal Box with Kenneth Barnes. Auntie Blanche came to see me in *The Cassilis Engagement* and, God bless her, pronounced me excellent as a society matron and a raucous old woman in a red wig. Fortunately, I did not invite her to see me as Polonius. I wore a flowing white wig, a full beard that reached to my bust, and a voluminous green velvet robe with very wide sleeves. When I made the gesture which indicated that borrowers, so unfairly, were in heaven, my sleeve fell back revealing my still childish, stick-like arm up to the shoulder and my unusually small hand (a journalist once described my hands as 'elfin'). A voice in the auditorium said, 'Look at her hand!' and all the students in the audience exploded into laughter. The rest of the scene was a riot of amusement except for those of us on stage and Miss Chester in the prompt corner, thumping the stage with her crutch and murmuring balefully, 'The fools, the fools!'

My last performance was in *The Merchant of Venice* in which Miss Burnett had awarded me one act of Gratiano. Unfortunately, my Nerissa was Dorothy Webb, over a foot taller than I was. The audience found us pretty funny, but I did not repeat my *tour de force* as Polonius.

There were no classes during the last weeks of term and we spent our spare time watching the performances of other divisions. There was one play which enchanted me, *Prunella* by Laurence Houseman and Granville Barker, which for many weeks was a sort of secret country into which I could retire from the unhappiness of life at home. Often I saved the thought of it until I was in bed, so that I could have something to look forward to all day.

By the end of term every corner of those two old Gower Street houses had become valuable to me and I found it hard to believe I would never come back.

Students could have a verbal or written report on their work. I had chosen to have a verbal one and went both to get it and to say goodbye to Kenneth Barnes. It was then he told me how narrowly I had missed failing at the entrance examination, but he hastened to add I had turned out better than was expected, and that if I would take up character work he thought he could see 'a way out' for me. I can remember the tone of his voice and his anxious expression. He knew something of my circumstances and must have been distressed to have on his hands a girl who could ill afford the Academy fees and was physically unsuited to the stage of those days. I wasn't ugly, I doubt if I was even plain, some photographs show me as quite attractive. But I was a little odd, my head was slightly too large for my small stature, my whole personality quite unlike that of the normal pretty girl of the period. And the theatre did not welcome little oddities except as character actresses.

Not that I realised this at the time and, though I thanked Kenneth Barnes for his advice, I had no intention of taking it. No character actress I; my sights were still set on my two favourite parts; Juliet and Lady Teazle. Anyway, it was a comfort that Kenneth Barnes said he would welcome me back when I was able to return.

Auntie Bertha had recently come from Manchester to take charge, so there was really very little I could do for my mother except to keep her as cheerful as possible, which was not easy as I was so abysmally miserable myself. Soon I worked out a set of mental refuges: *Prunella* for the last thing at night, and during the day strictly rationed dives into Compton Mackenzie's *Sinister Street*. And for a time my mother persuaded me to go to a weekly matinée at the Coronet Theatre, Notting Hill, where Miss Horniman's Company was playing. But though I counted the days to this, once I got there I would find myself imagining her suddenly worse, and me not with her, so I gave up going.

One trouble was that, though there was little nursing to be done, Auntie Bertha was of such boundless energy and ruthless conscience that she continually created work for herself, Charlotte and me, once saying that it could not possibly be right for us all to be sitting down at the same moment. Though enormously kind, she was not conducive to peace and my mother eventually asked me if I could manage alone. I was sure I could, so dear Auntie Bertha returned to her left-alone husband, though with every intention of coming back to us before long. She considered me far too young to have to face so much responsibility.

Sad as they were, I was grateful for the next five or six weeks for my mother and I recaptured an intimacy we had hardly known since her second marriage. There was still little for me to do. Charlotte ran the flat and looked after my stepfather, not that we saw much of him; though still using my bedroom, he had fully recovered and was out many evenings—I suppose; the blank in my memory about him still operates.

Each morning I arranged flowers in the numerous delicate silver vases my mother loved, lowered the green sunblinds and then sat in the pleasantly shaded room to read aloud or talk—it was mostly talking as my mother could no longer get interested in books. She was worried because she had not been able to help me much over becoming grown-up. Once she said with sudden anger that I must never believe anyone who told me that women could not expect physical pleasure from marriage—astonishing frankness from a woman usually so reticent about sex, and very gratefully received by me. But for the most part we talked about how to improve my appearance. I must choose clothes that made me look taller—'try for a long line and avoid fussy trimmings, especially round the neck'. One day she sent me to a hairdresser, who gave me a Marcel wave and dressed my hair with thirty-three hairpins. It felt like ironmongery but the effect was good and, after that, I would sit struggling with it every morning while she offered encouraging advice.

On my eighteenth birthday, in early May, I found she had with Charlotte's help got together a large box of presents—silk stockings finer than I had ever had and all sorts of little luxuries. When I opened the box she wept and said she had not expected to be alive and Charlotte was to have given me the present. I really think she was distressed because her continued living had spoilt the surprise she had so carefully worked out.

Never before had she admitted that she was going to die and we quickly banished the idea, helped in doing so because we then became interested in Christian Science. An old gentleman, an acquaintance of my stepfather, asked if he might come and talk to her about it. He brought with him two dozen tulips which were like no tulips I had ever seen. They were very tall, with enormous blooms of strange colours, mauves, browns and blackish purples. They lasted for well over a fortnight and gave my mother extraordinary pleasure. I still have a vivid mental picture of them, standing on the bedside table with a copy of *Science and Health* beside them.

My mother found the book difficult but I did not; even after one talk with the kind old man I understood quite a lot. Since my confirmation I had decided that religion was meaningless for me, but here was a religion that seemed to me reasonable— except that I could never see it as a religion; to me it was simply a philosophy. As our elderly friend came frequently and explained very patiently, my mother understood better and was given new hope.

I went to one Christian Science service, but it set me back badly. (All my life I have been incapable of taking part in any mass worship without feeling there was nothing *to* worship.) And I was never fully to accept orthodox Christian Science. I find some of its tenets, and much of *Science and Health* ludicrous. And yet, and yet, I have gone on reading *Science and Health* and nothing has shattered my belief in its basic truth; indeed, without that belief I can't imagine how I could have got through life.

My mother was, of course, attended by a doctor, but she was now having no medical treatment and had always refused to take the morphia tablets he offered her; she was convinced these would mean the beginning of the end. So it was possible for our friend to get a Christian Science practitioner to attend her. Practitioners have the same effect on me as church services. But my mother's improvement was so marked that it astonished her doctor. Perhaps, if she had not been surrounded by people who believed her to be dying, she might yet have recovered. Even I was lacking in faith and all the more so because she was perpetually in pain.

The nights were the worst times. During the day there was sunlight, she could look at her flowers, watch people in the street and talk. But at night she could not sleep and I could not keep awake. She wept if a night nurse was suggested for she could not bear the thought of some strange woman near her, so we just had to manage as best we could. Around midnight, Charlotte would support her while I arranged her pillows— she slept sitting up; then the light was put out, the curtains drawn back because she liked the light from the street lamps; she would take a mild pain-killing tablet and I would try to get her to sleep.

She liked me to recite to her, bits of Shakespeare, odd verses I remembered from *Prunella*, the drowsy alliterative lines of *The Vision of Piers Plowman* which she found more soothing than anything else. Sometimes I sang songs which she had sung to me when I was a child. But sooner or later I always fell asleep and left her wakeful. She tried hard not to wake me, but often by three or four in the morning she would do so, pathetically apologetic. Although more than willing to get up, I was such a heavy sleeper that I felt as if drugged as I staggered round the kitchen, warming milk. She did not really want the milk, she only wanted someone to share a few moments of her interminable night.

I came to realise that during those lonely watches she thought continually of her youth and relived her life. It was not only death that she could not resignedly accept, but also the fact that life had brought her so little of what she had longed for. She had had an impoverished childhood, a brief romantic girlhood, those few happy years of marriage and then, from her middle twenties, only the hope that she could build a second happiness. Nothing since my father's early death had ever turned out right for her. She had never had the chance to do anything with her very real talents, never had a penny to spare. Her second marriage had been bitterly unhappy. She had always been courageous, but never philosophic; she had remained, temperamentally, too young for philosophy. And this youth of spirit made things harder for her now.

Her early romanticism lingered and even intensified during her illness. One evening when I was alone in the flat with her there was a violent thunderstorm and she asked me to draw the curtains back and put the lights out so that we could watch the lightning. (We had done this ever since I was a tiny child.) There was a terrific thunderclap and, at that very moment, her heavy box-mattress which had a water-filled rubber bed on top of it and was thus of great weight, slipped from one side of the bed-frame to the floor so that she lay at an angle which put her in danger of falling out of bed. The mattress must have been shifted when the bed was made and the accident seemingly had nothing to do with the storm—though for a moment we both thought the bed had been struck by lightning. It was impossible for me to lift the mattress and to move her would have caused her great pain, so all I could do was to rush out and get help. Before I left she asked me to turn the lights off again and my last glimpse of her was as she lay at that most precarious angle with lightning suddenly illuminating her face.

It seemed as if every neighbour we knew was out but at last, after dashing through the rain, I located a helpful married couple. We found her bright-eyed with excitement and she was cheerful and even amusing while the bed was set aright again. Afterwards, when I praised her bravery, she said 'The storm helped so much.'

Early in June Auntie Bertha came back. This did not make things easier as, by then, my mother and I were working hard at Christian Science, which was made more difficult by the presence of someone who did not believe in it. Not that Auntie Bertha was antagonistic; she followed her usual practice of giving all religion a wide, though respectful, berth—adopting a sort of let sleeping dogs lie attitude. She thought, one felt, that there *was* a dog, but not one she had been introduced to, and her attention might provoke it. But when Auntie Blanche, an orthodox churchwoman, insisted that my mother ought to receive Holy Communion, Auntie Bertha (who had once said to me, 'They say if you don't take it three times a year, God won't let you *in*') felt it might be just as well. My mother made no objection. She was not too keen on Communion, but gathered that a clergyman would pray for her recovery and said she would be glad of anyone's prayers. So one morning Auntie Blanche brought a rather nervous young man who made elaborate preparations, intimated that Auntie Bertha and I should put on hats (Auntie Blanche already had hers on) and started his service. But he did not, as we expected, pray for the sick; he prayed for the dying and when my mother heard this she collapsed. He took the sacrament on her behalf and was then hurried from the room. And later I fear that I said some very angry words to him. I don't know whose fault it was—possibly

Auntie Blanche's—but personally I blamed the whole Church of England and never had any more to do with it, or any ritualistic form of religion. And if Auntie Bertha was correct in her surmise that without Communion one could not get into heaven, I will remain, eternally and unrepentantly, out.

My mother never recovered from that shock and, despite our assurances that it was a mistake, thereafter believed we were now waiting for her death. And that afternoon the doctor insisted that, against her will, she should be given some treatment by a professional nurse. This proved painful, also my mother felt that, by forcing it on her, the doctor had weakened her faith in Christian Science. Coming on top of the morning's catastrophe this was too much for her. She became angry and at last demanded morphia, which she took furiously and scornfully. Soon she was asleep and though I was glad to see her peaceful, I felt that the vital spirit that had sustained her for so long had been withdrawn, leaving her—as the doctor then told us—almost on the brink of death.

However, she awoke next morning quite clear-headed and was soon able to conduct a surprisingly business-like conversation with me, as if offering last minute advice before starting on a journey. She particularly advised me to stick to Christian Science. She said she had come to it too late, and didn't fully understand it but she felt it was true. In the early afternoon my Aunt Nan and my uncles arrived from Manchester. She was grateful to them for coming, especially as she felt they would be a comfort to me. (She had earlier arranged that I should return to Manchester with them after her death.) I, too, was grateful though I think I took family solidarity for granted. When my uncles had gone to find a hotel, she said she would take some more morphia tablets. After she had taken them I sat alone with her in the summer evening feeling these might be the last minutes we should ever share, longing to say something which might help her. We had often discussed the possibility of immortality and once I had quoted to her some of the beautiful lines from Shelley's 'Adonais' which more or less summed up what I believed:

> He is made one with Nature; there is heard
> His voice in all her music, from the moan
> Of thunder, to the song of night's sweet bird . . .
> He is a portion of the loveliness
> Which once he made more lovely.

She liked this because she loved music and Nature, but she really longed for a personal immortality which would include reunion with the dead. The best I could manage now was 'I'm sure there'll be *something.*' She said she was, too. The minutes drifted past. After she became drowsy she murmured, so quietly that I could barely hear, 'Dodie has been the best daughter any woman could want.' Those were the last words I heard her say. I think she meant them to be.

She died in the early morning. At the end of our little road the sun was rising and, through the wide bay window, I could see its dazzling brilliance behind her head. She was quite unconscious, but for sometime had been a little restless, as if searching for something. As I waited beside her I would not, if given the power, have called her back for I knew that life had little more to offer her. She had never accepted middle age and would have hated old age. Her prolonged youthfulness of spirit was really the enemy of content. I was all the happiness she had known since my father's death and every day I was becoming more absorbed in my own interests. I could never have sacrificed my life to her and she would never have accepted such a sacrifice, for she had a horror of parents who hang on to their children. Sitting there holding her hand I knew that, dearly as I loved her, I should have had little more to offer her. I accused myself of selfishness, but instinctively knew that my attitude was normal. But I now think that such analytical thought and such clear self-knowledge at such a moment were very far from normal.

There came a moment when my aunts whispered that she was going from us. Her restlessness had ceased and now it was as if a veil was lifted from her face. She opened her eyes wide and looked supremely herself. And then she looked surprised, and delightedly surprised. For a second her eyes were alight with happiness. Then she was dead.

My aunts, who had watched at many family death-beds, looked at each other quickly. Then Nan said, 'We were hoping that would happen for you.'

I am told that death often brings such a moment. I only hope it brings as much comfort to the dying as to those who watch.

IV

Manchester Consolations

By nine o'clock my aunts were taking me out into the already hot day to order flowers and help me buy mourning. None of us approved of it and my mother had particularly disliked it yet, only the previous day, she had advised me to wear it for a few months to avoid criticism which might hurt me. One thing in its favour is that the purchase of it occupies the mind, and the full tide of emotion is held at bay for a little while by the worry of choosing and fitting. My own case was especially difficult because I was too small for stock sizes, my aunts knew nothing about London shops, were horrified by the prices and insisted that everything was too old for me. But during the morning we managed to find one alterable dress at my mother's favourite shop, Bourne and Hollingsworth. While the fitter was at work I saw that my worn-out aunts were sitting side-by-side fast asleep. I began to laugh and they woke and started to laugh too, while the young fitter looked shocked and embarrassed.

We trailed around London for the rest of that exhausting day and only late in the afternoon did we find anything else possible for me—a much befrilled taffeta coat and skirt soon to become my pride and joy. Then we crawled home, too tired to feel much emotion. My uncles were waiting for us and Charlotte provided an enormous meal. We all ate, surprisingly ravenous.

My mother had been placed in her white drawing-room; she lay already surrounded by flowers and looking astonishingly like photographs taken of her in her girlhood. My aunts and I sat with her for a while and then, when my uncles had gone back to their hotel, we helped Charlotte to drag the double-bed mattress from the bedroom so that we could sleep across it on the dining-room floor. None of us could bear to go into the bedroom.

True to family tradition my aunts and I did not go to the funeral, but afterwards we helped scatter my mother's ashes in Richmond Park. She had asked that this should be done and also asked that her name should not be engraved on any tombstone so that no one should ever remember her in connection with a grave.

The day after the funeral it became necessary to have a discussion with my stepfather. My mother had left me all she possessed, but this was little more than the furniture of the flat, which had been bought with her money. She had, however, persuaded my stepfather to sign a deed that he would gradually repay the money, and he pointed out that, if he did, he ought to be allowed to keep the furniture. My uncles and I at once agreed, but I was determined not to let him have her piano, which she had owned long before she met him—indeed, before I was born. He insisted that removing the piano would take ten shillings a week off the rent of the flat if he let it furnished. A devastating row blew up and all the bitterness I had been storing up came out. My uncles calmed me down and Uncle Harold reminded me, privately, that we were so many of us against my stepfather. They were extremely forebearing to him, particularly considering what had happened to the large sum of money they had sent to pay for my mother's first operation. A famous surgeon had performed it for nothing, so the money had gone to the races and hadn't come back.

Eventually my stepfather promised to send the piano, the little armchair given to me by my uncles when I was nine, my books and some other personal possessions. But I refused to leave for Manchester until the piano and chair were on their way—and it was as well I did, for none of the other things were ever sent to me. I lost all my books, except for a few particularly valued ones which I packed in my trunk.

As I hope not to mention my stepfather after this chapter I will outline my further relations with him.

I only met him again once, some fifteen months later, during

My Mother, 1911

My Auntie Madge ('Nan') and her children, Esmé and Ronnie, that 'astute boy.' 1912

St Paul's Girls' School, Brook Green, Hammersmith

35, Riverview Gardens, Barnes

Phyllis Morris

As Katharina in *The Taming of the Shrew* at the Academy of Dramatic Art

As Hortensio in *The Taming of the Shrew* . . . looking 'like *both* the little princes in the Tower'

The Lounge

Exterior. The Three Arts Club, Marylebone Road

1915, as Low Sung in *Mr Wu*

Evelyn Laye, aged fifteen, as I knew her in 1915

my first stage engagement. I was in a musical comedy, touring London suburbs. One evening a note from him was brought to my dressing-room saying he would call for me after the show and take me out to supper. I had barely finished reading this when I was sent for by the leading lady of the company, who had always been particuarly kind to me. She told me she had heard me being enquired for at the stage door by 'a very bad man' with whom I must have nothing to do. On hearing this was my stepfather, she stood her ground, said he was notorious and frequently seen hanging round stage doors—thus indicating one failing I hadn't known about. Of course I had no intention of going out with him but, at the end of the show, I did bring myself to tell him so with reasonable civility. As I remember he made some sickening remark to the effect of, 'You and I ought to help comfort each other, kiddie.'

A year or so later my uncles at last took legal steps to recover what he owed me and he was ordered to pay by instalments. He defaulted so often that it was ten years in all before the matter was finally settled and even then I only got a proportion of the money and no legal expenses. But seven years after this, when my first play was successfully produced, he was on the telephone the next day asking me to meet him—offering a boxing match as an inducement. I declined—politely, I hope—and went on declining many pressing invitations. In my whole life there has been nobody else to whom I have remained unforgiving and I might, quite conceivably have forgiven his behaviour to me. But never, never could I forgive the misery he had caused my mother.

My uncles had promised that I should go back to the Academy in the autumn but, as our train steamed out of London, I felt I was going into exile, grateful though I was for the wall of family affection that surrounded me. Still, I quite liked the idea of a few months in my uncles' Whalley Range house. I was glad not to have the bedroom my mother and I had shared, which had been taken over by Uncle Arthur. The room he had vacated was small and much overshadowed by the almond tree whose top-most twigs I had so often looked out on from the cistern room, but I became fond of it—mainly, I think, because I slept so well there and with a clear conscience. For months I had felt guilty about sleep because it meant leaving my mother alone and wakeful.

My uncles had asked their housekeeper to 'feed me up' and she proceeded to press vast quantities of food on me. She was a kindly woman devoted to the dog, Peter, and to frequent cups of tea, to which Peter also had become addicted. At least five times a day he could be heard nosing his bowl round the kitchen, whereupon she would happily put on the kettle. Over-fed, he was developing a middle-aged spread but still took my uncles to their trams in the morning. He was pleased to see me, but not ecstatic.

I have always been surprised I did not suffer more after my mother's death. Perhaps this was because I had for so many months been prepared for it and of course it was a comfort that all unhappiness, both before and during her illness, was over for her. Also I was helped by a letter I found, written by her five years earlier at a time when she seemed to fear she might die suddenly. Addressed to a child it was written very simply, but it contained much good advice on how to bear the loss of her, much of it based on her own experiences after my father's death. She told me never to look ahead in sorrow but to say, 'I will just get through this day', and then to fill up each minute with little occupations. And she concluded with instructions she had repeated only the day before she died: to blot out all memories of her as ill and to remember her as well and happy—'and now perhaps among the wild flowers we so often searched for'. (And we never did find any.)

My days were now certainly full of 'little occupations'. I was given breakfast in bed and I then dressed with extreme care in my new mourning. (I added a cloth coat and skirt, price one pound, which can hardly have been so faultlessly cut as I then thought them.) I spent nearly an hour doing my hair, with its full complement of thirty-three hairpins, and taught myself to make fashionable 'tango curls', which I moored to my face with spirit gum.

Once dressed I sometimes went for a walk, but most of the

fine old houses I remembered had now been replaced by rows of nasty new ones. I preferred to settle down in the dim drawing-room, with my mother's piano (how glad I was I'd rescued it) and the tall mahogany bookcase I had known since my earliest days. I particularly enjoyed opening its keyless doors by a little finger inserted in the keyholes. As in childhood, I dragged the heavy Shakespeares out and lay on the floor reading them, still entranced by the Kenny Meadows illustrations. There were many calf-bound volumes of classical music which I strummed away at; and in the drawers at the base of the bookcase, almost too heavy to pull out, were all the sentimental songs accumulated by the family over half a century. I found these saddening. Really the music I enjoyed most was Ragtime. I had several collections and banged away for hours. Why did it give me so much pleasure—an excited pleasure? I suppose it was my equivalent of present day 'Pop' music.

My uncles, who had no conventional ideas about observing a period of mourning, took me to some entertainment almost every evening. And I had many invitations. I spent some days with my father's brother, Uncle Tyrrel, and his family. They no longer kept goats, but had two pet pigs called Parma Violets and Eau de Cologne, and my cousin Leila was collecting Ella Wheeler Wilcox in limp suede. I only hope I wasn't sneery about this. Another invitation was from the Watts sisters, those friends of Edwardian musical evenings, who took me to Strat-ford-upon-Avon for a week. The theatre, alas, was closed but the atmosphere was exciting. It was during that week I had a last outburst of grief about my mother. I cried almost all through one night, obsessed with the thought I should *never* see her again. After that, I was on the way to full recovery. Perhaps it was because the sadness faded so soon that my happy memories of her have remained so vivid. And I have never ceased to imagine her reaction to clothes, books, happenings. . . . With all her romanticism, she loved modernity—how greatly she would have appreciated a permanent wave. (She once said that in Heaven she was counting on curly hair.) And how I wish she could have known radio and television. After twenty years or so, the sound of her voice faded from my memory's ear. But after fifty years I still hold mental discussions with her.

On my return from Stratford I decided I must do some solid work, so I polished off two long short stories (around ten thousand words each) and a one-act play which was inspired by *Prunella*, though my Pierrot, Pierette, etc., were simply people at a fancy-dress ball. I never attempted to place any of this work, but when Uncle Harold bought me a book on film technique I wrote a film scenario, typed it at his office (my first brush with a typewriter) and sent it to a film company named Hepworth, using the pseudonym 'Charles Henry Percy', a combination of three characters played by Fred Terry.

How did I get time for all I did that summer? I still have the impression of months and months of recuperative peace. But actually, it was only six weeks after my mother's death that war was declared. Only for a few days had I known it was a possibility. Then, around eleven o'clock at night, when my uncles and I were returning from supper with Auntie Bertha, we saw newsboys with placards saying, 'England at War'. I told myself I should remember this moment all my life, but I felt no surge of patriotism. Fairly recently I had, with pride, coined the phrase, 'Patriotism isn't love of one's country, but hate for everyone else's' and decided I was an internationalist. I hadn't chosen a good year for it.

At first the war seemed as unconnected with me as the dimly remembered Boer War. What made far more impression was my first visit to a ballet; Anna Pavlova had brought a company to Manchester. Someone had told me that ballet could be as moving as great music or great poetry. So far, I had come by little great music, but I did know the strange shiver great poetry sent through me and I went to that ballet in high hopes. Only when the Holy Ghost failed to descend on me at Confirmation had I felt as disappointed. I believe it was a poor company, but I have seen plenty of fine ballets since and, though I have greatly enjoyed the music and the decor, it is really painful to me to see dancers on their points, only little less painful than watching acrobats. I bitterly regret this.

Early in September I did at least notice the war, because

my uncles began to wonder if I ought to postpone my return to the Academy as it would be a waste to take my training at the wrong moment. However, they left the decision to me. I asked how long they thought the war could last and Uncle Eddie said: 'Well, not beyond Christmas because business can't stand it.' So I decided to go back to London as planned.

My uncles were lending the money for my fees and living expenses; apart from the money my stepfather owed me I could count, at twenty-one, on a few hundreds from a paternal great-grandmother's will. They were distressed not to give me their money outright, but they were now in a poor financial position. The department for which Uncle Harold had been a velvet buyer for so many years had not long ago closed down, leaving him to start anew in middle age. He, like his brothers, had become a manufacturers' agent and was barely established. Now all their agencies for German goods were worthless. But they repeatedly assured me there would always be a home for me and, at least, a dress allowance. (Actually, my debt to them was discharged by some seemingly almost worthless shares my father had left—which, years later, sprang up in value.)

I was to stay in London with the mother and sisters of my old Whalley Range schoolfriend, Violet, with whom I had kept in touch. She, after the family migrated to London, had taken a job in Canada but hoped soon to return. Her mother asked one pound a week for my entire board, including sandwiches to take to the Academy. It now seems ludicrous that my uncles and I thought this pretty expensive.

A few days before I was due to leave, Messrs Hepworths wrote to tell Charles Henry Percy they would pay three pounds ten shillings for his screenplay if he would re-type it, with only one scene to a page, cut out some of the sub-titles, and offer them a fresher title than *Maisie Manages Things*. I dashed to Uncle Harold's office for the re-typing and sent the script off with the title, *Schoolgirl Rebels*, which they eventually used. Three pounds ten shillings! Marvellous—and the first money I ever earned.

On my last evening Uncle Harold said he wanted to have a serious talk with me, so I sat on his knee, as so often in childhood. After a vague preamble he said he supposed I knew about certain things. I helpfully assured him that I did, so he contented himself by advising me to have nothing to do with strange hospital nurses. Again those sinister nurses, and the fact that my hardheaded uncle took them seriously, made me wonder if the Argentine really was full of kidnapped girls. His final remark was, 'Well, well, you're like the young chickens—all your troubles ahead of you'.

But there I disagreed with him for it seemed to me that, with my mother's death behind me, no other troubles could be very menacing.

All the family came to see me off at the station and my aunts wept. Then Nan said, '*You're* not crying, you hard-hearted thing,' then added that she was very glad. '*We're* too soft.' You need a bit of hardness to get through life.' But I did feel a little 'soft' as I waved goodbye, not so much for my weeping aunts as for my non-weeping uncles. My aunts' lives were full; it was my uncles who would miss me most. I knew what it had meant to 'the boys' to have me in their home again.

I had lunch on the train, a last treat from Uncle Harold, and then wrote a poem, on the fly leaves of a complete Shakespeare I carried in my handbag—a singularly silly Stratford purchase which could only be read with a magnifying glass. The gist of the poem was that 'if love could last' I would willingly give up my pursuit of 'a phantom fame.' I then told myself coldly it was pointless to worry about love lasting when it hadn't even started. What I really meant was that I hoped it soon would.

I spent the rest of the journey gloating about my return to London. I had planned to arrive on a golden afternoon and drive in a taxi to Piccadilly and then all round the West End, looking at theatres and listening to the whirr of the traffic, which I found so romantic. Unfortunately Violet's mother, when she met me, assured me it was not practicable to go from St Pancras to Hornsey via Piccadilly and to take a taxi would be extravagant to the point of lunacy. So we went by tram, its whirr was not romantic and, when we reached Hornsey, I felt I was more in the provinces than I had been in Manchester.

I never explored Hornsey fully and have no wish to insult the whole locality, but the part I stayed in was just rows and rows of tiny, respectable, elderly houses. From the first I felt depressed and somehow peculiar; this wasn't my London. Violet's mother and sisters were most kind, but I went on feeling peculiar. I had only to look out of my bedroom onto all the little, autumnal back gardens to fear that life held nothing whatever for me.

The day after I arrived I went to Oxford Street to buy winter clothes, taking my whole quarter's dress allowance: five pounds—I had fixed that figure myself and thought it princely. I had looked forward to this, but it proved a miserable business. Never before had I bought clothes entirely on my own. In the end, I shopped in Selfridge's Bargain Basement and bought an imitation, black pony-skin coat for two pounds five shillings; a black velvet 'Spanish' sailor hat for five shillings, and another black velvet hat, like a small bandbox with three bows on it, which cost one shilling and eleven pence. (Kind friends at the Academy said this last was so odd that it just might have cost three guineas. No friend was ever kind enough to say a good word for the coat which, when I became a touring actress, was referred to by the company as 'the landlady's coat'.)

A couple of days later I set out to recapture the London I longed for and walked around the West End for hours. But I unwisely chose a Sunday and, with all shops and theatres closed, found myself depressed. And then, even more unwisely, I took a bus to Barnes and walked past all the little shops I had known so well, the circulating library from which I got *Sinister Street*, the chemist whose headache powders my mother thought miraculous, until the miracle ceased to work. I could not face walking along Riverview Gardens, but I stood on Hammersmith Bridge and looked back at the drawing-room window. Then I realised I was deliberately harrowing myself, which was exactly what my mother wouldn't have wished. I would never again come back, never do anything to remind me of those years in the flat—except that I must keep in touch with Charlotte (which I did until she died as an old woman).

I got back to Hornsey feeling low—but I was cheerful enough

when I started out for the Academy on a brisk October day. The war news must have been bad because it had actually made some impression on me and I remember telling myself I really ought to be worried about it. But I wasn't. I jumped off my bus and strode along thinking of nothing but the glory that was Gower Street.

All the friends I had made in the spring had now left, but I soon had a new set and, again, they were the wealthiest and best dressed girls. Considering my inexpensive clothes and general insignificance I can only put this down to their kindness of heart. It was bliss to be hanging my Spanish sailor in the attic cloakroom, to be eating Bourbon biscuits in the basement common-room (slightly embarrassed by the curling sandwiches Violet's mother had so kindly sent with me) and to be rehearsing in the Stage Room. I was with Miss Burnett again and we were doing *The Morals of Marcus* in which the heroine was a small, dark girl with a foreign accent. I was the only small, dark girl in the division and I was a whale on foreign accents, so I did not see how I could fail to win one act of the part.

Soon after the term began, a Mrs Hannan, an old friend of my Auntie Blanche (at present fulfilling a life-long ambition to go round the world) wrote asking me to visit her. I had met her several times and knew that her husband had been a playwright and novelist, so I was delighted when she suggested I should join them as a paying guest, all the more so when she told me her husband often got boxes for theatres (though only when plays were on their last legs) and would give me introductions to managers. Her house was in a fairly dreary street of what she called North Kensington and I called Shepherd's Bush, but the locality did feel to me like London, which Hornsey never did. So I arranged to leave Violet's mother; I explained it was all in the interest of my career.

The trouble with the Hannans was that they wanted not a paying guest, but a paying daughter. They wished me to sit by the fire between them, night after night, reading straight through Mr Hannan's forgotten novels. I found them dull, but he was a most intelligent man and very kind. Mrs Hannan could be kind, too, but she continually criticised me and I began to feel I should have to move. But if I showed signs of restiveness a box for some Saturday matinée was arranged and she reminded me of those introductions her husband would give me when I finished my training. So I stayed on, sometimes on friendly terms, sometimes much irritated. One serious drawback was that my attic bedroom was so badly lit by gas that I could not read there. The only pleasant thing I remember about it was a picture of a cat, with a napkin under its chin, remarking 'Waiter, bring me a mouse'.

I was soon faring badly with my parts at the Academy. My rival for an act of the small, dark foreign girl was a tall beauty with red-gold hair named Lewisa, one of my particular friends. She was rich and had no intention of going on the stage but, unlike most such girls, she was a clever actress and, in spite of her unsuitability, won the part in fair fight, leaving me with only a small character part. In Miss Burnett's second play, *Paolo and Francesca*, I was again in competition with the lovely Lewisa, for several parts, all of which she won. This time she insisted on giving up the best one and also persuaded Miss Burnett (whom she knew very well, being a private pupil) to let me play the part, 'Nita', right through the play, an unheard of luxury. I still feel grateful to that generous girl, possibly the only girl I met at the Academy who could have made a great success had she become a professional.

'Nita' was a charming part, both light and dramatic; one of the few parts that I was ever good in. But I did not get through the performance without a contretemps. I had recently become friendly with a girl named Barbara Noel, the daughter of Conrad Noel, the famous Socialist Vicar of Thaxted. She was playing Francesca in Act Two and had invited a family friend, a Naval Commander, to come and see her—I spotted his gold braid soon after the curtain went up. Barbara had charm, but not even a red wig could turn her into a beauty; and although my hair was stiff with pearls I was hardly a riot either. We had a scene in which we discussed the fatal effects of women's beauty, which culminated when I picked up a mirror and, following Miss Burnett's instruction, flung myself into an exaggerated attitude and remarked exultantly: 'We cannot choose, our faces *madden* men.' At this the gallant Commander let out such a hoot of laughter that the entire audience became demoralised.

Still, I did make a success and in the written report I had that term Kenneth Barnes said that, despite previous fears, he had noticed 'a sense of the stage and a sureness of touch which should go far towards opening the door to success, even in these troublous times'—God bless his optimism.

Towards the end of the term I saw a commotion in the entrance hall of the Academy, centred round a weeping girl. She was short and rather pretty, despite a marked resemblance to a Pekinese, two cherries dangled from the brim of a small hat over a markedly snub nose. On hearing she was crying because she had just won a scholarship, I wondered if she was quite right in the head. Nothing told me she was destined to become the best woman friend of my lifetime.

V

The Three Arts Club

During the Christmas holidays, in Manchester, I wrote a second screenplay, Hepworths having written twice to Charles Henry Percy almost beseeching him to send them some more of his work. They didn't like it when they got it, and my script came back soon after I returned to the Academy. (I didn't earn another penny from my writing for sixteen years.)

I had now moved up into the Upper Middle Division and there I met the girl who had wept because she had won a scholarship; her name was Phyllis Morris. (Actually, she did not accept the scholarship as her father was quite happy to pay her fees and the runner-up could not have continued at the Academy without a scholarship.) I think I first became interested in her when I found she wrote poems. She and I thought these resembled the work of Walter de la Mare, but one of her sisters described them as 'too twiggy'. Phyllis had a great sense of humour and a highly belligerent nature; we have now been bickering cheerfully for over half-a-century.

I had some good parts that term, including one act of Mrs Arbuthnot in Oscar Wilde's, *A Woman of No Importance*. Fisher White, an excellent actor, directed this and gave me a valuable criticism of my acting. It was during the dress rehearsal in the Stage Room, after I had been giving my all to a long speech culminating in:

> Leave me the little vineyard of my life; leave me
> the walled-in garden and the well of water; the
> ewe-lamb God sent me, in pity or in wrath. Oh
> leave me that. George, don't take Gerald from me.

Mr White called me to the front of the stage and said, 'Miss Smith, I have been under the impression that you were as utterly devoid of talent as it is possible for a human being to be. I now realise that a tremendous amount is going on inside your head; but nothing, nothing is coming over the footlights. What your acting needs is a little more mmf'. The noise 'mmf' was accompanied by a most expressive thrusting gesture. I knew exactly what he meant, but only very, very rarely did I come by any 'mmf'.

Another memory I have of Fisher White is when I came on as Hortensio in *The Taming of the Shrew*, in a black outfit I had found in the Academy wardrobe, he said: 'Dear Miss Smith, could you go away and come back looking less like *both* the little princes in the Tower?'

Before I was due to go home for Easter my much-loved aunt, Nan got a separation from her husband and came, with her two small children, to live with my uncles. This meant that I could only be given a camp-bed put up in the cistern room. Life had become anything but restful. My aunt, in spite of having a good maid, worked from morning till night and I felt I must insist on helping her. My uncles' housekeeper had been able to cope quite easily single-handed, so I never understood why Nan had to work so hard. And she always loathed housework. For years she had made a success as a traveller for her husband's business (though she couldn't prevent him bankrupting himself). Now the poor dear was back at housework and also felt she and her children would be a burden to my uncles. Fortunately they were now doing better in business and were planning a move into a larger house, further from Manchester, at Ashton-on-Mersey. They assured me that one very pleasant room was to be mine entirely. But though I loved my aunt and was fond of her children, I regretted I should never again be on my own with my uncles.

I had only been home ten days when a telegram came from Kenneth Barnes offering me thirty shillings a week for a three weeks' engagement, as general understudy and stage manager of a company of Academy students who were to present Pinero's sketch, *Playgoers*, at some suburban music halls. This venture had begun as an entertainment for Army camps and some agent had (misguidedly, one feels) booked it professionally. I telegraphed acceptance, received a script the next morning, and was then escorted to the station by an almost cheering family.

There were six women and two men in *Playgoers* and, as I was to be general understudy, I decided to learn the entire play—and pretty well knew it by the time I reached London. It was fortunate I learned the men's parts as well as the women's because, though Austin Trevor understudied the leading man, I had to understudy Austin, the idea being that I could play his part as a little boy. The sketch was about a well-to-do young couple who decided to take their cook, parlour-maid, house-maid, useful-maid, kitchen-maid and odd-job man to the theatre, with supposed-to-be amusing results.

Phyllis Morris was in the cast and, after the first rehearsal, I went to tea with her at the Three Arts Club, where she was staying. I sat in the lounge eating watercress sandwiches feeling this was my spiritual home, but Mrs Hannan was being particularly impressive about her husband's influence with London managers so I did not dare to leave her.

We opened at the old Euston Music Hall, said to be a tough house and *Playgoers* was anything but a tough play. As I stood in the prompt corner, seldom prompting quite loud enough, I heard a sort of rustling noise in the auditorium. The resident stage-manager said to me, 'That's the bird, dear, and if it gets much worse I'll have to bring the curtain down'. Fortunately, Phyllis was about to burst into loud comedy tears and the audience found these funny. And as she had several more such outbursts we just got through. After that, we built up her part but, all week, we were on the edge of disaster. And on Saturday night, when one of the cast had to remark, 'Strikes me we're in for a precious dull evening', there was a loud shout from the gallery: 'So are we.'

It was at that performance that the stage manager went to separate two fighting stage hands just before our sketch was due to end. I gazed frantically at his complicated switchboard. How did one get the curtain down? He returned only just in time to stop me bringing down the Fire Curtain.

After our opening night at Euston, I had found a supper of cold chicken waiting for me in my attic. I had lit myself through the sleeping house by a candle that was left out for me, so I did not light the wretched fish-tail of gas, but ate my elegant supper by candlelight, telling myself I was not yet nineteen and was already earning my living on the stage. When I told Phyllis about my chicken supper we decided we would one day share a flat and a French maid, named Celeste, who would supply exquisite suppers when we returned from playing important parts in the West End. For many years we talked about Celeste, whenever we were particularly hungry, imagining the meals she would supply. She was a *princesse lointaine* of maids, never to materialise. And never again was there any supper awaiting me in my attic. Later I was told this was because I hadn't expressed thanks for the first one. I fear I simply accepted it as being in place of the dinner I was usually given.

Our second week of *Playgoers* was at Tottenham and at the first performance Phyllis discovered she had come down to the stage without her lucky ivory pig. She kept the curtain down while she went up four flights of stairs to get it. The house waited and much of the stage manager's language was quite new to me. The pig presumably went off duty a couple of days later when Phyllis had such a bad female pain she felt incapable of playing. I visited her in her bedroom at the Three Arts Club to be given helpful hints as to how I should play her part. She didn't seem particularly ill to me but by then, she told me, she had bullied a doctor into giving her morphia. She never did take kindly to pain and, if morphia was not available, would often call on God to release her from life. I got used to this over the years.

While putting on my make-up that night I told myself that reference books of the future would state, 'Dodie Smith made her first appearance at Tottenham Palace' (which owing to that dogged researcher, John Parker, *Who's Who in the Theatre* eventually did). My role, that of the Useful Maid, was hardly glamorous as I had to have a dead white face and my front teeth blacked-out. The audience didn't find me as funny as Phyllis but they weren't such a noisy audience as at Euston;

just sepulchral. Phyllis was back next day but during our third week, at Chelsea Palace, two other girls were too ill to play, fortunately on different nights. I got through quite well, even though we had rowdy audiences. I evolved a theory that to quell rowdiness you must make more noise than the audience. There is an opposite school of thought that believes you should drop your voice to make an audience listen. That wouldn't have worked with Chelsea Palace audiences. As things were, I may not have amused them much, but I did seem to stun them a little.

After Chelsea, *Playgoers* ended. (Why it ever started—and got star billing—I never could understand.) The Academy re-opened and I achieved the grandeur of being in the Final Division. And in June, I at last moved to the Three Arts Club. (The three arts were Music, Drama, Painting.) I felt a little guilty about this because, though Mrs Hannan had often been very unpleasant, she had sometimes been kind; also I had come to realise that my pound a week was of importance to her. Then, on my last morning, she reminded me that it was the anniversary of my mother's death and said that any change I made today would be unlucky. I thought this so unkind that I stopped feeling conscience-stricken. I needed no reminder of my mother's death. I had been thinking of her ever since I woke up; and I went on thinking of her on my way to the Three Arts Club, feeling she would have liked it as much as I expected to.

It was an impressive, five-storey corner-house in Marylebone Road, opposite Madame Tussauds, with a fine lounge over-looking a high, walled garden with tall plane trees. There was also a Members Only Room, known as the Green Room; a basement dining-room and about eighty bedrooms and cubicles. I could only afford a cubicle—even that was seventeen shillings and sixpence a week, with breakfast—but it had a large window with a plane tree brushing against it, and from the first I liked it better than any room I had ever had. There was good weathered-oak furniture from Heal's (not that I had then heard of Heal's) and an air of modernity that would have pleased my mother. The cubicle partitions started a foot above the floor (so that shoes were apt to wander into neighbouring cubicles) and ended several feet from the ceiling. One could hear every sound made by occupants of even distant cubicles; yet there seemed to me to be a pleasant feeling of privacy. Perhaps this was because I was on my own at last, instead of being a paying guest.

Phyllis was now living at her Brighton home, coming up to the Academy every day, so there was no one I knew at the Club; and as she had warned me that members were stand-offish, I rather feared they would be like the girls of St Paul's School, but older and fiercer. So I was surprised to be received with friendliness. When I got back from the Academy, that first day, I found a laundry list in my cubicle with such high prices that I felt I must do my own washing. It had always been done for me (recently by Mrs Hannan's foundling maid, said to adore her, but frequently in tears), but no doubt I could soon learn. So I armed myself with a small piece of scented soap and went down to the laundry, in the basement.

I had barely got started when a pleasant-looking girl came in and, as there was only one washing place, said she would wait until I finished. But after watching me for a few minutes she said it would be quicker if she did my washing, and I was more than willing. Eventually she rolled my things and her own in a towel, said she would iron them later, and took me up to have tea in her room; her name was Nina.

She shared her room with a large, Irish girl, known as Owl; and their friend, whom I met that day, was called Pixie Shackleton. Name and all, Pixie was a schoolgirl's dream of a heroine. She had flaming red hair, a pink complexion, small but strong features and piercing blue eyes. She would have been pretty had not thick red eyebrows met over her nose. She was small, slim and took size one in shoes and, as she could rarely get these, her too-large shoes were always falling off. She was studying music, played the piano well, had a beautiful contralto speaking voice, and a laugh that might have been the guffaw of a guardsman.

Pixie and I struck up the kind of romantic friendship which had never before come my way. With Phyllis I perpetually bickered, argued, competed. With Pixie I held soulful conversations on the Club roof, watching the sun set over Baker Street Station (where Chiltern Court had not yet risen) and wondering what life had in store for us. We saw ourselves as highly temperamental women, liable to be involved in stormy love affairs.

The roof was my favourite part of the Club. It was large and flat, with a wrought-iron balustrade, and several stone gables on which it was possible to sit or even lie back, looking up at the sky. Some washing was generally to be seen, flapping in the breeze and here and there long-suffering residents of the fourth floor had chalked notices saying: 'Don't practice tap-dancing here. Follow the arrow.' But if you followed the arrow you would find a message from someone else saying: 'Go away'. And if you wanted to practice dancing, you took not the slightest notice of either message.

The fourth floor had an atmosphere of its own, being less changed from its original state than other parts of the house. There were no cubicles, only attic bedrooms. The Club ghost was said to haunt the fourth floor exclusively, with its headquarters in the large attic shared by Nina and Owl. I was told that anyone playing the piano there was liable to see streams of blood running down the music. I played hard and hopefully but had no luck. The fourth floor bath was unlike any other in the Club, being an enormous old porcelain one, very slippery. To get into any of the hot-water bathrooms one had to put tuppence in the slot on the door. So often the water was not hot that we all felt entitled to a free bath if we could get one. Doors would be propped open by chairs and if some wandering housekeeper protested, she was liable to be told, 'That bathroom owes six people tuppence.'

One sight common to all landings was that of the nightly queue of kettles waiting on the floor to be moved up onto the gas-ring. Sometimes there would be a yell from a kettle-remover that the gas was expiring and she certainly wasn't going to put a penny in the slot. It was bitter to be the owner of the next kettle. One was not supposed to do any serious cooking, but I once saw a cabbage cheerfully boiling on a landing.

I gradually got to know many other Club members, but I

spent most of my evenings with my first friends. We were definitely in the lower ranks of members. In the dining-room we sat at a table by the door known as 'The Odds and Ends Table'. By the fireplace was 'The Music Table', known to everyone who did not sit there as 'The Museum'. In the window was the glamorous 'Star Table' where the actresses sat and repelled newcomers. The art students occupied a table in the middle of the room—most of them were mature ladies who seemed likely to remain students for the rest of their lives. There were a few successful exponents of each of the three arts the Club served; but on the whole we were an impecunious lot. I was extremely happy.

Things were going well at the Academy, too, for owing to the illness of another girl I had come by the second act of Nora, in *A Doll's House.* Austin Trevor and I spent all our spare time rehearsing the famous flesh-coloured stockings scene, in passages and on staircases if we couldn't get a class room. Dear Austin at eighteen was a remarkable Doctor Rank, just about dropping to pieces with decay. I decided I must make a dress to play Nora in and, without any pattern or any knowledge of dress-making, cut wildly into five yards of pale grey Crystalline, costing a shilling a yard. Pixie helped with the sewing and we relied much on safety-pins. The dress, trimmed with grey swansdown, was really quite pretty. I wore it with a sort of Elizabethan ruff of white tulle; I favoured ruffs, believing that they framed the face.

The weekend before I was due to play Nora I went to Thaxted with Barbara Noel for the Church Festival her father held every summer. I remember that we changed from the main-line train on to a little local toy-railway and then walked across fields, climbing several stiles. It was my first visit to that unspoilt part of Essex and it seemed to me that never before had I seen so much sky. I was enchanted by Thaxted, with its great church towering above ancient houses, its windmill and the lovely vicarage garden. The vicarage itself was a trifle bare; Barbara said her father had recently taken most of the carpets and some of the furniture to the church. He was a very original and likeable man, with a great sense of humour. I learned that he had offended some of the village mothers by referring to their perambulators as 'spawn carts'. On the day of the festival he preached an unusual sermon, much of it about the holiness of dancing.

Folk-dancing and music played a large part in the Festival—Gustav Holst was there, I remember. And so was the Commander who had laughed when, in *Paolo and Francesca* I had referred to my maddening beauty. And there was a lady who walked about carrying one lily. But best of all I remember the village girls, in the evening, singing the White Paternoster on the vicarage lawn and then dwindling into the summer twilight waving white handkerchiefs.

The whole weekend gave me so much pleasure I longed to write about it and once tried, and failed, to build a play around it. Not until fifty years later did I at last make use of it in my novel, *The Town in Bloom*, greatly changed but, for me, finally discharging a debt.

The only slight cloud over that Thaxted weekend was my knowledge that the performance of *A Doll's House* was only a few days distant. I remember saying to Barbara, 'You see, to play Nora is such a tremendous responsibility'. She fully agreed.

However, all went well at the dress rehearsal. Miss Burnett approved of my dress and said my performance had 'thrilled her'—unheard of praise, coming from her. And old Alfred Bishop, who had once said I ought to be allowed to go on the stage only if prepared to starve, had promised me to come. He was an actor, not a manager, but my prestige was increased.

On the great day the first act went well though Phyllis, as Nora, was only considered reasonably good. The second act started; I was more excited than nervous and began very well. And then I saw that the chair I had to sit on for the 'flesh-coloured stockings' scene was not there. I didn't need it at once, but I had to think out what I was going to do without it.

Should I carry one from the back of the stage? Should I sit in one placed well down-stage and thus be in a hopeless position for the scene? While I thought this out I went on saying my lines, but mechanically, not living my part at all. I knew this—but I could not stop worrying about that missing chair. And when the moment came I lacked the courage to carry a chair from the back of the stage, and meekly sat in the down-stage chair, presenting to the audience only one ear and part of a profile. It was an impossible position and made things hard for Austin, too, as he could not now avert his face from me for certain changes of expression. As for my changes of expression, they could only be done with the back of my head. And half-way through the scene my face-framing ruff got loose from its moorings and hung down my back like a fat white caterpillar. Our daring flesh-coloured stockings scene went for nothing, and I was so unnerved that when I at last got out of that wretched chair and danced the Tarantella, I seemed to crash into every piece of furniture on the crowded stage. When, at the end of the act, Cyril Raymond as Helmar arrived and demanded: 'Where's my squirrel?' it was a totally despairing squirrel who hurled herself at him.

The curtain fell to very mild applause. Miss Burnett, coming out of the prompt corner, said, 'Whatever happened to you, dear? You were so good at the dress rehearsal.' Coldly—for it was she who was responsible for the setting of the stage—I explained about the missing chair. She said briskly, 'Let that be a lesson to you. Always make sure any chair you need is in position'. A truly outrageous remark which I resent to this day.

The third act Nora did little better than I did. Over a quarter-of-a-century later I met her in Hollywood (she had for many years been married to that famous Dr Watson, Nigel Bruce) and we recalled our failures as vividly as if they had been made in front of all the crowned heads of Europe. She reminded me that only Phyllis had won—a little—praise from old Alfred Bishop. Well, Phyllis was certainly more like a squirrel than we were, though even more like a Pekinese.

Soon after my debacle in Ibsen, I was wandering with a fellow student through some back streets near Tottenham Court Road one late afternoon when I saw my film-play, *Schoolgirl Rebels* advertised outside a dingy little cinema. The box-office girl said it had just started so we went in.

The film was about some schoolgirls who, to punish an unpopular mistress, posed as ignoramuses when questioned by

an Inspector. The ringleader later found she had misjudged
the mistress, visited the Inspector and put things right, just
in time to save the mistress from dismissal. Hepworths had
cast the film—as I had modestly suggested—with three of their
stars: Chrissie White, Violet Hopson and Stewart Rome, and
stuck to the story closely. But some of the comedy had been
much exaggerated and, each time this happened, I was furious
and longed to explain to the audience. At the end there was
a surprising amount of applause which, instead of pleasing me,
embarrassed me horribly. I rushed from the cinema, closely followed by my companion, who had hoped to see the show
through for her money. She told me my face was bright scarlet.

A Doll's House had been a half-term performance and, once
it was over, I became obsessed with the knowledge that my time
at the Academy was nearly up. How was I to get work? One
or two students had got jobs—notably Eva le Gallienne—but
most of us did not even know how to look for jobs. Kenneth
Barnes seldom had the chance to place students and, when he
did, naturally chose the most brilliant ones and I certainly
didn't rank as one of those. However, he gave me helpful advice
on how to write to managers.

I wrote letter after letter without getting one interview, often
without getting an answer. (I was always to remain grateful to
the American playwright, Walter Hackett, who in the midst
of rehearsals for his first play in London, found time to send
me a handwritten, regretful postcard.) To add to my depression,
Phyllis got herself a job. She wrote to Henry Ainley, then playing in *Quinney's,* and asked him to help her get into the company that was about to tour the play. Ainley replied that it was
nothing to do with him and she must apply to the management.
So she turned up at the theatre during an audition and said she
had been sent by Mr Ainley. This got her respectful treatment,
but the only job available was to understudy two important
parts, one of them elderly, and she was told she wasn't old
enough. On my advice, she made herself up as an elderly
woman and went down again. The management succumbed—
and Mr Ainley, when she wrote and confessed she had made use
of his name, wished her luck. She was to get the stupendous

salary of four pounds a week! And she always had an allowance
of three pounds a week from her father. How I envied that
allowance.

One morning when I had no classes my first Club friend,
Nina, said she would take me to see some musical comedy
agents. She was hoping to become a concert singer, but needed
work badly and thought she might take a job in a chorus. I
didn't fancy the chorus, but thought I might get a part and,
though I had never had a singing lesson, was more than willing
to sing *Down Vauxall Way* to anyone who cared to listen. So
we trailed round the West End clutching rolls of music. I hadn't
known about agents and it made me feel like a professional
just to wait in their offices, even if one didn't get seen. And
the offices were interesting, many of them in odd little back
streets, in ancient houses, their atmosphere that of a fast-
vanishing London. At one old house near Covent Garden we
went up a graceful staircase, past long-empty niches, until we
reached an agent who heard us sing and, then and there, offered
both of us chorus jobs at thirty shillings a week. We were so
excited at being offered anything that we accepted.

But almost instantly we changed our minds. To tour in a
chorus would be a dreadful waste of my Academy training, and
Nina had visualised a West End chorus. So we sent the Owl
down to explain and offer herself in our place, though without
any luck. Owl was rather on the heavy side for a chorus lady.
And on my next free morning, Nina and I went to an agency
near Leicester Square, run by a Captain Lestocq who looked
very dashing in his uniform. He said he would send us cards
for auditions, Nina's for musical comedy, mine for a straight
play. My card came only a few days later and instructed me to
bring a song. Surely, in a straight play, I shouldn't have to
sing?

A few minutes after I arrived in Captain Lestocq's outer
office, I realised I had been sent what should have been Nina's
call for a musical comedy audition. I managed to get in to see
Captain Lestocq and explain. Should I telephone Nina? He
said it was too late and he would like me to try for the job
myself. The project in hand was to be a revival of *Kitty Grey*,

which was to have a West End cast and play round London suburbs for two months before touring, and the chorus was to be paid the unusually high salary of two pounds a week. I was then introduced to the manager who would be presenting the company. He was N. Carter Slaughter, once famous in melo-drama as Tod Slaughter, particularly for playing Sweeny Todd, the Demon Barber. He asked me what experience I had. I could only mention the Academy which had always made agents groan, but went down well with Mr Slaughter; he said his wife had been there. Later I discovered he thought I meant the Academy of Music.

The audition was held in a nearby rehearsal room and I was much impressed by the assembled chorus ladies, most of whom wore very smart dark suits and spotless white kid gloves. I had recently spent much of my quarter's allowance on two white voile dresses, such as my mother had favoured for summer wear. The one I had on that day would have graced a garden party and so would my large black hat trimmed with forget-me-nots, but neither of them were right for London. I knew this, but don't remember minding.

The accompanist was late and some girls accompanied them-selves. Captain Lestocq asked me if I could do this.

I said, 'Well, I can, but I use actions in my song'. Then remembering what serious songs the girls had been singing, I added, 'But perhaps you don't like actions'.

Mr Slaughter said he would welcome a few actions and I had better wait till I could be accompanied.

I returned to my place. The girl next to me said, 'Beginner, aren't you? Only beginners use actions.'

As soon as the accompanist arrived I was called. This time I had provided myself with a new song, 'Cinderella, the Kitchen Maid'. The accompanist, used to playing *Until* for contraltos and various songs about roses for sopranos, started off at too slow a speed which was so catastrophic we had to stop and start again. We got on better then, but in the second verse the music fell off the piano. By the time it was retrieved I had forgotten the words, but managed to make up something resembling them. Then, as I reached almost the end of the second chorus, I realised that I had not used one action! The last lines were something like:

> Then, you see, as she fled from the Palace door,
> Well, she somehow became once more—
> Cinderella, the Kitchen Maid.

I stretched my arms downwards as far as they would go, put one hand on top of the other, palms downwards, and looked down with an expression of extreme modesty, ended the song on a high note not indicated by the composer, and made a demure curtsey. All this was intended to be whimsically charming, but it was greeted with a roar of laughter from the assembled company. Captain Lestocq and Mr Slaughter were still laughing so hard when I went over to them that they seemed incapable of speech.

'Wasn't that awful?' I said, feeling it best to be cheerful.

Captain Lestocq said not at all, it had been very nice; and Mr Slaughter said he was going to give me not the chorus, but a nice little part. I would only be paid two pounds a week, like the chorus, but this would be increased if I made a success. A contract would be sent to me. I have no idea how I expressed my pleasure at this surprising news, but everything I said seemed to convulse these two men. I can only imagine I was a blessed change after the stately chorus ladies. The one who had called me a beginner gave me anything but a loving look when I went to pick up my handbag.

'They gave me a part', I said airily, as I turned to go. At the door, I looked back and waved gaily to Mr Slaughter and Captain Lestocq. They seemed to think this was nice of me.

Rehearsals were due to begin very soon and I was anxious in case Kenneth Barnes refused to let me leave the Academy before the end of the term. But he gave me his astonished blessing. His astonishment was natural, seeing that most of his star pupils had not yet sighted work (some of them never did sight it). It was a bright moment for an ugly duckling who did not yet know how good she was at talking herself into a job, and then acting herself out of it.

From then òn my memories of the Academy are vague. I recall no farewells to the building, fellow students or teachers—though I do remember that one of the nicest teachers, Norman Page, insisted on vetting my contract. My friends at the Club also fade out of my mental picture. Now I see myself in a rehearsal room near Oxford Circus. A greyish light filters through a dirty glass roof, foxed Victorian pier-glasses reflect me most unflatteringly. The principals are dowdily dressed and friendly, the chorus smartly dressed and unfriendly. And over everything broods a most unglamorous atmosphere. I feel lost and ill at ease. The Stage, it seems, is not going to be quite what I expected.

VI

'Kitty Grey'

I never again encountered the musty atmosphere that hung over rehearsals for Messrs Bransgrove and Slaughter's revival of *Kitty Grey*, so perhaps it emanated from the piece itself. Although the musical version had been produced as late as 1901, it derived from an earlier straight play which derived from an even earlier French play. And now, in 1915, it suggested an elderly lady skittishly telling naughty stories. It was about a puritanical wife who is shown how to hold her husband by the kind-hearted actress to whom he has turned for amusement. Daisy le Hay played the actress; Ethel Newman, a white-haired spinsterly lady who could look extremely pretty in a blonde wig, played the wife; Leonard Mackay, was the husband; and there was a comedian named Wyn Weaver, victim of a famous Tree story. Mr Weaver was alleged to have approached the celebrated actor-manager remarking, 'Sir Herbert, my name is Wyn Weaver'. To which Tree, with a glassy stare, replied, 'Why?'

Two of the nicest members of the cast were Sebastian Smith and his wife, Lindsey Grey; he played the rakish King Ernest, who rioted among the bathing belles of Biarritz, and she was Kitty Grey's dresser. Finding we shared a surname, they frequently referred to me as their daughter.

I was cast as Sadie, a dashing American, extremely modern (circa 1901). I sang, in a quartet, that I made little bets, smoked cigarettes, and rode a motor car; and I strode round shaking strong men's hands so hard that they winced. As I was only just over five feet tall and had such particularly small hands, I hardly made this convincing.

From the beginning I realised I was entirely miscast, but I

might perhaps have made a better showing as the hearty Sadie
had not Mr Slaughter and his kind wife been determined to
keep me 'soft and young', as they phrased it. Except for one
entrance in a riding habit, I must always wear white. During
our first week of rehearsals I was invited to Mr Slaughter's
office to see about clothes and arrived expecting to meet some
well-known dress designer. Instead I was ushered into a dim
room where rows and rows of dilapidated dresses hung on racks.
Mr Slaughter proudly told me he had recently bought up the
entire wardrobe from the Duke of York's Theatre.

'Here's just the very thing for you', he said. 'One of Miss
Vanbrugh's dresses.' He handed me a wilted mass of white
satin and lace.

Honoured as I have always felt to have made my first appearance (I didn't feel the Useful Maid at Tottenham Palace counted) in a dress of Irene Vanbrugh's, I cannot feel that it was
heaven-sent for me. To begin with it must have been nearly a foot
too long, Miss Vanbrugh being tall and the dress dating from
a period when hems touched the ground (they had now saucily
climbed up to the ankle). And shortening ruined its proportions.
There was a high, boned neck and an elaborately draped bodice.
It had undoubtedly been a lovely dress in its heyday, but that
heyday had been long, long ago.

I needed a second dress but there was nothing else white, so
Mr Slaughter said the wardrobe mistress could 'run me up
something'. (She did; it was trimmed with rosebuds.) He then
led me into another room where there were rows of shoes looking as if they had been vacated by very tired feet. I was relieved
to think that none of them were liable to fit me, and told Mr
Slaughter that I took a size two.

'There's a nice size four here,' he said, handing me some
once-white doeskins which had a trellis of straps across the
insteps. 'If they're too large, just shove some paper in the toes.'

He then found a pair of black riding boots which were inches
too long, but also agonisingly narrow. I plucked up courage
to ask if I couldn't have some *new* footwear, but he looked
quite shattered and advised me to take what he suggested
before he let the chorus loose on the wardrobe. I realised that

the musical comedy world was not the exquisitely dressed world I had expected.

At least my riding habit was to be new, pale grey cloth and, at the first fitting, rather promising; I fancied myself in those breeches. But with it I had to wear a hard, black bowler hat. I protested that, at Biarritz, I should wear a soft felt, white or pale grey. I was told that unless I wore a hard bowler the audience wouldn't know I was in riding kit. That bowler was unlike any other I ever saw; it had an enormous crown and a very narrow brim. And it was much too large. Only my ears prevented it from descending on to my nose.

I might have protested more about my clothes had I been doing better at rehearsals; nobody bullied me, but even kind Mr Slaughter asked me if I could not be a little more 'dashing'. One day after I had been rather freely criticised I was sitting gloomily on a table watching the chorus march round in one of their numbers. They had always been so frigid to me that I was surprised to see one girl give me a dazzling smile every time she passed. I hastened to smile back and, when there was a pause in the rehearsal, she came and sat beside me and set herself to cheer me up.

She was a tall, handsome girl with a resemblance to Gracie Fields, though with stronger features and darker hair. She was elegantly dressed and overflowing with high spirits. We became friends at once and she invited me to share theatrical rooms with her and her sister (also in the chorus) when the show opened at Croydon. She was always called Gwendo.

I found it hard to understand why such a glamorous creature was in a touring chorus, but I was to learn that her elegant clothes were usually made by herself and freely secured by safety pins; that she had scarcely enough money to last through rehearsals and that her high spirits had to stand up to ill-health —she was frequently smitten with appendicitis pains. She had an unusual background, being the daughter of an English soldier of high rank and a Gaiety actress who eventually made a second marriage, to a Frenchman, and brought up her three daughters of the first marriage in France. Gwendo not only spoke English with a French accent, but also had a completely

French outlook and always spoke of the English as if they were a race both foreign and incomprehensible to her. Her main objection to them was that they were hypocrites. The men, while appearing kind to the point of fatherliness, were in reality 'just makin' up to you'. (Presumably her habit of dropping all final g's derived from her long-dead father's world.) The women, while posing as pure and easily shocked were, in her phrase, 'All whatlets'. I asked if she thought I was a whatlet, but she seemed fairly convinced I was respectable—'Though even with you one can't be sure. Perhaps all the time you're foolin' me.'

Her own respectability had led to trouble with managers who, encouraged by her high spirits and sometimes outrageous remarks, formed the wrong impression of her and then resented being rebuffed. She said it had been their own faults. 'They shouldn't be so fatherly. In France one knows where one is. The men are always after the same thing, but they're honest about it.'

Life with Gwendo was extremely noisy and wherever we went people stared at us. I once tried to tone her down in a tea-room, on which she said, 'Oh, oh, oh, my little friend Sadie is rebukin' me. That is what I like about you, Sadie, you are so well brought up.' I was always called Sadie in the company.

But even with Gwendo to cheer me up I would almost have welcomed death when the first night was on us; at last I knew what it was to feel really nervous. I shared a dressing room with Mrs Sebastian Smith and, arriving ahead of her, found there was one fairly good mirror and another, much larger, which was cracked and almost covered by an engraved adver-tisement for Bass. The Bass mirror seemed to me unusable, so I imagined Mrs Smith and I would share the other and set out my make-up in front of half of it. But when she arrived she said, 'Oh, you have it all, dear. I always say the girls who have to put on a pretty make-up need the best place', and cheerfully settled herself in front of Bass. Only later did I realise there are rigid orders of precedence in dressing-rooms and that I should have waited and given her, as the far more important actress, first choice.

I went down to the stage long before I was called and stood

listening. It was Bank Holiday and there was a large and quite appreciative audience. After a few moments there was a roar of laughter and I remember how odd this sounded to me, as if someone had turned on a laughter machine, not like individual people laughing. The longer I listened the more impossible it seemed that I could ever mount the steps to the rostrum and make my entrance. I wondered what would happen if I slipped out and disappeared into darkest London. Then I began to torture myself with the idea that, as soon as I got on the stage, I should start using bad language including several words I believed to be obscene, though I'd no idea what they meant. Suppose I shouted them? During those few minutes I worked myself into a state of nerves that did me lasting harm, for I never again stood waiting for a first entrance without experiencing, if to a lesser extent, something of the same feelings. That night, too, I formed the habit of touching wood, usually the frame of some piece of scenery, and had to go on touching it until I heard my cue.

I had a singularly difficult first entrance in *Kitty Grey* for I was supposed to give a ringing laugh off-stage, at which someone on-stage had to say, 'Here's Sadie!' To laugh loudly at absolutely nothing is extremely difficult but, when my cue came, I gave one last, violent swallow, then threw my head back and did my very best. Nobody said, 'Here's Sadie!' While the stage waited, the stage manager dashed from the prompt corner and said, 'Louder, dear—they haven't heard you.' *Could* I laugh louder? I achieved a noise that would have done credit to the Demon King in pantomime and at last heard the blessed words, 'Here's Sadie!' Then, urged by the stage manager, I mounted to the rostrum and stepped into sight of the audience.

Everyone on stage turned to work up my entrance. I stood there and delivered my first line: 'What, you three together and no fighting? Gee, I *am* surprised!' I had been told this would get a laugh and I must wait for it. I waited. The audience didn't think the line any funnier than I did, so it was in dead silence that I descended the few steps to the stage; that is, dead silence except for a curious popping noise. All the press-hooks with which the breeches of my riding habit fastened below the knee popped open, one after the other, leaving the breeches flapping above the tops of those agonising boots.

During this scene my hat came down to the bridge of my nose, my stock flapped up and stuck out under my chin like a white goatee beard and revealed a large triangle of pink flesh, and I twice tripped over my enormous riding crop. (Gwendo said it was the size used by the Cavalry.) I was thankful to get off-stage and do a quick change into the wardrobe mistress's white *chef-d'oeuvre* trimmed with rosebuds.

Mercifully I did not appear in Act II and my only catastrophe in Act III was when I caught my heel in the lace of Miss Vanbrugh's dress while dancing in the quartet. Quick action by Leonard Mackay just prevented me from falling. I remember nothing about the second house—we were playing twice nightly—but at the end of the evening there was a general feeling of success. Mr. Slaughter came into the dressing-room and embraced Mrs Smith warmly (her comic duet with Wyn Weaver had, as they say, stopped the show.) He kissed my hand and said I had been 'very sweet'.

Mention of Leonard Mackay, a particularly nice man, reminds me that he gave me some advice which I was never to forget. At our Croydon dress rehearsal he led me to the front of the stage, pointed up to the Gallery, and said: 'On our first night there will be a little boy up there who has been saving up for weeks to come and see us. He will be in the very back row— and if he doesn't hear every word you say, he will be bitterly disappointed. Never, never forget the little boy in the back row of the Gallery.' I never have forgotten him and though, as an actress, I may have erred against him I never did when, so many years later, I become a playwright. Again and again during rehearsals of my plays I went to the very back of the Gallery to make sure every line was audible, and I never did so without remembering Leonard Mackay's little boy.

I could not enjoy playing the truly appalling part of Sadie; it was badly written and I had trouble with the American accent. (In vain did Ethel Newman advise me, 'Just force it down your nose, dear.') But I greatly enjoyed sharing theatrical digs with Gwendo and her sister, particularly supper after the show, when for the first time I met that staple of my diet during my touring years: Heinz Baked Beans. I was also regaled, by Gwendo, with the doings of the chorus: 'But *what* whatlets, Sadie! You wouldn't believe.' But she was fairly guarded in her conversation and sometimes pulled her sister up: 'That's enough, Vera. You mustn't shock Sadie.' Vera eventually decided to join one of the whatlets and leave Gwendo and me on our own. And Gwendo, encouraged by me, ceased to censor conversation and gradually enlightened me in various useful ways. In this way she was abetted by Mrs Sebastian Smith who once remarked, while we were dressing, that it didn't seem right that anyone so innocent as I was should be orphaned and on the stage. I have always remembered the tactful way she explained the peculiarities of some of our very pleasant chorus boys: 'Well, dear, it's really rather sad. It's just that they mistake themselves for girls.'

During the week we played at Kingston, Gwendo decided a fringe would suit me. The idea came to her while I was still in bed and she instantly approached me with scissors. I protested; very few people were wearing fringes. But she firmly got on with the job, then assured me it was a success and I looked 'very French'. I too liked the fringe and went on wearing one for over thirty years.

The week we were at Walthamstow there was a Zeppelin raid. There must surely have been earlier raids but, presumably, I had been too occupied with my own life to take much notice of them, and was utterly astonished when the call-boy knocked on our door and, instead of calling us for Act III, shouted: 'Zepps! All downstairs, please!' I was dressed, but Mrs Smith was without her skirt; she had on a large hat trimmed with Cockney ostrich feathers, a funny tight bodice and white calico knickers through which she had recently threaded magenta ribbon, 'just for a change'. In our excitement, we couldn't find her skirt and she seemed to prefer the risk of death to going downstairs without it. Fortunately it turned up a few seconds before the dressing-room lights were turned off.

When we got down to the still-lighted passage at the back of the stage we found that the chorus had not been as modest as

Mrs Smith; some of them were near-nude. The stage manager
was vainly urging them to go back for some clothes. Our leading
lady, Daisy le Hay, threw a protective arm round me and drew
me into her dressing-room, closing the door against the lights.
We groped our way to the wide open window, drew back the
curtain, knelt on her theatrical basket and looked upwards.
The Zeppelin now seemed very close indeed; silvered by searchlights it looked quite beautiful.

'It's coming right over the theatre now, dear.' said Miss le
Hay, 'so I must close the window', as if closing the window
would keep the nasty bombs out. I entertained no such illusion
and thought it quite likely that I was going to die. And I
remember thinking: 'And I don't feel at all frightened. How
astonishing!'

The Zepp passed without dropping any bombs on us and
soon we went back to the lighted passage and found that the
chorus had gone back to dress for the third act, which shortly
rang up. Throughout its progress distant bombs could be heard
and, each time one fell, a handful of the audience walked out,
but most people stayed. After the curtain fell, Ethel Newman
indignantly complained to the stage management because her
dressing-room lights had been turned out. She said she hadn't
been able to find her gloves—'And Germans or no Germans, I
do not play the last act without gloves.'

The raid ruined our business for the rest of the week so the
management said we must play an extra matinée, but we should
not get paid extra for it. The chorus asked me if I would lead
them in a protest about this and, rather flattered, I agreed. So
the previous evening we approached the stage manager and only
when I had been arguing with him for some time did I realise
every member of the chorus except Gwendo had deserted me.

'Never expect anyone on the stage to back you up about anything,' said the stage manager, and then broke it to me that as
Miss Newman had refused to play the matinée I, as her understudy, would have to go on for her. The part was enormous but I was rather good in it—I knew this from Gwendo,
who had watched me rehearse; I could believe her because she
had never made any bones about telling me how awful I was

in my own part. For the matinée I was told to use Miss Newman's dressing-room and wear her clothes. The dresser was
just handing me some elaborately frilled pink knickers, necessary for a dance done in a very short skirt, when Miss Newman
arrived in a blazing temper and told me to use my own underwear. As I had never yet risen to anything more dashing than
black silk knickers with elastic at the knees, I was prepared to
fight for the pink frills, but before we got to the struggling
stage the stage manager arrived to say that, as there were only
seven people in the house, they were being given their money
back and there would be no performance. Miss Newman
eventually forgave me. (And soon after that I took to making
very fancy underwear.)

The next week we were to play Woolwich and Gwendo said
the Arsenal would be an ideal target for Zeppelins and she
wasn't going to sleep anywhere near it. We must get rooms
in London; both of us favoured the Baker Street district. We
hunted all Sunday and only late in the evening did we find some
we could afford, in Marylebone Road. The landlady said they
belonged to a regular lodger who was on holiday and had given
her permission to let them. We could stay on for three weeks,
after which our provincial tour would start. The rooms were
furnished with antiques and the sitting-room walls were covered,
right up to the ceiling, with rows and rows of old engraved
portraits, Tudor and Jacobean. I must have spent hours staring
at them. And I wondered if the rightful owner of these most
unusual rooms would be any too pleased they were now the
refuge of two struggling actresses.

By our first Thursday we were pretty well penniless actresses,
for fares to Woolwich and meals in restaurants (the landlady
would only supply breakfast) had used up almost all our money.
Indeed, we had so little to eat that day that Gwendo fainted in
the dressing-room that night. No doubt I could have borrowed
from Mrs Smith but I didn't want to; and Gwendo assured me
she could raise enough from the chorus to take us through
Friday. (We should be paid on Friday evening.) But she only
got enough to pay for our next day's fares. We couldn't afford
our usual supper of sandwiches from the coffee stall in Maryle-

bone Road, but Gwendo found a threepenny tin of Heinz Baked
Beans in her suitcase and we dug a penknife into it and speared
beans out one by one. Then, on Friday morning, it occurred
to me that I might raise money on some of the little pieces of
jewellery I had with me.

I went out and asked a policeman to recommend a nice
pawnbroker. He sent me to Messrs Attenborough who were
delighted to give me one pound on a pearl and aquamarine
brooch. They would have given me more, but I saw no point
in accepting it as I only needed to get through the day and
fully intended to redeem the brooch. I then fell for a second-
hand wristwatch which had SADIE on its green suede strap.
It seemed to me dirt cheap at ten shillings, so I bought it.
Gwendo and I could get all the food we needed for the day
on the remaining ten shillings.

During the next two weeks I pawned every bit of jewellery
I had with me, always intending to redeem it because it had
been my mother's. I never did. And Messrs Attenborough
declined to advance me one penny on SADIE, probably because
she wouldn't go. They pointed out they'd never said she would.
I became quite attached to the shop and the assistants started
to laugh as soon as I came in.

The worst part of those weeks was the travelling as air raids
had dislocated suburban trains. I remember being on a Clap-
ham Junction platform at one in the morning and asking myself
if I really liked being on the stage. And I could assure myself
that I did—except for the awful moment before my first
entrance each night. And I was particularly looking forward
to starting the provincial tour.

And then the blow fell. On the first night of our last suburban date, at Brixton, I was alone in the dressing-room, during
Mrs Smith's busy second act, when I was visited by Wyn
Weaver, who was the general manager of the show as well as
the chief comedian. He informed me that the management,
wished to dispense with my services. I was to be given a fortnight's salary and leave at the end of the week, before the tour
started.

During my life I have often found that bad news, for the

first few minutes, can have a stimulating effect; could it be that all one's mental forces rally to hold the news at bay for just a little longer? I remember becoming very gay and heartily agreeing with Mr Weaver's opinion that I had been miscast as the boisterous Sadie. We parted cheerfully; and the minute he went out of the room a load of misery descended on me which was like a physical weight on the solar plexus. I sat there staring at the naked electric bulbs, telling myself again and again that I must acquire a sense of proportion. 'This seems to matter now, but it doesn't really. In a few years you'll look back on it and laugh.' But I went on feeling it was the end of the world.

Next day I went to see Mr Slaughter, who was as kind as always, said he'd liked my performance and hadn't wanted me to be dismissed. But Mr Weaver, who was to be in sole charge of the tour, had insisted. At the theatre that night I found there was considerable indignation, as I was to be replaced by one of the chorus girls who was a friend of Mr Weaver's. She was a gentle, nicely-mannered girl to whom Gwendo had actually given the benefit of the doubt as to being a whatlet, so possibly the aspersions that were being cast were not justified. But she seemed unsuited to the part. Gwendo, who had already seen her rehearse, said she was no better than I was.

'Was she worse?' I asked hopefully.

'Well, not actually *worse*, Sadie darling. I'd say you were both equally bad.'

For the rest of that Brixton week I looked feverishly for work. I heard that there was a little boy's part going in a Lyceum melodrama and there was an audition on Friday. Before going down to it, I counted all the engravings in our sitting-room and told myself if there were over a hundred I should get the part. There were a hundred and one! I visualised arriving at Brixton that night with the news that I had landed a West End engagement. But when I stood on the Lyceum stage a voice from the dark auditorium said: 'You don't look consumptive enough.' I said I could make up to look consumptive, but the voice said: 'We want someone who looks consumptive to start with. Next, please.'

While I was taking my make-up off on Saturday night, I

wondered if I should ever put it on again. Mrs Smith did her best to cheer me up, but she had to admit that it was a bad time to be out of work, with all the autumn tours already started.

Poor Gwendo was miserable at starting off without me; we had planned to have such fun on tour. I sadly said goodbye to her on Sunday morning, then packed my clothes. The rightful owner of the hundred and one engravings was due back that evening and the landlady was already busy shooing out all traces of actresses.

VII

'Mr Wu'

At least I had somewhere to go; the Three Arts Club was only a couple of minutes' walk. I had seldom given it a thought during the past two months though I had once asked Gwendo if she would like to have tea there. She shudderingly refused, appearing to think it was some house for Female Correction.

Now I was thankful to get the cheapest grade of cubicle, at ten shillings a week. It was a gloomy, windowless little box and I felt pretty low as I unpacked there. None of my summertime friends were still at the Club, but I was rather glad about this as I did not want to tell them what had happened to me. Nor did I wish to tell my uncles while I still had some money in hand; nearly a pound of my last week's salary, plus two weeks' salary in lieu of notice, in all, nearly five pounds. Could I, if I cut down on food, make that last a month?

On the Monday morning I set out to visit agents. I had on a black turban hat with an eighteen-inch feather sticking straight up at the front; I believed this gave me height. My thin navy suit had a sort of Eton jacket, cut away to reveal a bright red blouse. It was a grey, chilly October day and depression must have lowered my usually magnificent circulation, for I remember feeling very cold indeed.

I went first to Captain Lestocq who, as agent, was entitled to one week's salary from me. So far, I had only paid him six shillings and he now refused to take any more. He said my performance had not warranted dismissal and, if it had been good enough for two months in London suburbs, it was quite good enough for the provincial tour. But he couldn't help me to get work as the Army was now claiming all his time and he was about to close his agency. He did, however, give me the names of some other agents.

The first of these I went to was a Miss Enid Baird who told me to go at once to another agent, Lee Ephraim, who was in need of a conjurer's assistant. And as I had won Miss Baird's sympathy by telling her how hard-up I was, I felt I must at least investigate this job, little though I fancied it. Mr Ephraim turned out to be not an ordinary theatrical agent, but one who looked after the interests of some well-known music-hall stars. It was one of these, a famous conjurer, who needed an assistant.

I got on well with Mr Ephraim (and was to like him better and better, over a period of many years). He told me the salary would be four pounds a week—double my *Kitty Grey* salary! I began to feel tempted. He then said I would have to wear tights and asked me to tell him, frankly, how my legs were. Someone had told me that agents might ask to see my legs and I was determined to be professional, so I said briskly, 'Would you like to look at them?' He said perhaps he'd better.

I was wearing high, cloth-topped boots so when I raised my pleated skirt to just below my knees all Mr Ephraim got was a glimpse of four inches of shin. He said that was very nice, but with tights, it was above the knees that counted. So I daringly revealed my knees and the elastics of my black silk knickers.

'Look dear,' said Mr Ephraim, embarrassedly, 'you take your legs to a photographer and get them photographed all the way up, and then come back to me.'

I said I would, but the minute I was out of the office I decided I couldn't. Apart from not wanting to assist a conjurer, I could hardly have myself photographed bare-legged, and I'd no idea how to get hold of tights. So I went back and said I didn't really think the work would suit me.

Mr Ephraim shook his head sadly. 'What a pity! You might easily keep that job for ten years. Not much safe work like that to be had.' Knowing how feckless I could be with my hands, I doubted if it would really be safe work for me—or safe for the conjurer.

The next day I went to see an agent named Akermann May, who astonished me by saying he had just the thing for me. He scribbled an introduction. 'Take this to Martin Henry, in Bow Street. By the way, are you wearing very high heels? Most of you girls do.'

I assured him I wasn't.

'Then you may be just a bit too tall for this part. It's a little Chinese girl, in *Mr Wu*.'

I now assured him that my heels *were* high (as indeed they were) and that I had elevators in my boots. He laughed and said, 'Well, if Mr Henry says you're too tall, take your boots off. I'm serious about that, dear. It might just get you the part.'

Martin Henry's flat was near Bow Street Police Station. I rang the bell hopefully but got no reply and, though I went back three times that day and once the next morning, I still couldn't get in. So I returned to Akermann May who told me just to wait outside the flat till Mr Henry arrived. 'Even if it takes you till midnight. He's bound to come home sometime.'

Back I went to Bow Street. Still no answer to the bell so I sat down on the cold stone stairs. As it was only a small block of flats not many people came in and out; if I heard anyone coming I sprang up and rang Mr Henry's bell, so that it would seem I had only just arrived. But if the same person saw me twice I felt I was being looked at suspiciously. By mid-afternoon I was ravenous so I dashed out and got a cup of tea and some buns; the café was close enough for me to keep an eye on the entrance to the flats. Then I settled down on the stairs again. There wasn't much daylight and less as the afternoon drew on. Eventually I went to sleep and Mr Henry, coming up the dark staircase, fell over me.

He took me into his flat, made sure I was free to start the following Monday and then said he thought I might do for the job, especially as I had dark hair and a fringe, and could thus play a Chinese girl without wearing a wig. Then he fell silent and I thought he was looking dubious. I feared he was thinking I was too tall.

I said quickly, 'Would you like me to take my boots off?'

'I should hate it,' said Mr. Henry. I doubt if he. ever knew why I had made the offer.

He then said I could have the part, which was only a few

lines, but I would also have to understudy the part of Mr Wu's daughter, which was a very good part indeed. The salary would be thirty-five shillings a week. Being under the impression Mr Henry was merely someone connected with the company, probably the stage manager, I said, 'Wouldn't the Management make it two pounds?'

'They certainly wouldn't,' said Mr. Henry, who was himself the Management.

I accepted the job and was told to go to Kingston-on-Thames that night, to see the play and introduce myself to Frank Royde who was playing Mr Wu and was in charge of the company. He gave a superb performance, making Mr Wu far more evil than Matheson Lang, who created the part, had done. Indeed, when I went round to Mr Royde's dressing-room I was surprised to find he was a normal, pleasant human being. I happened to mention I was to understudy Nang Ping, Mr Wu's daughter, and he asked me to keep that to myself for the moment, as the present understudy was a very young girl whom he wanted to give the experience of a few rehearsals before breaking it to her that she was much too tall for the part. I met her at next day's rehearsal. She was Evelyn Laye, then aged fifteen.

Other people I particularly noticed at that rehearsal were Haidee Gunn, Frank Royde's wife, who played Mrs Gregory, the part created by Lilian Braithwaite; a Scotswoman, Lola Duncan, who played the faithful Chinese maid, Ah Wong; and Helen Saintsbury—always called Dolly—who most brilliantly played Mr Wu's daughter. At the end of the rehearsal she suggested that Evelyn and I should share rooms with her the following week in Birkenhead. Everyone was friendly. How miraculous that I had landed a new job so quickly!

And then, on the Saturday, I started one of my typical, ghastly colds with sore throat, streaming nose and every bone in my body aching. The Sunday train journey was deadly and when we reached Birkenhead it was already dark and there was a thick fog. Dolly Saintsbury had not booked rooms ahead, so we started out to hunt for them, escorted by Dolly's faithful admirer, Edgar Norfolk, one of the kindest men I ever met and a very good actor. After a few enquiries we realised getting rooms for us three girls together was going to be difficult and Dolly decided she would live alone and we should fix her up first. Eventually we left her planning supper in front of a roaring fire; theatrical landladies whose rooms were still unlet on Sunday were apt to light alluring fires. Evelyn and I went out into the fog again, accompanied by kind Edgar; Dolly said she would lend him to us. Around ten p.m. we found rooms, but no roaring fire and no supper. Edgar had a room booked which, if the worst came to the worst, he would have given up to Evelyn and me—and slept I can't think where.

I was so ill next day that I could barely crawl to the theatre, but I somehow managed to get through my part—I had very little to do except listen sympathetically to Dolly's beautiful performance as the ill-fated Miss Wu. What I remember best is the impression made by Evelyn Laye. She wore a white muslin blouse and a white satin skirt which stuck out over her stomach, and she had on a most unskilful make-up. As the young English girl, she had about eight lines and I cannot say she said them well; she adopted a fruity, contralto voice. But such was her enchanting prettiness that a box of chocolates and a note from an officer arrived for her in the first interval; followed by a second note, from a second officer, in the second interval. Lola Duncan, who was an old friend of Evelyn's family, insisted that the notes should be ignored and wanted the chocolates to be returned, but Evelyn and I said this would be discourteous and bore them home in triumph.

Evelyn was a mother to me all that week giving me breakfast and supper in bed and coercing me to eat vast quantities of onions boiled in milk which, she said, were good for colds. She happened to notice I was reading Dumas' *The Queen's Necklace* and asked what it was about.

I said, 'Marie Antoinette.'

'Really?' said Evelyn. 'Who were they?'

The next week Dolly decreed that Evelyn should live with her, so Lola Duncan and I shared rooms and got on splendidly. We were in Lincoln and the town was completely blacked out. One night I walked home from the theatre on my own—my part was finished long before Lola's—and got temporarily lost in the hilly streets of ancient houses leading up to the great Cathedral. There was no traffic at all and townsfolk, walking in the middle of the street, occasionally glided by me carrying lanterns. I felt I was back in the middle ages.

Eventually Dolly decided I should share rooms with her, and Lola and Evelyn should live together. Why did we always do what Dolly decided? I had preferred living with Lola, but living with Dolly was reasonably pleasant, provided you gave her the best bed, the best armchair and waited on her hand and foot; she had a talent for drawing unselfishness from people. She was small, dark, pretty, wittily amusing and highly talented; but already, at nineteen, she was the victim of a self-destroying egoism. I found that not only on the stage did I spend my time listening sympathetically to Dolly. Her private life had been one long series of woes. Ill-treated as a child, victimised in her career, persecuted by admirers—and now enemies put pins in her grease paint. (There *was* one pin, but I always thought she put it there herself.) She was often shaken by hatred for some member of the company, though I never knew of anyone who did her harm—certainly Evelyn Laye didn't and Dolly hated her almost continuously. Poor Evelyn, the least hateworthy of people. (And as things eventually turned out, poor, poor Dolly.)

I usually shared a dressing-room with Evelyn so we saw plenty of each other. We only had one quarrel, about who was the senior member of the dressing-room. I was 19, had four lines (in Chinese) and was paid thirty-five shillings a week. Evelyn was 15, had eight lines (in English) but only received thirty shillings a week. Eventually we asked the stage manager to arbitrate. He said it was a dead heat. In that case, we asked him, whose name was to come first on the allocation note he pinned to our dressing-room door every week? He undertook to alternate the order and honour was satisfied.

This matter was treated dead seriously and well it might be, for in almost all the companies I was to be in, there was trouble about the order of names on dressing-room doors. And some time later there was a shattering row about it. Lola and Dolly usually dressed together and though Lola was some fifteen years older

than Dolly and a highly experienced actress, there was no
doubt that Dolly's part was the more important so her name
had to come first. On one occasion when we all four had to
dress together, the stage manager accidentally made out the
list on the dressing-room door as follows:

> Miss Duncan
> Miss Saintsbury
> Miss Smith
> Miss Laye

With biting irony Dolly said to Lola, 'You are apparently the
leading lady of this dressing-room this week, so you will wish
to choose your place first,' and then sent the dresser with a
furious message to the stage manager. Before he arrived, Lola
had slipped out and altered the list so that it read:

> Miss Saintsbury
> Miss Smith
> Miss Laye
> *but*
> Miss Duncan

For this, Dolly did not speak to Lola for a month; and the
stage manager was furious that anyone had dared to alter his
list.

Not long after Evelyn and I had our mini-quarrel, the news
was broken to her that her job of understudying Mr Wu's
daughter had been given to me. She was broken hearted and
sobbed on my shoulder, which meant she had to stoop considerably. I remember her saying, 'I do understand, but it's bitter,
bitter. You don't know how it hurts.' I pounded her on the
back and said I thought she ought really to go into musical
comedy, adding kindly, 'With your looks, you might do quite
well.'

Late in the autumn we played Bolton and I managed to
stay with my family, now moved to Ashton-on-Mersey in
Cheshire. I liked the house and the locality, but the bedroom

alleged to be mine was really my cousin Esmé's; she had merely moved into her mother's room for the week. And already there was a gap between me and the family. I loved them all, but for me, now, home was a mixture of theatre dressing-rooms and theatrical lodgings. And I found it difficult to talk about my life. Nan, especially, would have been interested in even the smallest details, but I gave her very few. The public, I think, is always interested in the theatre world and the theatre world instinctively tries to keep to itself. It was a relief when the week was over though neither then, nor ever after, did I leave the family without feeling both sad and faintly guilty.

Soon after that Dolly decided to marry Edgar Norfolk, though she always said *I* decided it. Almost every day, during interminable monologues, she would ask me, 'Shall I marry Edgar?' to which I always answered 'No'—for I felt no one who really wanted to marry would ask such a question. But I was finding it harder and harder to live with her; it wasn't only her selfishness that irritated me, it was also her conceit. One day I happened to mention that many of the most fascinating women in history had red hair. She went straight to a looking glass, examined her black hair carefully and then said: 'I knew it! There *are* red lights in it.' Quite suddenly I was through with Dolly. But I hadn't the heart just to walk out on her (how well I understand men who murder their wives in preference to leaving them) so, instead, the next time she asked: 'Shall I marry Edgar?' I said, 'Yes!' and invented some good reasons. That evening she said to Edgar, with winning naivety, 'Dodie says I'm to marry you. So I shall.' Living with her might be my idea of hell, but it was Edgar's idea of heaven, so I didn't feel guilty towards him at the time.

Free of Dolly, I lived on my own and very pleasant it was, but I felt lonely on Christmas morning. Dolly was with Edgar; Evelyn was with a young admirer, heavily chaperoned by Lola. And my landlady asked me to go out for my meals. So I took a train to London—we were somewhere near—and spent a day and night at the Three Arts Club. There were few people there and at dinner in the evening I found only three members in the dining-room. They were sitting at the august Star Table when I meekly settled at the Odds and Ends Table behind the door. I heard one of them say, 'We must ask that child to join us,' which she instantly did. She was a music member named Joan Vincent, considerably older than I was, and we never became close friends but again and again, during my years at the Club, she was suddenly *there*, doing me some kindness, offering some piece of advice, or seeming almost uncannily aware of some moment of great importance to me.

The next week we played Coventry and, late on the afternoon of New Year's Eve, my landlady's husband burst into my ground floor bedroom already drunk and brandishing a carving knife. He demanded that I should shake hands with him, which I very hastily did. When I mentioned this at the theatre Lola said I must not sleep in that house again and two young men in the company went back with me after the show. To avoid ringing the bell we climbed through my window and they kept guard while I packed. Judging by the noise in the kitchen the whole household was now drunk and no one heard us all escaping. I then saw the New Year in with Evelyn and Lola, in a depressing bedroom with one flaring gas jet. Lola, who had provided whisky-and-water, drank 'To Scotland'. Evelyn drank 'To those we love'. I just drank—and very nasty it was.

Shortly after this Evelyn's father joined her, which left Lola free to share rooms with me. In spite of the fact that she was so much older than I was, I found her a wonderfully good companion with a remarkable sense of humour—which she certainly needed, as she had many worries in her private life and suffered almost continuously with neuritis; not that she ever complained, and I only learned about her worries by tactful questioning.

Our days had a pleasant pattern. We breakfasted late, strolled to the theatre to look for letters, changed our library books at Boots (a town without a Boots was a dead loss), met members of the company for morning coffee at cafés and pottered about until a late lunchtime. Lola paid a daily visit to the local Catholic church (I enjoyed this and lit many candles to St Anthony, reputed to be good at job-finding; I should eventually need his services and, anyway, I liked to see the candles flickering). Often there was a Cathedral to be seen, more often an old market square, and always the interest of new shops. These were particularly fascinating in the older towns for so many of them had been converted from old private houses and thus enshrined layers of the past—eighteenth-century, Jacobean or even Tudor.

Lunch was followed by a nap for Lola. Hardly ever in my whole life have I taken an afternoon nap. Then there was a rather low high-tea—seldom more than an egg—before the theatre, where almost always some devastatingly interesting incident occurred on stage: someone dried up, someone got a laugh in the wrong place, or failed to get one in the right place, Lola stepped backwards into the lily pool—and stepped out again without a flicker of surprise marring her imperturbable Chinese expression, and so on. And in the dressing-room some delightful new feud started, or Dolly described someone's atrocious behaviour to her and what she was going to do about it. But what I enjoyed most was supper after the theatre, with Lola in a really expansive mood.

She was the least catty of women and had a real horror of scandalous gossip, but she did not think that just *telling* things about people, in a sympathetic, understanding way, came into the category of spreading scandal. And I soon discovered the mere mention of some well-known member of the theatre world would cause her to reel off the most intimate details of that person's life. It wasn't advisable to ask her direct questions as she was then liable to say, in a slightly holy voice, 'I don't think I'd like to tell you that, dear, not about one of my closest friends.' The thing to do was to wait until after supper and then, having poked up the fire and put a few cushions to ease Lola's neuritic back, just to toss names into the conversation. Then, with any luck, she would go on talking until two in the morning. She said that I always woke up after midnight and there was certainly plenty to keep me awake; during my stage career I was frequently meeting people for the first time whose lives were an open book to me owing to information received from Lola.

Vividly though I remember theatrical rooms they have, by now, a conglomerate personality for me, and certainly they closely resembled each other. Almost always the sitting-room walls were hung with photographs of the landlady's dead relatives, so enlarged from small photographs that they had the blurred look of spirit photography. On the mantel there would be artificial flowers and china kittens peeping from china boots. There was often a toneless piano with faded silk behind its fretted panels. Plush tablecloths, Nottingham lace curtains and aspidistras were seldom absent—and if they were one felt nervous. Uncluttered, well-aired rooms might indicate a landlady who wasn't used to professionals and would refuse hot suppers at eleven p.m. and be mean with the coals. I became extremely fond of the plushy, stuffy rooms and, to this day, feel they would be good places to write in.

Bedrooms were less appealing, lacking in personality and icy in winter. I suspect the beds were hard as bricks, but I could sleep on anything in those days and only worried about the sheets being clean. Had they not been, we should probably have walked out; dirty sheets were rarely found in theatrical lodgings as landladies lived by recommendations and any such heinous crime would have wrecked their reputations. Most of them were the proud owners of Visitors' Books full of compliments, ranging from the dignified entries made by aristocrats of the touring world, such as:

'H. H. Corrington Crossthwaite desires to express his extreme satisfaction on this (his fourth) visit.'

to the more ebullient:

'Thanks to Ma for good cooking, comfy beds and everything O.K. A home from home. All the best from the Crazy Collinis. Trick cyclists and accordionists. Not forgetting Tommy. What price Ma's jam roll?'

Bathrooms were the worst drawbacks in theatrical rooms. We seldom accepted lodgings that had no bath but, having got one, we were apt to be squeamish about using it. So often layers of paint were peeling off and the brass taps were covered with verdigris. And bathrooms were liable to be full of old clothes, bits of broken furniture, and large mysterious bundles that didn't look quite dead. One shuddered at all this by the light of morning; but sometimes at night, by the flickering light of one candle on a decrepit wicker chair, the sinister surroundings seemed to give an added comfort to the hot water and one achieved a macabre cosiness.

The oddest bath I was ever in was at Hull; it shared a ground floor back-room with the landlady's son's bed and a bicycle. Hot water was achieved by filling the bath with cold water and then lighting a row of gas burners under it. Despite the serious air raids on Hull, the landlady had not put up any curtains at the window so one had to take night-time baths in the dark, except for the eerie blue glow from under the bath. There one sat, thinking about being boiled alive. Actually, the water never got very hot; what did was any part of the bath not covered by water, so one repeatedly burnt one's elbows. To set one further at ease there was no lock on the door and the landlady's son kept clomping about in the hall, admonished by his mother: 'Mind, Bert—the lady's *in*.' One night after a loud knock on the front door, the landlady dashed in to say that the military police had seen a light coming from the bathroom. She managed to turn the gas jets off and tell me to lie low in the bath before they appeared at the door and assured themselves that the room was in pitch darkness.

In that house of lightly-boiled lodgers there was a little maid-of-all-work whom Lola and I pitied. I gathered she worked from six a.m. to midnight for only a few shillings a week. We decided to leave her a really generous tip. The week's bill was higher than I expected and the tip would mean cutting down on my regular weekly savings. Still, when I thought of this poor girl, younger than I was, condemned to a dreary existence, she was more than welcome. She accepted the tip politely, if not exuberantly; then, seeing us off to the station, remarked, 'Eh, miss, how I should hate your life.'

Mention of much-raided Hull has reminded me of one air raid we experienced, which made a lasting impression on me, though not because of the raid itself. A few days earlier Lola had happened to say she had never been in a raid and wondered how she would react. She thought she would find the danger stimulating, as I had at Walthamstow. And we were both sure that Dolly would have hysterics. When the raid occurred—just after the show finished—I saw at once that Lola was badly frightened, though she said nothing about this until afterwards. But there were no hysterics from Dolly; never in all the months I knew her did I see her behave so well. She comforted the terrified dresser, was particularly nice to Lola, made a tour of dressing-rooms to see how everyone was feeling and, finally, during the worst part of the raid, went by herself to the very top of the theatre to see if any gas jets had been left on any-where. It all *could* have been just a performance, but both Lola and I thought that the courage and consideration were genuine.

Most of the time she was as infuriating as ever and rather more so after she married. One evening, at a time when she was being particularly unreasonable with her devoted young husband, she decided to harrow him by fainting on stage soon after the curtain rang up on Act I. I say 'decided' because her faint was so obviously histrionic, as was her piteous wail when carried off into the wings: 'Where am I? Where am I?' But what mattered to me was that I at last got a chance to play her part, though in the most difficult circumstances. The curtain was rung down, the play began again and, as there was no one to play my part, I just had to do without myself and make some tricky cuts. But I managed well, got through the long emotional scenes safely, and achieved a satisfactory scream before falling at the feet of the vengeful Mr Wu, when he makes his first terrifying appearance at the end of the act and discovers his daughter has betrayed his honour with an Englishman.

Frank Royde rewarded me with a laconic 'Well done!' but when he decided to give Dolly a week's rest he did not let me go on playing her part. Instead, he engaged an actress who had played it before and would only need one rehearsal. No doubt this was easier than rehearsing someone in my part and in the three parts I understudied. All the same, I was furious and said I would leave at once. Mr Royde told me that if I left without giving two weeks' notice Mr Henry would 'fight me'. How Mr Henry was going to set about fighting a thirty-five shillings a week actress I didn't know, but it sounded formidable; and, as Mr Royde then told me how much he admired my beautiful performance of my four lines in Chinese, and how he relied on me as an understudy, I gradually calmed down. I don't wonder he relied on me for, as well as understudying Dolly, I understudied Lola as the Chinese maid, and also a coolie; and one day I managed to play two of these parts as well as my own. It meant fantastic quick changes of both costume and make-up (pretty make-up for my part, yellow and elderly for Lola's, brown for the coolie including arms and legs). This was on a Saturday, when we were giving a matinée as well as playing twice nightly, so by the end of that evening I had played nine parts practically non-stop.

After many weeks with Lola I decided I ought to live alone and try to work at writing. This meant I could only afford what landladies called 'a combined'. Such rooms had the usual bedroom furniture, plus an armchair and table for meals and were, as a rule, only patronised by the lower rungs of the profession, or elderly actors and actresses pathetically anxious to save. To me, any loss of prestige was more than compensated for by being able to go to bed by a fire. I could enjoy my supper (Heinz Baked Beans three nights a week, Heinz Spaghetti three nights a week, and on Sunday whatever the landlady had by her, usually an egg) without the dread of a plunge into an ice-cold bedroom hanging over me, and I could go to sleep by firelight. Those combined rooms left me with a life-long devotion to bed-sitting-rooms—which was instantly frustrated when, eventually, I began to make money. Now I come to think of it, never in my well-to-do days have I been able to achieve the luxury of going to sleep by firelight.

I lived extremely cheaply, and even more cheaply when sharing with Lola as we often got a sitting-room and bedroom—sometimes two bedrooms—for as little as ten shillings a week. Combined rooms might go up to six or seven shillings a week. Old touring hands usually did their own catering, but we always left it to the landlady, and even so, our total bills were seldom more than fifteen shillings each. Woe betide the landlady who made a charge for 'use of cruet'. I generally had a whole pound of my salary left and despite the fact that I bought a new suit, a dress, hats, shoes and any amount of junk—such as eight miniature brass candlesticks for my dressing place, and numerous hideous mascots—I saved sixteen pounds on that forty-weeks *Mr Wu* tour.

Salisbury, Canterbury, York, Bath, Exeter, Ely, Peterborough, Chesterfield, Norwich, Nottingham, Newcastle, York, Goole (where *was* Goole?) . . . the names come crowding back to me, so often accompanied by some vivid memory, of sight-seeing, theatres, lodgings, incidents: bargain-hunting in markets, walks in the country, finding some bluebells. Many years later, touring England by car, I often tried to find some of the dozens of theatres I played in, but seldom could. And, if they did still exist, they had been degraded into cinemas.

We went to Ireland and Scotland, too. For the crossing to Ireland, with its dangers of torpedoes, Lola offered every member of the company a St Christopher medal that had been blessed by the Pope (it must have been fiddling work for His Holiness; they were considerably smaller than a threepenny-bit). For the night journey from London to Edinburgh, a compartment was allocated to Lola, Evelyn and me. Lola and I reclined luxuriously with a whole side each. Evelyn Laye, as the junior, was firmly relegated to the floor; Lola kindly lent her a rug.

Sunday train journeys were fairly bearable if one had booked rooms ahead, but if they were still to find, one began to feel very low as the afternoon waned. We always seemed to be taking a whole day, with several changes of trains, to travel a distance any self-respecting crow could have covered in a couple of hours. Again and again we found ourselves waiting on a platform called 'Sandy' and I never could believe there was any place attached to it. After an hour or so there, I used to get a curious living-in-limbo feeling and have sometimes feared that, after death, I may find myself on Sandy platform with no rooms booked for the night.

In the Spring, Martin Henry offered Evelyn a leading part in a touring revue at the princely salary of three pounds a week, which I greatly envied. Shortly before she was due to leave she and I were sharing a large dressing-room with Dolly and Lola and, for once, we were all on good terms with each other. One evening Dolly was making a swansdown-trimmed bed-jacket (she had a passion for swansdown), Evelyn was pretending to be the heroine of a melodrama with a bundle of clothes as a baby, and I was putting on character make-ups—my *chefs-d'oeuvre* were a Vampire, Charles II and a Streetwalker. Lola, who was lying back in the deck-chair she travelled with because of the neuritis in her back, said: 'I've been wondering what sort of futures you three girls will have.'

We all looked at her with interest; she was impressively sibylline in her Chinese make-up, black wig and black clothes. But she would say no more. I could, however, pretty well guess how she rated our chances of success and she wasn't very impressed with mine. She believed Evelyn's beauty would help her in musical comedy but thought that Dolly, with her combination of prettiness, charm and great talent had by far the best chance. And I think we all felt the same, not excluding Dolly.

Around seventeen years later, when Evelyn Laye had for many years been a star and I had become a successful playwright, I read in my morning paper that an actress called Helen Saintsbury had shot herself. She had been found dead in bed, wearing a swansdown-trimmed negligée. I had been out of touch with her for many years and now could only learn that she had been generally dissatisfied with life (her marriage had long since ended). What had cancelled out all her charm and talent? Perhaps it was her ever-present resentment of people and of life in general. Someone had always done something to Dolly and she was going to 'show them'. Perhaps at the end she was showing the whole world. But that lonely death must have called for great courage. I was glad, then, to remember her courage during the air raid when she had not only been courageous, but also most gracefully considerate.

Evelyn's part was taken over by a friend of Mrs Royde's, named Elsie Routledge, who had never before acted professionally. I was asked to look after her. She was very young, small and round, with enormous blue eyes; and within a couple of days I realised that she was perfection as a companion, always

cheerful, sympathetic, interested in life, and seemingly unconscious of her extraordinary unselfishness. Happy touring days,
like happy countries, are short on history so I have few memories
of my last three months in *Mr Wu*, though the music of the
revue, *Bric-a-Brac*, which we continually strummed and sang,
can still evoke for me the sunshiny atmosphere. And I do recall
that Elsie's fiancé, a naval officer, brought an early copy of
Rupert Brooke and read the poems aloud to us. Another
memory: Elsie was teaching me to fox-trot in a theatre
dressing-room when we heard the news of Lord Kitchener's
death at sea. We paused long enough to say, 'How awful', then
went on fox-trotting, while Lola, whose life was dominated by
dread of the casualty lists, looked at us with envious disapproval.
When she married, Elsie gave up the stage and vanished from
my life, so she remains for me young, charming and untouched
by time.

I approached the end of the tour with complicated feelings:
excitement at the thought of returning to London, dread of
being out of work, and regret at the break-up of the company.
The last night in the dressing-room had a poignant quality—
there we were, so closely associated for forty weeks, and after
one more train journey we should all be on our own. Lola
said touring was an odd business, only rarely did you make a
lasting friendship. We all swore that this time we would keep
in touch and Lola and I arranged to lunch together in a week's
time, to make a good start.

But when we met we were already absorbed in our new
interests, and though I was to meet her quite often over the
years, and Evelyn too, we were never back on terms of close
friendship. I was to find, again and again, that each theatrical
tour had a small, intimate world of its own which, once left,
could never be re-entered.

VIII

'Ye Gods'

No one I knew well was staying at the Three Arts Club when I got back there, but the next day, while I was having tea in the lounge, in walked Phyllis Morris whom I had not seen for a year. She had got bored with her well-paid job as understudy in the tour of *Quinney's*, left it and taken a holiday. Now she was moving into the Club, preparatory to looking for work. She was wearing a loud black-and-white check suit which suggested she was a bookie, large patent-leather boots with fawn cloth tops, and an exquisite, white silk, Dolly Varden hat. The hat had been given to her by her mother and was intended for garden-party wear, but it had cost three guineas and Phyllis was not going to wait for a garden-party.

Instantly we were back on our old footing of friendship and eager to tell each other about our tours. The Club lounge was a beautiful room with cream walls, grey carpet, magenta silk curtains, cream wicker chairs and many little red lacquer tables. The whole of one long wall was taken up with windows looking on to the walled garden; the afternoon sun, filtering through the leaves of the great plane trees, bathed it in a subdued golden light. Sitting with Phyllis, eating elegant cress sandwiches, I suddenly felt extremely happy and completely at home. Already the tour of *Mr Wu* seemed to be in the distant past.

When it was time for dinner, Phyllis announced that she was going to sit at the exclusive Star Table. It was, she pointed out, the actresses' table and we had been acting for almost a year, which probably few members could claim. So down to the dining-room we went and settled at the window table. Nobody struck us, but several members looked as if they would like to. However, we talked loudly about our tours and Phyllis mentioned impressive plans she had for future work, and gradually our fellow diners began to talk to us with civility and even a touch of wistfulness. After a few more meals we felt ourselves to be accepted and among the élite of the Club.

Before starting to hunt for work I bought myself a new outfit, a navy blue suit with a large white collar and a large sailor hat with streamers; I saw myself as a frank, skipper's-little-daughter type. Phyllis went in for sophisticated dressing and announced that she was going to specialise in Marie Tempest parts, a decision on which no manager ever saw eye-to-eye with her. She said she was also going to specialise in playing children, but was damped when after she said to an agent, 'Have you any children's parts?' he said, 'Why? Have you a child?'

As well as visiting agents, we pestered stage-door keepers, who could sometimes oblige with useful hints. At His Majesty's Theatre stage-door we discovered that experienced dancers were needed for a show about to go into rehearsal called *Chu Chin Chow*. I felt it was useless for me to try, but Phyllis fancied herself as a dancer; and as for experience, it was her habit to invent fictitious past engagements. So down she went to the audition. She informed me later she had begun a neat little dance, but had been stopped by a man's voice from the auditorium telling her that wasn't the kind of thing that was needed.

'What we want', said the man, 'is a dance that will lure men.'

'So', said Phyllis, 'I took off my jacket, rolled up my sleeves and I lured like mad.' She gave me a little exhibition, which looked like a cross between snake-charming and shadow-boxing. 'But it didn't work. Of course you can't do really good luring in a shirt-blouse.'

Anyway, we thought *Chu Chin Chow* sounded awful and most unlikely to run.

As I was still out of work at the end of a fortnight, I decided that a picturesque style of dressing might appeal to managers more than my rather brusque sailor outfit, so I made a very full, black taffeta dress. With this I wore my hat with streamers, a long black silk scarf, and a three yard sash, so that when the wind blew I fluttered from head, shoulders and waist. I finished this outfit just in time for the audition for the tour of *Ye Gods*,

a farce in which there were nine women so I had hopes of
landing something. But my heart sank when I found the stage
packed with girls, most of whom were applying for the one part
I really wanted, that of an hysterical parlour-maid which,
though not the official lead, was much the best woman's part.
I had put my name down for it with the manager, Bernard
Hishin, but doubted if I had much chance.

To both my surprise and horror I was called before anyone
else. Bernard Hishin was there, also the agent Miriam Warner,
and Charles Windermere who played the lead in the London
show and was to direct the tour. I read a few lines, then came
to the hysterical scene.

I said, 'You don't want hysterics now, do you?'

But they certainly did, so I let off some piercing screams.

Someone said, 'And now you have to lie down and kick.'

Painfully conscious of all the girls watching in the wings, I
took off my hat, gloves and scarf, put them on the stage with
my bag, then flung myself down, beat the stage with my hands
and kicked in all directions.

'Kick higher,' said Mr Hishin.

'Scream louder,' said Miss Warner.

'Laugh and cry at the same time,' said Mr Windermere.

They stood about a foot away from me, inciting me furiously
—I shouldn't have been surprised if they had thrown their hats
into the ring. This orgy went on for several minutes and then I
was allowed to get up and restore myself to order. After being
told I should be written to, I departed fearing I had made myself
a laughing stock, but one of the waiting girls said to me: 'You've
got it,' and some hours later a none-too-pleased Phyllis, who
had also been trying for the part, arrived back at the Club and
said no one but me had been allowed to read it.

Two days later I was sent for to sign my contract at Bernard
Hishin's office and emerged with it into Shaftesbury Avenue in
such a stage of bliss that I was nearly run over by a bus. The
idea of being killed in my hour of triumph harrowed me so
much that I recklessly took a taxi back to the Club where I
had tea with extra sandwiches and basked in congratulations.
I doubt if ever in my entire life I have felt more exalted than

after winning that part of Polly Brown in *Ye Gods* at three pounds a week.

Among the girls who congratulated me was Joan Vincent; she had befriended me on my lonely Christmas day. She now advised me not to return to the Club at the end of my tour. 'This place is full of failure. Already people envy you for getting work. They'll steal your luck. Go somewhere else.' She was dead serious and rather impressive but, if anything, she made me feel more self-satisfied. It was pleasant to be young and lucky and envied—if I was—by girls of whom I was still slightly in awe. Vincent—most girls at the Club were known by their surnames, though I never was—saw she was making no impression, so shook her head and departed. I was to remember that conversation in later years.

Ye Gods was still running in London and I went night after night, swollen with pride when the man in the box-office smilingly handed me my free seat. There was a little tune played in the intervals which became tied up with my happiness. I never discovered its name and I never have, though I still sometimes hear it played on the radio. Always it transports me back to the stalls of the Strand Theatre in 1916.

Rehearsals, which took place in the London set, began soon and I enjoyed them, except for my first entrance. I had to run full-tilt down a staircase carrying a tray, and I had always been bad at stairs, having fallen down them twice as a child. I was assured that it didn't in the least matter if I fell down them now, as the audience would think it was part of the play; I was supposed to be under a love spell. So were seven other women, but the spell hit me first and I had most of the fun; I had to clasp the leading man (Ivor Barnard) round the knees, then kiss him madly and almost throttle him, have raging hysterics and finally be carried off, fighting and screaming, by the comic butler. The poor man was little bigger than I was and very stout, and though I only weighed seven stone he found it difficult to lift me. The other men tried to teach him—and me—the knack of it, which largely depended on my leaping into his outstretched arms with more confidence than I felt.

After about a week Charles Windermere, at the end of the

morning rehearsal, said to me: 'We shan't need you this afternoon, dear—or tomorrow.'

I said, 'The next day, then?'

'We'll let you know.' He turned away to someone who was
waiting for him. I walked away, out of the stage door and into
the sunny Strand, utterly stricken. They were getting rid of
me.

I had reason for believing this. At the beginning of rehearsals,
a young girl had been playing the leading man's fiancée, a poor
part but, officially, the leading woman's. One day she said to
me, 'It's nice to be the leading lady. They've told me I can
have tomorrow off.' The next day, a far more experienced
actress (Estelle van Gene) was the leading lady and the young
girl was seen no more. And now . . .

I went back to the Club and lay on my bed, then went over
rehearsals in my mind, trying to recall anything that would
prove I hadn't been liked. Was it because I couldn't run downstairs fast enough? And I had been criticised once or twice. The
more I thought about it the blacker things looked. By mid-
afternoon I felt I couldn't live through the night in this state
of suspense. Better to know the worst.

I got up and bathed my swollen eyes—I had been weeping
freely—and went back to the Strand Theatre, where I hung
about until I saw the company leave. Then I hurried down to
the stage where I found Charles Windermere putting his papers
together. He said cheerfully, 'Hello, do you want something?'
A torrent of words poured from me. He stopped me and told
me to start all over again and say it slowly. When he finally
gathered what was worrying me he said, 'Go home, you silly
girl. You're *engaged* for the part. You've got a contract, haven't
you? And you're quite good. It's just that we're rehearsing the
curtain raiser now and you're not in it.' And then, to fill my cup
of relief to overflowing, he added, 'If you want something to do
tomorrow, you can go and get your photograph taken for the
front of the theatre.' He scribbled an address for me and said
the management would pay.

Oh, noble Charles Windermere (dead in 1955 at the age of
82). My job was safe, praise had been lavished on me, my

photograph was to appear outside theatres! The world was a football at my feet.

We opened in the pier theatre at Colwyn Bay and all went well. I got on happily with the whole company and was enjoying the tour very much when, after only a few weeks, I was laid low.

The day we reached Norwich a cluster of spots appeared on my face. They were like no spots I had ever seen; indeed, they were more like blisters. The next day there were far more and I doubted if it would be safe to make-up over them. I went to a chemist who said he had never seen anything like them in his life and I must at once go to a skin specialist. He gave me the name of one.

I set off in abject misery. For I had suddenly decided what was the matter with me. It was leprosy. Someone had recently told me of the story of a girl who had some peculiar spots, went to a doctor, was given something to drink, and woke up in a glass case tied on to the stern of a ship (a sort of nautical trailer, presumably) on her way to the Leper Islands. And she never came back. I was dying—an old, forgotten woman on the Leper Islands before I got to the doctor.

He was an imposing doctor, with a richly furnished consulting room. I looked him straight in the eye and said, 'Is it leprosy?' He said, 'It's chicken-pox, my good girl, and you are infecting my premises.'

I cannot say he was a sympathetic doctor; his one idea was to get me out of his house. And he would not tell me where to go. He said no hospital would take me. I mustn't stop on in my rooms, infecting people. Hadn't I a home? I said I had relations in Manchester but there were children there. 'Out of the question, anyway. You mustn't travel anywhere by train. Really, there's nothing I can suggest.' He looked as if he hated the sight of me.

I sank down on his beautiful pile carpet and wept copiously. 'Get up, get up,' he said, 'You're infecting my carpet now.' But he seemed to relent a little and said there was just a chance the Norwich Isolation Hospital might take me as they had a ward of glass cubicles where different infectious diseases could be nursed together. 'They don't take chicken-pox, but I might persuade them. You can come back here at six o'clock and see.'

I asked what I was to do all day and he said sit in a park as far away from people as possible. I went out of the room feeling like a pariah.

I found the stage manager at the theatre and warned him my understudy would be needed. He thought it doubtful the management would keep my job open for me. After that I spent a long, hot afternoon doing my best to avoid people. When I went back to the doctor he was much kinder—I could well understand how the arrival of a ragingly infectious girl in the middle of a busy morning must have annoyed him. He said he had arranged everything. An ambulance would call at my rooms in half an hour. I had to take a tram—feeling guilty—and then run like blazes in order to get back in time.

At the hospital I was found to have a high temperature and began to feel very ill indeed; up till then I'd been mainly conscious of misery. The Sister came to interview me and expressed surprise that my face was only decorated with spots. She said, 'I thought all actresses painted their faces.' Apparently she also thought all actresses dropped their aitches, for I later found she had taken down my address as 'The Three Hearts Club'. She said my green nightdress would probably give me arsenic poisoning, but I could wear it until my friends at the theatre brought me more of my clothes. I suppose a few days' arsenic poisoning didn't count.

After she had gone, I lay back in a rather dismal twilight and took stock of my surroundings. All the glass cubicles opened on to a garden and had a door and a fairly large window set in a brick wall. All the interior dividing walls were of plate glass. On my right were children recovering from scarlet fever; in front of me was a diphtheria case. I could see typhoid and cerebral fever patents a little further away. (I had one of the end cubicles so never felt people were staring at the back of my head.) Fortunately, all my fellow-patients were approaching convalescence and I did not see anyone suffering. But it was queer to feel that so many varied germs were so close—I feared they might come in on the nurses' uniforms. Suppose I caught one fever after another and had to spend months and months in hospital? Thinking of the curtain ringing up at the theatre with my understudy playing, I felt very, very low.

Just before I fell asleep it struck me that I was, indeed, in a glass case—if, mercifully, not trailing behind a ship on my way to the Leper Islands.

Two days later a deputation from the company arrived to say goodbye to me; our two leads, Ivor and Estelle, who were about to become engaged, and half a dozen others. They stood outside my window, gesticulating, because I could not hear what they said, and finally my nurse opened the window just wide enough for them to push an envelope through. It contained three pounds ten shillings which they had generously subscribed. They also left me some of my clothes, but most of those travelled on with the company—though I still did not know if I should get my job back.

My chief memory of the next weeks is of acute and humiliating hunger. My temperature fell almost at once, but I was kept on milk for a couple of days; then I was told I was to go on 'full diet' and looked forward to masses of food. But I found that full diet consisted of three thin slices of bread-and-butter and a cup of tea for breakfast, a tiny helping of meat, or fish, and vegetables for lunch, and three thin slices of bread-and-butter for tea—the last meal of the day. Twice a week there was a rice pudding after the main course at luncheon—and I would have fought any one for that rice pudding—and very occasionally I was given an egg for tea; but the scarlet fever children next to me looked at it so wistfully that I could hardly bear to eat it.

Knowing that the hospital was quite free, I asked my friendly nurse if I could pay for more substantial helpings, but she said it was out of the question. She did, however, buy me large amounts of plain chocolate to be eaten by night when lights were out. Had I been seen eating it she would have got into trouble. Anyway, I couldn't have eaten it under the eyes of my hungry little neighbours (all the patients I could see were children). I would have liked to give them some, but my nurse said it was too risky. So all day long I counted the hours until I could get at that chocolate.

It proved impossible to borrow books locally in case I infected them, but my nurse found some tattered books which could be destroyed when I finished with them. Anyway reading was none too easy as my little scarlet fever neighbours sang loudly during most of their waking hours. Of their two favourite songs, one began with 'The Zepps are coming, can't you hear the crowds roar?' and the other concluded, 'Remember, you'll always find a friend in the girl you cast aside.' The one blessing I could count on was my nurse, who came in to cheer me up whenever she had a spare moment. Though no beauty, others as well as myself must have appreciated her for she had got herself engaged to three men at the same time. Hearing about them was a constant joy.

Our business manager had been told by the hospital that I should have to remain for three weeks and the London management had promised to keep my job open for this period. In the middle of the third week I asked what day I should be leaving and was told by Sister that I should have to wait a little longer than three weeks, but I could, in another couple of days, get up. Till then I had not set foot to ground—and when I did, I instantly collapsed. I could not have believed that less than three weeks in bed could do that to one's legs. After that, I was allowed to practise walking, on a strip of garden outside the cubicles and was reasonably steady in less than a week, but still was not allowed to leave. According to Sister, one was infectious with chicken-pox until the last crust was off one's spots, and there were three crusts on my back which obviously had no intention of moving. Sister (not one of my favourite characters) said gaily that she had known one girl who retained one infectious spot for six months.

'But I shall lose my job,' I wailed. And after I had been in hospital for over five weeks I got a letter to say the job could only be held open for one week longer. My dear nurse told me not to worry and proceeded to wash my back rather roughly. 'All crusts off now," she reported, grinning. 'You'll be out on Saturday.' (After the production of my first play, *Autumn*

Crocus, she arrived out of the blue to congratulate me, having remembered my insignificant name for fifteen years. She had married one of the three fiancés and was a happy as she deserved to be.)

I finally left the hospital one bright autumn morning and no doubt experienced all the emotions of a prisoner released; but all I can remember now is thinking of food. I prowled ravenously round Norwich until eleven thirty, feeling that I could hardly expect a meal to be served earlier than that. Then I went into a large restaurant and ordered roast beef. The waitress eyed me curiously and said she would see if there was any ready, then returned with an underdone plateful. I attacked it fiercely and then had some more. At last, after pudding and coffee, I felt un-hungry for the first time in six weeks. I then went to tidy up and after one look in the glass I knew why the waitress had eyed me curiously. In the hospital my only mirror had been the tiny minimising one in the top of my powder box, so I had no idea how bad the chicken-pox marks on my face were. I now saw them in their full glory. There were six really deep, bright red pits, including one huge triangular one on the end of my nose. I looked truly appalling. And to cheer me further, I was now smitten with indigestion—for the first time in my life.

I caught an afternoon train to London and spent the night at the Club, avoiding members as much as possible. The next morning I went to a doctor, who told me frankly that a neglected *small-pox* case could hardly look worse than I did. He said there was one chance in a hundred that the marks would go away; otherwise I was marked for life. So it was in no gay mood that I rejoined the company at Guildford. I reported to the theatre, then went to find a room.

That night everyone was kind to me, but people were obviously horrified by my looks. I decided I must always live alone. But after a few days a girl named Violette St Claire, who had joined the company during my absence, asked if I would like to share with her and another girl we called Flapper, because of the part she played. (In that *Ye Gods* company I was always called Polly, as in *Kitty Grey* I had been Sadie, only in *Mr Wu* was I called by my own name, as I could hardly be called Low

Sung.) I said I preferred to live alone and did so for another week—at Croydon, close enough to London for Uncle Harold, up on business, to come and see me one morning. It was obvious that he was appalled by my scars. And later in the week my landlady and her husband came in and stood hand in hand while they offered to adopt me. They said had their daughter lived she would be just about my age now and they could not bear to think of me, an orphan, out in the world all alone. I hoped I showed enough gratitude when refusing their very kind offer. They finally assured me I could always count on a home with them.

Thinking this over, I decided they must have been motivated by pity for my appearance and I attributed the same motive to Vi (as Violette was always called) and Flapper when they again asked me to live with them, and again I refused. But on Saturday night when Vi discovered I'd still got no rooms, she announced there was an extra bedroom in the house where she and Flapper had booked rooms and I could at least *try* living with them. She would see that I was properly fed which might help my continued indigestion. So eventually, after they had both sworn they were not simply taking pity on a scarred pariah, I grudgingly consented.

It astounds me now that I could have been so ungracious, and that Vi, often diffident, could have been so determined. She was a slight, dark, attractive girl in her middle-twenties who had been on the stage since a child, both as an actress and a dancer. She had done a tour of South America (without the good offices of a hospital nurse with a hypodermic syringe) and was the complete professional. And it was typical of her that she disliked her own professionalism and admired my lack of it. She did all the shopping, housekeeping, writing for rooms, etc, and would take sewing out of my hands and do it herself.

Life with Vi and Flapper (a most agreeable girl) was too comfortable for me to remember much about it. My indigestion departed as I got used to a normal amount of food and my spots quickly paled, though the deep indentations remained. One day I bought a pot of a vanishing cream called Ven Yusa which my mother had greatly liked. It was (and still is, I believe)

a pleasant, reasonably-priced cream, but I feel sure its manufacturers don't claim curative properties for it. However, from
the moment I began to use it my scars began to disappear. I
continued to plaster my face with faith and Ven Yusa, and
after several weeks only the one on the end of my nose
remained. Even that was unobtrusive and eventually dwindled
away.

Early in December we had a week out, during which I stayed
with Vi in her mother's house at Hendon. Although the tour
was going out again after Christmas, I felt I ought to look for
an even better job and was encouraged to by Vi—rather to my
surprise as I imagined she would miss me if I left. The first day
I went the round of the agents, Arthur Gibbons offered me the
schoolgirl's part in *The Rotters* by H. F. Maltby and I was
jubilant; for though the salary was the same as I was getting
I loved the part and the play was much better than *Ye Gods*.
Vi rejoiced with me and then told me she had known I was to
be replaced after Christmas as a girl friend of one of the backers
of the show was to have my part. I was indignant, but what did
it matter now? I'd got a fine new job—and on the first day
I'd looked for work.

As a reward to myself I ordered, at a shop near Oxford
Circus, a silver cigarette case with a match box attached,
costing just over a week's salary; I had recently taken to smoking, with highly sophisticated gestures. I had to pay in advance
but was assured that my money would be refunded if I wasn't
satisfied. When the cigarette case came, there was no matchbox
and my request for my money was met with a blank refusal.
In a violent temper, I rushed out into Oxford Circus and told
my story to a policeman on point duty who was surprisingly sympathetic, considering the traffic that was piling up behind him.
He sent me to a police station where I was received with even
more sympathy. A burly policeman seized a telephone and,
after some truculent words to the shop, said, 'Well, now. The
magistrate's just going into court. Shall the young lady go in
and tell him, or shall she come back for her money?' A moment
later he hung up and said cheerfully, 'That's all right, miss.
You go and get it.' I asked him if I really could have gone to

the magistrate and he said, 'No, miss. You could not. But we use a little bluff now and then. When in doubt, always come to the police.'

I had already formed a high opinion of the police, having written a letter addressed to 'The Police, Cambridge' in which I asked if they could do anything about a coat I had sold to a landlady (appropriately, the imitation pony-skin called by the *Mr Wu* company, 'the landlady's coat'), accepting her promise that she would send me ten shillings for it, which she had failed to do. Possibly this is not quite the sort of job the police are paid to do, but the coat was quickly returned, with an angry letter saying: 'You sent the police to my house.'

Instead of the cigarette case I gave myself a new handbag. I favoured a box-type resembling a miniature dressing-case, with gilt fittings. I had a whole dynasty of these bags, which could be bought for a little over a pound, and I called them all Anthony. The new one, blue morocco, was Anthony II. It once flung itself open at a busy crossing and the policeman on point duty held up all the traffic while he helped me to collect its scattered gilt fittings. Very, very kind to me the police always were.

IX

Spring Evening

When I left *Ye Gods* I had one of my fiendish colds so was thankful to have booked a cubicle at the Three Arts Club and be able to crawl into bed there. Soon after I did so, Phyllis Morris walked in, wearing a black hat with a life-size yellow-kid chicken on it. She was back from a tour of the Camp theatres. We had been completely out of touch, but were at once best friends again and she was noble about getting me hot drinks, hot water bottles and nearly asphyxiating me with Friar's Balsam—not that any cold of mine ever yielded to any remedy known to man.

Still, I was well and in good spirits when I went off to the first rehearsal for *The Rotters*, wearing one of the newly fashionable coat-frocks; mine was black velvet trimmed with white rabbit. But from the beginning things went badly. An atmosphere of gloom pervaded the cold, ill-lit rehearsal room over a public house. The producer seemed to dislike me and when Arthur Gibbons came in for a short time he didn't give me a smile. When I arrived for the next morning's rehearsal I was told to go to his office, where he informed me that I was hopeless for the part. He had only heard me rehearse a few lines, but that was enough to show him that my voice was too mature. I said if he wanted a child impersonation, I could do one but he insisted he must have a naturally high voice such as his wife's; she would now replace me.

He told me he had liked me so much as a person he had wanted to give me the part and thus made a mistake. It was probably true, as we had always got on well; he was an agent as well as a manager and I had often visited him. Anyway, I thanked him for the two weeks' salary my contract called for and bore him no ill feeling. We parted sadly.

Christmas was only a few days off, which somehow intensified my misery. As well as losing the job, I had been made to feel so old. I had seen myself as still something of a child, rather a Barrie-esque character. Now, at twenty, my voice was 'mature'. Perhaps my appearance was too. I walked along the wintry Strand very near tears—then suddenly adopted a devil-may-care attitude, hurried to the little Wardour Street shops and spent the whole of my two weeks' salary on clothes.

Fortunately the Club was not deserted that Christmas and I now had plenty of friends. There was a fancy dress party and a play in the lounge on Twelfth Night, in which I somehow came by the leading part. But once the holiday season was over I had to face the fact that I was workless; and now my luck deserted me. I hunted for several weeks of bitter weather without even the sniff of a job.

Early in February I called on Bernard Hishin, still the management of *Ye Gods*, hoping he might have some new play in hand. He was sympathetic about my fiasco in *The Rotters*, but had nothing to offer me. Then he said, 'Still, come and see me next week.' This was so often said by managers and agents just to get rid of me that I barely felt the second visit worthwhile, and was astounded when Mr Hishin said he would move the girl who had replaced me to another company and I could have my old part back. He then asked me how much he had paid me.

'Three pounds,' I said, fully expecting him to cut this down now I was crawling back after failure.

He said he'd make it three pounds ten shillings, this time. And I think that was the most generous gesture ever made to me during my entire connection with the stage.

Even with a raised salary it was a little ignominious to return to a company I had left so cockily, but I was cheered by a 'Too delighted for words' telegram from Vi and Flapper. The mention of that telegram brings me the most vivid mental picture of my Club cubicle, the telegram lying on the bed and a pair of high black leather boots standing by the wardrobe. (Why I ever bought a black leather pair I can't imagine, as my friends and I thought boots only had sex appeal if their tops were light cloth. White tops were the most dashing of all, but considered fast.) Those black boots carry my mind to an incident they had a share in weeks later.

We were at Stockport, in snowy weather. One of my colds had lingered on and on and Vi perpetually fussed telling me to wrap up. One night, as we walked back to our rooms after a fresh fall of snow, I said I was sick of being coddled and was going to try hardening myself. I flung off my coat, hat and gloves, undid the neck of my dress and finally unlaced those high black boots. Vi, picking up my clothes, nearly wept with dismay; even Flapper, who was equable as well as agreeable, was anxious. I strode on heedlessly, the high tops of the black boots flapping widely, the long black tongues slapping the snow. I scarcely like to mention the unlikely fact, but by next morning my cold had completely gone.

At the earliest hint of Spring in the air I became restive and kept saying 'something' would have to happen or I should go mad. Flapper, though less violent, agreed with me; and by 'something' we made no bones about specifying a young man—one each. Vi already had romantic, and not very happy, preoccupations, but did her best to help us. According to her, if one wanted notes sent round by officers, one had to invite them by skilled eye-work. To me, the auditorium was always a vast black void and the idea of looking at anyone in it seemed most reprehensible. Also in my scenes I was the centre of interest and could hardly gaze enticingly at the audience. It then occurred to me that I had one chance, during my hysterical scene, and when I flung myself down for it that evening, screaming loudly, I directed a winning glance at three young officers in the front row of the stalls. And I kicked higher than usual, with reasonably good black silk-stockinged legs.

The result was instant. A note came round in the next interval. True, it was addressed not to me but to our leading lady, Estelle van Gene, but it asked her to bring me out to tea next day with 'one other young lady'. It was a very correct little note. Estelle was now married to Ivor Barnard, who had joined the Army. She had no interest in tea with officers, but had no intention of doing me out of an invitation and we invited Flapper as third. Later in the evening our business manager, Frank Bell, got wind of our proposed party and expressed dire disapproval. He was a charming, humorous man who had always been particularly kind to Vi, Flapper and me. He told me a harrowing story of some chorus girls he had known who went out to what they thought was a perfectly innocent tea, felt sleepy and slipped into a doze—and nine months later gave birth to babies. I said I hardly thought similar fates could overtake us in a Hastings tea room.

Our officers turned out to be three pleasant Canadians; Flapper and I thought their accents and their habit of talking about baby-carriages, band-concerts and street-cars were enchanting. We had a hilarious tea; I choked and was told my eyes were fascinating when bloodshot. Then our friends came to the play again that night and we went out to supper with them, in spite of Mr Bell's gloomy prophecies.

The next week two of our young men followed us to Eastbourne, Flapper's and mine; the eldest had dropped out, as had Estelle van Gene. We went roller skating, took taxi drives, put pennies in the slot machines on the pier, ate vast meals and laughed continually. Frank Bell, softened after meeting our respectable young men at the stage door, said my walk had developed a noticeable elasticity and he was right. Had I known how, I would have bounced instead of walked.

The truth was I had never felt so cheerful in my life. I had become obsessed with the idea that I was unattractive to men. I was twenty and had never had anything approaching a love affair. True, I wouldn't have looked at any of the young men I had met on tour, but I still found it depressing that none of them had looked at me. Now someone I really liked was showering flowers and chocolates on me. I told myself I wasn't in love, and I intended to quell my young man if he tried to kiss me (actually, he never even got as far as holding my hand except in roller skating), but there was no doubt about the elasticity of my walk.

My walk-improver said he would follow me to Folkestone

the next week and I bet him a box of cigarettes he wouldn't. He was to come on Tuesday but failed to arrive. Flapper, who had been expecting her young man too, was philosophic, but I plunged into misery, played sentimental songs, and analysed my feelings to patient Vi, always insisting that I wasn't *really* in love.

'Well, if you go on like this when you're not in love, God help you when you are,' said Vi and begged me to come to the pictures. But I hung about the house, hoping for a telegram. On Friday I decided to pay my bet of cigarettes, with which—in the teeth of Vi's opposition—I sent an insulting letter.

From Folkestone we went to Golders Green where I was soothed by an explanatory letter from my Hastings young man, saying he would come to London the following week and see me; he knew that the company was due for a week off. Although I thought about him during most of my waking hours, I had now acquired the habit of casting an interested eye on audiences and on Friday night this was fully reciprocated by a particularly good looking young man whose uniform was new to me. At the end of the show his card came round with the message, 'Would you like me to wait for you? Don't be long. Canadian Sergeant.' I thought this cheek, particularly from a sergeant, also Mr Bell was there ready to take me home—I was staying with him and his wife that week. The stage-door keeper was waiting for a reply so I scribbled, 'Sorry, impossible tonight.' Mr Bell said, 'Good God, Polly, why did you say " tonight ". He'll be hanging round the theatre tomorrow.' A similar idea had occurred to me when I wrote the message. But he wasn't and I forgot all about him.

I stayed at the Club for my week out and wrote inviting my Hastings young man to dinner there. I can't feel it was a good idea for he looked scared from the moment he entered the hall. I bore him with pride to a guest table—never before had I entertained a man at the Club—and the battery of female eyes seemed to deprive him of both appetite and conversation. I rallied him vivaciously but it was no good. He simply said: 'I'm terrified.'

After that gloomy meal he took me to *Hanky Panky* at the

Empire and I doubt if we laughed once during the show—and certainly not during the intervals. As the evening wore on I tried being provocatively scornful—girls in novels so often made a success of this—but my young man remained kind, quiet, rather red in the face and entirely unforthcoming. As he finally saw me up the steps of the Club I asked him point blank what was the matter with him. He said, 'Gee, Polly, didn't you ever have a mood?' and dashed into the night.

I was plunged into such despair that I decided I really was in love with him; when the tour re-opened the following week I could talk of nothing else.

Vi told our fortunes by cards every day and we went to every fortune teller we could find. One of these told me I should have no success until I was over thirty and then it would be as a writer, not as an actress. 'So you might as well sit back and store up things to write about.' I was not impressed with her; but I am now.

Distressed at the money we were paying to fortune tellers Mr Bell bought us a crystal ball and suggested we should use it ourselves. None of us had any luck, though I gazed into it for hours usually sitting under the dining-room table as I felt more psychic there. Our Nottingham landlady found this most dis-concerting and said I seemed a very peculiar girl.

My worst time of day was when I woke in the morning and lay listening for the post, for I continued to hope there would be a letter from my lost young man, forwarded by the Club. After three blank weeks the Club did send on a letter, but it wasn't the one I was waiting for. It was, however, distinctly interesting, addressed in green ink and with OHMS printed on the envelope, and from the Canadian Sergeant who had sent me his card at Golders Green; when replying I had thoughtfully written on one of my theatrical cards which had the Club address on.

It was a long, very well-written and rather impertinent letter. In addition to being a Sergeant (a Staff-Sergeant, hence the governmental envelope) the young man appeared to be a com-poser and the dramatic critic of a Toronto paper. He said he had spent three weeks trying to get a legitimate introduction to me and had enquired vainly in various theatrical quarters, including the Green Room Club (never one of my haunts).

I remained faithful to the Hastings lieutenant for at least a couple of hours, then wrote to the Golders Green sergeant asking him to call on me at the Club on the following Sunday evening—we were to be in London for a week, playing at Stratford. Vi disapproved; she said there were things in the letter which deserved a snubbing. But I was snubbing no man who had enquired for me at the Green Room Club.

So on Sunday, April 22nd, 1917, on a pale Spring evening, I was called from the Club dining-room to receive my guest. I remember that he looked abnormally large standing in the hall; he was over six foot tall and rather heavily built. One arm was in a sling, owing to a recent innoculation, and the club porter was solicitously helping him off with his coat. He was dark, good looking in a square-jawed, blunt-featured way, with a particularly well shaped mouth. He wore pince-nez. In my first glance there was something I did not like about his face and I was conscious of a slight revulsion. This feeling occurred every time I met him, but was always lost within the first few minutes.

I took him into the lounge, where there was a bright fire burning. It was still quite light and the chilly Spring sky seen through the budding plane trees had not yet been shut out by the heavy magenta curtains. There was a bowl of hyacinths on the table near which we sat. There were few people in the room.

I ordered coffee. It was then around seven o'clock. I have a vague impression that the room filled up, then emptied again. Then the hall porter came in and coughed very irritatingly. A little later he returned and kicked the dying fire out. And finally he entered forcefully, clicked some lights off and said, 'Now, miss, it's after midnight. I've given you an extra half hour.' He was a good friend of mine but, at the moment, I loathed him for even existing.

After I had seen my visitor off I retired to my cubicle intent on re-living the whole evening. Out of the five hours' welter of conversation I can now only recall two passages. One was when, after he had happened to mention the wife of a friend, I asked him, with magnificent casualness, if he was married. He said,

'You wouldn't be friends with me if I was, would you?' He so obviously expected a negative reply that I gave one, though not even a harem of wives would have held me at bay. He said, 'Well, I'm not, so that's all right.' Later in the evening he asked if I would ever be willing to give up the stage. I said I couldn't imagine it. He said, 'You see, I might one day ask you to marry me and come to Canada!' I said I was afraid it wouldn't be any use, at which he said, rather too cheerfully, 'Well, don't worry, I haven't asked you yet.'

Lying in bed I wondered if I could chalk up a proposal, or could he be said to have unpicked it? Anyway, I had plenty to gloat over and the fact that so much had happened at a first meeting made me feel almost fatally attractive. Of course *I* wasn't in love, I was the sought-after, elusive one—had I not instantly declined the proposal, even if it hadn't quite been one? I could still hear his voice, with its faint Canadian accent, see his slightly sardonic smile. What a large man he was! A Canadian sergeant's uniform was attractive, with its high, straight collar, quite unlike an English sergeant's. There had been a whiff of iodoform from the bandage on his arm, which had got mixed with the scent of the hyacinths . . .

I had every intention of going on gloating for hours, but after a short time I was smitten with a severe stomach ache; I was soon to learn that, with me, romantic excitement was frequently overtaken by this unromantic complaint. In vain I tried to continue the recapture of the evening; the stomach ache seemed determined I should think of nothing but itself. It grew so acute that I asked myself if I would even give up my new romance in order to get rid of the pain? I would not, I said firmly, and the stomach ache got worse. I then wondered if there was anything else I could offer to give up if, well, not exactly God, but *something* with power over stomach aches, would take it away. Had I any sin on my conscience? The only thing I felt remotely guilty about was crystal-gazing; it wasn't thought well of by Christian Scientists. I undertook that, if the pain would go, I would never look in the crystal again. Almost instantly, the stomach ache departed. But I was too worn out to do any more gloating, I just wanted to sleep, and sleep seemed something

I should never again achieve. I became conscious of loud breathing from other occupants of cubicles, lumps seemed to have arrived in my bed, my ears ached from being laid on. (Do other people's ears resent wakefulness as much as mine do?) At last I remembered I had a bottle of aspirin in the top drawer of the dressing table. I groped for it in the dark and took two tablets. I slept.

Morning revealed that sleep had been induced not by aspirin, but by cascara. After that, I threw both bottles away and tried sticking to my Christian Science, which had been slipping since my weeks in the Norwich hospital.

Later that morning, when I was sitting in the lounge, the girl named Vincent who had warned me to leave the Club before my luck left me, came and said she was sorry she had butted in the previous evening. I asked when she had butted in. She said she had noticed that my new friend and I seemed to be getting a trifle oblivious of our surroundings and had felt it tactful to ask me to hand her a magazine from the table near me. 'And you looked straight at me and said, "Go away!"'

I had no recollection of this whatever.

Every day that week I travelled to the Stratford theatre by bus. The same ride had been tedious when I was playing in *Kitty Grey*, but now it was a peaceful opportunity for basking. Along the route there was a soap factory which smelt so disgusting that Gwendo and I had always held handkerchiefs to our noses while passing it. Now I sniffed the air cheerfully, telling myself that the consciousness of beauty in which I felt bathed was proof even against soap factories. Those late afternoon rides, when Spring seemed to emanate even from bricks and mortar, remain forever gilded in my memory.

On Monday night I handed the crystal, wrapped in its black velvet, to Vi and gave her my share of it. I was in a grave, almost holy, mood as I told her about my Sunday evening.

'Polly's in love,' she said to Frank Bell, when he came to see us in an interval.

'What, again?' said Mr Bell.

I gave him no answering smile. 'This,' I said, 'is different.'

Unfortunately for me, it was.

X

The Man of Principle

I never did fully understand the goings-on of that infuriating
man who so thoroughly muddled up my early twenties and
erupted in frantic cables as long as ten years after. Phyllis, who
interviewed him once in an effort to straighten things out, said
she found him, 'very attractive, brilliantly clever and completely
unscrupulous'. She added that she was not going to see him
again in case she tried to get him for herself, a truly noble piece
of self-denial on the part of a girl who had once coined the
phrase, 'All's fair in love and work.' Not that I actually recall
her swiping any girl's man or any girl's job.

'Unscrupulous' seemed to me unjust, considering that most
of my difficulties were due to his high principles. Quite genuine
ones, I believed. The trouble was that they were intermittent.

He was twenty-eight, an Englishman who had gone to Canada
in his early youth, when he had spent some time on a ranch—
falling off horses, he said, until he learned to stay on them. He
had then gravitated into towns and the business world. (I
never quite knew what business.) Composing music and jour-
nalism were side-lines. I never understood why he had enlisted
as he disliked England and was intent on getting back to Canada
just as soon as the war was over. His extreme short-sight had
kept him from active service, though he sometimes harrowed
me by saying he was hoping to wangle his way to France.

He had an unusual surname and two admirable Christian
names, but he liked to be called by a nickname acquired in his
ranch days; this was 'Bud' and I found it hard to take. Our
Hastings Canadians had been called Bob, Dave and Hank. My
friend Pixie had recently married a Canadian called Ern; all
these names sat naturally on their owners, but the assumption of

'Bud' by a highly sophisticated man somehow embarrassed me. The odd thing about its assumer was that he combined sophistication with extreme sentimentality. For that matter, he was inconsistent in many ways and particularly in matters of taste. As a musician, for instance, he was highbrow enough to despise Gilbert and Sullivan, but could be moved to tears by a song called 'Dear Old Pal o' Mine'.

I hardly think the Canadian Staff got much work out of him that first week I knew him, for a letter written in green ink and covering at least three pages of foolscap awaited me every night at the theatre. I sat in my dressing-room replying, tiresomely interrupted by having to play my part. For some reason we could not meet all week, but there were telephone conversations as well as letters and by Saturday we had worked up a first-class quarrel; I think he accused me of accusing him of insincerity. On Sunday morning he rang up to know if we should call the whole thing off, or if he should come and see me at once, before I left for Plymouth. I hastily invited him.

Again I was conscious of that faint revulsion on first seeing him and, though it wore off, I never liked him so much when he was there as when he wasn't. The lounge, mercifully, was deserted that sunny morning but we only had time for a few minutes' talk. After we had resolved our quarrel, he said he was now quite sure about his feelings and they would last for ever. What about mine? I indicated that I was more than interested, but far from sure. He made me promise that, if I did discover I was in love with him, I would at once write and tell him. He then escorted me to the station and I was torn between pride at having such a large, good-looking man in tow and embarrassment because he wasn't an officer; had he been, I might have been surer of my feelings, snob that I was—but so were all my friends.

At Plymouth enormously long letters in green ink came every day and were satisfactory until the end of the week, when my twenty-first birthday occurred. I was still in bed, gazing at a patch of sunlight on the wall and wondering what he would send me (he had assured me he was going to send a present) when the landlady brought in a brief note which completely shattered my day. It was cold and stilted. He apologised for not sending a present, saying he did not feel competent to choose one. The fact that he suggested we might choose it together when I returned to London soothed me not at all—the rest of the letter was too chilling.

The girls were particularly kind to me all that lovely May morning and at the theatre there were letters from all my family. I had read somewhere that the best cure for unhappiness was to be kind to other people, so I wrote long and affectionate letters to everyone at home. Nan told me afterwards that my uncles were greatly touched by them; Uncle Eddie said he would keep his always. Every day I grew further from the family; I knew it saddened them and I felt guilty. But the thought of their having any real share in my grown-up life somehow embarrassed me. I was always glad I wrote those letters on my twenty-first birthday for I did manage to express some of the gratitude I felt for my happy childhood. (It was getting happier and happier in retrospect.) For my birthday, my uncles were letting me choose a white fox fur, neither they nor I having realised that white fox in the daytime was fast becoming a sign of an older profession than the theatrical.

At supper that night I announced I was giving up smoking. Vi had been begging me to for weeks, holding up her stained fingers as an object lesson. I think I was vaguely trying to bribe God, but I also felt that smoking didn't go with being in love, which surely I must be, seeing my misery over that letter? As I rarely smoked anything stronger than gold-tipped *My Darling* cigarettes, I wasn't making much of a sacrifice and I rather think that decision was the one thing for which I ever had to be grateful to 'Bud'.

I answered the chilly letter by asking what was the matter and, after several miserable days, got an affectionate reply, though not one word of explanation. Letters now came daily again and I was happy. We were in Newport, Monmouth, by then and I used to get up early and go for walks by a very small canal which had a large number of locks, a nursery rhyme sort of canal.

I was now almost sure I was in love and felt I ought to keep my promise and write and say so; but the tour was to end in another week and Vi strongly advised me to wait until I got back to London. We then heard that the tour had been extended for three weeks in Ireland. Four weeks of undeclared love was more than I could possibly bear—and had I not given my word? I spent a few more introspective days, read a novel about Canada discouragingly full of snow and bears; bravely faced the necessity of giving up my career (the girls had to listen to me facing it) and finally, in Swansea at half past five in the morning, sat up in bed to write my declaration, my first love letter.

Prior to that, my letters had mainly been about the fascinating subject of my own character; I remember writing that it had been formed by Bernard Shaw. Looking back on myself, I can't feel Shaw would have been pleased with his handiwork.

There was a rehearsal that morning and I posted my letter on the way to it; I did think of waiting until I had read the letter which I expected would be at the theatre, but was bursting to get my declaration off. Having posted it, I felt light as air. The die was cast.

Frank Bell was sorting through the letters at the stage door. 'Income tax again, Polly,' he said, handing me my usual OHMS envelope. I retired to sit on the stairs and read it. And there Vi presently found me, so stricken that I had forgotten the rehearsal. It was a short, chilly, almost formal letter, mainly about the weather. Vi read it and had to admit that, coming after a spate of semi-love letters, it could only be intended to choke me off.

After rehearsal I went back to our lodgings and wrote to my Canadian saying I now realised he had seen what was coming and his letter had been an effort to prevent it and that, though I could not take back what I had written, I now wanted him to forget it. Having posted this I resigned myself to despair.

Those patient girls would have been willing to sympathise all afternoon, but I shooed them off to the pictures and sat alone at the window, gazing across a little railway line to the grey Welsh sea. I tried to read. I had been finding *Lorna Doone* a pleasant accompaniment to being in love, but it was less good to the blighted, though I found some small comfort in Lorna's faithfulness. She went on trusting even when she had no word from her lover for months. But no word was better than some words. She didn't have to go on trusting through casual letters about the weather.

Misery lasted from Tuesday till Friday afternoon, when a letter came, this time to our lodgings. He admitted he had tried to put me off, but said there was a reason for it, which he could not tell me until I was back in London. What he could tell me now, and did for several pages, was how happy my letter had made him. I sank to the ground and had hysterics of relief. I remember wondering if they were genuine, or if I was just enjoying myself.

In Cork there were letters waiting for me and they continued throughout the week, and during the next week in Belfast. They grew more and more affectionate, but there were several references to that mysterious something which had caused him to try and put me off. Most of my waking hours were spent in wondering what it was. Vi had said he must be married, but he had specifically told me he wasn't.

Then on Thursday in Dublin, as we were beginning an early lunch before the matinée, a letter arrived in which he said he had decided to tell me the truth before I got back to London, so that I could make up my mind about seeing him again. He had been married for years and, though he had only lived with his wife a few weeks, the circumstances were such that he doubted if he could ever get a divorce. After this bit of news, he asked me to stop reading the letter and see if I could still give him one smile. I looked up, across my congealing stew, and smiled what I thought to be a very beautiful smile, but it caused Vi to say, 'Good God, Polly, what's the matter?' I had barely told her before I was smitten with my emotional stomach ache. Mercifully it went off before we had to leave for the matinée.

My stage hysterics were a comfort; never had I given a better performance. The mood for them persisted when I got back to the dressing-room and Vi, who had her own love troubles, caught them from me. A character actress from the next dressing-room walked briskly in and slapped Vi's face until she recovered, then turned to do the same kind office for me. But I had switched mine off and was prepared to resist assault.

I woke up next day with a weight on my heart, but soon began to feel it might be an interesting weight. Could one just be friends with a married man, or, if not, what were the implications? I had always had an idea I might be fated to live an unconventional, tempest-tossed life; tragic perhaps but . . . interesting. I sent him a noble letter, saying I would decide about our being friends after we met and agreeing to be at the Club on Sunday evening when, he had said, he would telephone.

This was the last week of the *Ye Gods* tour. It was sad to part with Vi and Flapper, those sympathetic listeners to my troubles —but I was able to confide these to two friends at the Club while I was having Sunday supper, having by then been back less than an hour. After that, I settled down in the twilit lounge with an eye on the door through which the hall porter would come to announce my telephone call. And thus, though unaware of it as yet, I joined that forlorn band, the girls who waited for telephone calls. There were usually two or three of them in the lounge—you could tell them by their habit of jumping each time the door opened and, as their vigil wore on, a certain wild look in the eye. Awaited telephone calls so often fail to happen, as did mine that evening.

It was remarkable how soon my aloof, wounded-by-deception attitude wore off. After a couple of hours I was nervy, abject and fearful that he might be dead—drowned possibly, as he was now living, with two other Canadians, in a riverside bungalow near Hampton Wick. It turned out that he had merely been on the Thames, not in it, and nowhere near a telephone. He rang up next morning to explain this (without apology) and to invite me to have after-lunch coffee with him at Fullers in Regent Street.

It was still Nash's Regent Street, with Fullers in an old, cream-painted house of many little rooms; we had one on the top floor entirely to ourselves. I talked volubly and he was remarkably silent; eventually he suggested I should try a little silence too, as he just wanted to look at me. So we gazed at each other, holding hands; he was an impressive hand-holder. But I would not let him kiss me, partly because the waitress kept coming in unexpectedly and partly because it would have been my first kiss (stage kisses didn't count) and Fullers wasn't a holy enough setting for the rite.

We were to be friends; after the war he was to return to Canada and somehow get a divorce. Meanwhile, I was to 'trust' him. And to spend Thursday evening on the river with him. We parted at Oxford Circus (his Army headquarters were at Oxford Circus House) and I walked away in the warm June sunlight feeling quite cold with loneliness.

On Thursday morning I got a note to say he had been sent to Folkestone until Saturday. I was disappointed but not unhappy. From Saturday onwards I sat around waiting for a telephone call. For a week I did not leave the Club, though I took a little air on the roof sometimes, after impressing on the hall porter where I was. Perched up there I thought of all my talks about life with Pixie. (She had already started divorcing *her* Canadian.) Now I was in love with a married man, life was rushing at me. But I soon learned that it had stopped rushing. He wrote to say he had decided not to see me again; his principles would not allow it. That was the first appearance of those utterly infuriating, on-and-off-again principles.

I wrote, several times, frantically but was ignored. Then— and it was just as well as I was making no effort to look for work—I heard that *Ye Gods* was to tour the London suburbs for a couple of months and I could rejoin the company. I accepted thankfully; apart from the money it was a comfort to be sharing a dressing-room with Vi again. Urged by her I tried to cheer myself up by buying new clothes and spent seven guineas on a pleated, black georgette frock which turned out to be a dress one remembers for a lifetime. I doubt if I ever liked any dress better, even when I could afford to spend ten times as much. It was very plain, trimmed only with a row of flat jet beads round the neck and at the very high waist.

Far less dignified was a black-and-white check suit with which I wore high white boots, white gloves, my new white fox fur and a jade green hat trimmed with purple pansies. I added a purple velvet chinstrap. It was a most becoming outfit and would have been just right for Shaw's Darling Dora. Phyllis, now back at the Club, said I looked outrageous and if my Canadian saw that hat his principles wouldn't last five minutes. She was cynical about men's principles and said men only developed them when their inclinations weren't strong enough.

I wrote again, quoting this interesting remark and saying I would be outside Oxford Circus House next day at one o'clock. It was a very moving letter, which I'd filled with rose petals; this must have been fun for him when he opened it at his Army desk. Anyway, it did the trick. He met me and we went to a little Belgian café which was empty enough for us to hold hands. But his principles were unaffected by my jade hat, complete with chin strap, and he would not agree to see me again.

Phyl's hat that summer was tightly covered in dark gold satin. It was expensive and ladylike, but it was also exactly the shape of a child's chamber pot. I mentioned this and Phyllis added a golden 'waterfall' veil which, if anything, stressed the resemblance.

Summer wore on and I forced myself to look for an autumn engagement but without much energy. Much of my time was spent riding up and down Oxford Street on the tops of buses, hoping to see my Canadian through an upstairs window of Oxford Circus House. One day I saw him striding along Oxford Street, hurled myself down the stairs, rang the bell frantically and plunged past an irate conductor. But it was no use, and I ended by returning to the Club, to be consoled by Phyllis over tea in the garden. She suggested I should send a letter by special messenger and tell the messenger to wait for an answer, as waiting messengers could have an hypnotic effect. So I dashed off a harrowing description of my chase along Oxford Street and sent for a messenger—who presumably had some effect as Bud telephoned asking me to meet him next day.

I wore my admirable black georgette (in those days georgette and even chiffon were considered suitable for daytime wear) without so much as a touch of colour anywhere and I

felt I looked almost widowed. We went to a café in Regent
Street called The Dug Out where the waitress seemed determined to join the party, coming back again and again trying to
sell cigarettes, chocolates, scent. Perhaps it was her frustrating
effect, plus the soulful black dress (which he much admired),
which caused him to invite me to spend Sunday on the
Thames.

That Sunday is not one of the days I would care to relive.
It began with an enormous lunch in the riverside bungalow at
which two other Canadians and two other girls were present.
There was hot roast pork, which I had been brought up to
believe was sudden death in hot weather. Everybody but me
was very jolly; I was too busy facing ptomaine poisoning. After
the meal we made a gay party in a boat, that is, it was five to
one as regards gaiety; I cannot recall saying one word. I was
often shy at parties and that one seemed to me particularly
embarrassing; also I feared Bud was not going to allow me to
see him alone. However, just the two of us did return to the
bungalow for tea, during which he put his arm around me. I
instantly averted my head and said 'Don't, please!' For God's
sake, why? Perhaps it was an echo of the wretched child who,
though longing to be called for in Postman's Knock at parties,
would face any boy who did call for her with a chilly, 'I don't
kiss.' I feel sure a little persuasion now would have done
wonders, but that highly-principled man instantly sprang up
and said, 'Let's take our tea on the lawn, shall we?' I admit
he said it kindly, but it was one of his major mistakes.

After tea, we went out in a canoe and he seemed to know
everyone on a full river; it was gayer than ever. Later, on the
way to the station, he courteously remarked that he had never
enjoyed a day more. I said I hadn't, either; I should think we
were equally untruthful.

I reached the Club in time to watch the last of the sunset
from the roof. Then I lay back on the gable and bitterly
regretted 'Please, don't!' But I could soon make amends. We
were to meet again three days later, at Oxford Circus.

I arrived punctually and waited for over an hour. I then
wrote a temperate letter saying I must have mistaken the day.

No answer. I wrote again, saying I would be at Oxford Circus at the same time the following Monday and was sure he couldn't leave me to wait in the street again. But he could.

I felt it would be pleasant to pour out my woes to Gwendo, my friend of *Kitty Grey* days. I found she had left the stage and was now doing war-work; she had a good secretarial post in a Whitehall office. She came to tea at the Club and, as she had always disliked the idea of the place, I was glad to note that the lounge was looking its best and there were half a dozen beautiful girls present—showgirls, mostly. Gwendo surveyed them with a duchess-like stare and said, 'And these are your friends? All, all whatlets.'

She seemed equally disapproving of the girls she met at her work.

'Whatlets?' I asked.

She considered this, then said, 'No, one could not say that— they are of a different class; all very aristocratic. So beautifully dressed and so very, very ladylike. But in a few weeks they are coming to me and asking if I could tell them how to stop having a baby.'

She listened to my troubles with patience and then gave her opinion. I had forgotten how French her accent was.

'And you wish to know if he will come back? Then, my poor Sadie, I must tell you frankly that he won't. You cannot write a man passionate love letters, chase him along Oxford Street, send him special messengers and then say, "Please, don't!" What a thing to say! *Of course* he has gone for good.'

'But he said we could be friends,' I insisted.

She dismissed this as beneath discussion, then said, 'There is a French proverb which means, "A door must be open or shut." Either you must remain a pure little English girl—possibly the only one—or just make up your mind to be a whatlet. As he is married, there is no way in between. Come now, you shall learn that proverb in French, you have a very nice accent when you try. "Il faut q'une porte . . ."'

Her own virtue was still intact, despite many assaults on it. She had worked for an elderly and amorous Colonel who had offered her anything she liked for a Christmas present. 'And I chose the most wonderful thick woollen nightgowns.' These had kept her warm all that war-time winter, but had a chilling effect on her employer. Now she was working for a younger man who was most attractive and used a seductive hair lotion. 'So unfair of him,' she complained. Gwendo's virtue never sat easily on her.

As I escorted her to the front door, she paused by the notice board and saw that a member wished to let a furnished flat for thirty shillings a week. She said, 'Could we not take that together, Sadie?' I had discovered that a cubicle was no place for the lovelorn, so I said the flat would at least be a place where I could cry, at which Gwendo laughed heartily. It was the attic floor of an old house in Crawford Street; we took it for a month.

I at once wrote to tell my Canadian about it and actually got a reply by return of post. No, he couldn't come to see me there; he was getting transferred to Folkestone. He would ring me up before he left—which he did next morning, so early that I was still in my bath and had to come down damp in a dressing-gown. I stood on tiptoe in the stuffy telephone box— the mouthpiece was always too high for me—and implored him to see me but he was adamant.

'This is goodbye, then?' I said miserably.

'Oh, no,' he corrected me cheerfully. 'Only *au revoir*.'

I cherished the *au revoir*, but it now seems to me inexcusable. For a man, as well as for a woman, a door should be open or shut.

In a way it was a relief to know there was nothing I could do as I didn't even have an address I could write to. Gwendo and I moved into the flat next day and were at once faced with the problems of housekeeping. We were annoyed to find there was a shortage of sugar and I remember stirring honey into my tea and actually giving the war a few thoughts.

The chief drawback to the flat was the rubber bath. It was easy to fill it by means of a rubber tube attached to the little geyser over the kitchen sink, but emptying it was tedious. One had to bale out with jugs and finally empty it into the sink, a job which required two people. Gwendo always left for work before I had my bath so I had to spend the day with it unemptied.

We soon got tired of cooking ourselves meals and took to going out for them, often joined by Phyllis. I have a vivid mental picture of one of those meals. Gwendo was in black with touches of spotless white, Phyllis wore the golden chamber pot with the waterfall veil, I was in my check suit with its full complement of green hat, white fox fur and high white boots. ('But what a whatlet you look in that outfit, Sadie, dear,' Gwendo had remarked.) Phyllis had now, like me, developed married man trouble and we talked interminably about our sufferings. Suddenly she looked at me wrathfully and said, 'It's all very well for you. Oh, I daresay you're suffering, but it's all *mental*. I—' she struck herself fiercely on the chest—'I am suffering *physically*.'

Gwendo regarded her with hauteur and said: 'No, Phyllis, you are not. Not in Maison Lyons when we are eating poached eggs.'

Afterwards she told me she could not stand any more of Phyllis's love troubles. I said mine must be pretty exhausting, too.

'Oh, no, Sadie, dear,' said Gwendo. 'You see, yours are *funny*.'

Phyllis had again got a job to tour the Camps, under the auspices of the Navy and Army Canteen Board. I envied her as she would be working for Basil Dean whom I had admired since I was a child when I had seen him acting in Miss Horniman's Company in Manchester, and she suggested I, too, should try to get into a Camp tour. I got an appointment with an important official.

Phyllis said this was one time when I must not wear my green hat. Much stress was being laid on the respectability of the players engaged. 'What you really need are clothes that look "county"—tweeds and a velours hat.' She had recently acquired a formidable velours hat which was vastly unbecoming to her Pekinese features.

I intended to wear my black georgette, but on the day of the appointment it rained so heavily that I went in my black mackintosh and sou'wester. They were neither county nor glamorous, but no one could have said I didn't look respectable. The official who received me wasted little time on me: there were no jobs in any of the Camp Companies and he wouldn't even put me on the waiting list. But a week later Phyllis reported that a girl was urgently needed in her Company, she had given a glowing account of me and arranged for me to be seen. I pointed out that I'd already been seen and hadn't been liked.

'Well, you might see a different man this time,' said Phyllis. 'Anyway try. And wear your black georgette.'

But I had recently made an impression with my green hat and white fox fur outfit; an agent had tried to kiss me. To hell with looking respectable.

I saw the same official. After he had engaged me, I happened to mention that I had seen him before. 'Oh, no,' he said decidedly. 'You must have seen Captain Dean. I couldn't possibly have forgotten you.' He went on to tell me that all engagements were for a probationary month. 'That's so we can be sure you're a good girl. Are you a good girl?'

He said it playfully, very playfully. That was a good green hat; possibly a forerunner of Michael Arlen's.

I was given a feeble ingénue part in the farce, *Jane* (the first play I ever saw, when I was rising five, and I didn't like it any better now) and a middle-aged mother in *Niobe*—also a farce. We had a pleasant but feeble director and I was disappointed to see no sign of Captain Dean. We then heard he would be coming to evening rehearsals—a blow to me as I was still playing in *Ye Gods*. I had made it clear to my playful official that I should have to give two weeks' notice and he had waved this aside airily. But I gathered from Phyllis that Captain Dean was anything but airy when faced with an incomplete cast at his evening rehearsals, and when he did get to one daytime rehearsal he appeared to dislike my performance. I may say that only a man of depraved tastes could have liked it, as it was in ingénue parts that I achieved my low as an actress.

I telephoned Phyllis that evening and she reported that my

part had now been given to a girl named Henzie Raeburn. I feared this meant I should lose my job altogether but Phyllis said No, Captain Dean now thought I could be dressed up to play the very short part of Mr Pixton, a hen-pecked husband.

'It's because you're so small, dear,' said Phyllis kindly. 'Captain Dean thinks you could look very funny as Mr Pixton.'

I decided I would see Captain Dean and the entire Navy and Army Canteen Board in Hell before I would let the Army see me looking funny as Mr Pixton; but mercifully it was one of Captain Dean's more evanescent inspirations and I was left just to understudy in *Jane* and to play my part in *Niobe*. Captain Dean did not rehearse *Niobe* and a new director for it now arrived who decided I should be a young mother, not a middle-aged one. This meant that I had to provide new dresses at my own expense.

I then went to spend the weekend with Phyllis at her Brighton home. We returned on Monday only in time for the *Niobe* rehearsal so I did not go to the flat, nor could I before dashing off to some far-out suburb for *Ye Gods*. I telephoned Phyllis from the theatre to hear how the evening rehearsal had gone.

She seemed worried, 'I'm afraid Captain Dean said something very odd about you.' Some change in the cast of *Jane* had been discussed and the stage manager had mentioned that I was available. Captain Dean had then said, 'She can't come to evening rehearsals. Wash her out.'

Wash her out? Neither Phyl nor I had heard the phrase before. Did it mean I was going to get the sack? I returned to the flat sunk very low indeed.

I was to sink lower. As I stumbled up the narrow, unlit stairs of the old house I remembered that Gwendo had planned to spend the night with her sister; so the flat was in darkness. As it was lit only by gas we had a firm rule that matches must be handy on our top landing. I felt for them. No matches. There'd be some in the kitchen, near the gas-stove. I opened the door and was thankful for the gleam of moonlight through the window, but not thankful for what it revealed; the sink, the draining board and the table top were piled with dirty crockery. Gwendo must have had all her meals in during the weekend and washed up nothing. And then, on my way towards the matches, I fell into the unemptied rubber bath. It was the last straw—to a girl who had been baulked in love and had now been washed out by Basil Dean. I just had the strength of mind to get back on to dry land and then, sitting on the kitchen floor, I abandoned myself to weeping.

But as always after moments of abandonment, there comes the deadly time when one has to reclaim oneself. And by then, even the moon had passed me by. I fumbled my way from kitchen to bedroom and put myself to bed in pitch darkness. For I never did find those matches.

The next morning I went back to live at the Club. I had already paid my full share of the flat's rent and I left a note saying I'd settle for any expenses I might have incurred. I must say I quite liked the thought of Gwendo coming back to find the kitchen just as she had left it—only wetter.

XI

On a Donkey at Portsmouth

The Navy and Army Canteen Board Light Comedy Company opened unimpressively, at one of the Surrey camps. We played several of them, driving out each night from Aldershot, where accommodation was so scarce that we had to stay at the most expensive hotel, which cost more than the four pounds a week I was earning. Fortunately I still had some money in hand, but was indignant with the Government. Now that 'The Management' was the Government, one was almost always indignant with it.

After *Jane* had been launched, with very mild success, we concentrated on rehearsals of *Niobe* and were told Basil Dean was coming to the Sunday dress rehearsal to add finishing touches. Most of us were satirical about this as so little time had been spent on the play we doubted if we could get through it at all. And Captain Dean's opening address made us feel even more doubtful for he began by telling us he hadn't read the play and had no idea what it was about. He proposed to watch us perform it, in the hope that some bright ideas would strike him.

This seemed to most of us lunacy. The hero of my childhood's many visits to Miss Horniman's Company was toppling fast.

After listening to us for half an act Captain Dean stopped us and said he had begun to get the hang of things, and he didn't find the play very funny. I couldn't have agreed with him more. He then began to give people hints on how they should characterise their parts.

When he came to me he said, 'Now you, Miss Smith, have been puzzling me extremely. I thought at first you were the ingénue heroine and then you turned out to be the mother of a family. What you ought to be is the lone, lorn woman of the play.' He then said some of my lines for me in a lugubrious voice and told me to copy him. Mercifully, I was able to do so and, when we started to rehearse again I, for the first and last time in my acting career, found myself being brilliantly directed. The hero was on his pedestal again.

It was the most astonishing *tour-de-force*. Without knowing what line was coming next, or even how the plot was going to develop, Basil Dean proceeded to give ideas for characterisation, intonations, new movements, bits of new business and even occasional funny new lines. Such behaviour could have been wildly disconcerting, but again and again he would get us to repeat a scene and fix it. Sometimes he would say the pace had dropped and then go back and spot the line which had slowed things up. It was purely inspirational direction and the whole company responded to it; no one seemed to get tired though we went on for hours and hours. And gradually that dreariest of farces turned into a funny entertainment. It was a revelation to me what inspired direction could do to a play.

'Of course you won't remember it all, but you'll remember some of it,' said Captain Dean. He was in a magnificent temper most of the evening and the only person who got into trouble was Henzie Raeburn. She played a maid and had to draw curtains and switch on lights which she did with the heartiest good will, but this necessitated changes of lighting, and the electrician kept failing to synchronise these with her actions. Again and again poor Henzie was blamed. During these interludes all Captain Dean's bonhomie deserted him. I was to learn, in later years, that lighting a play is seldom conducive to bonhomie. And one has to remember that stage lighting *belonged* to Basil Dean. I sometimes feel there is a mistake in the first chapter of Genesis about who it was that first said, 'Let there be light.'

It was very, very late when we finished, but Captain Dean called each of us to him in turn for a detailed criticism which, in some cases, was fairly biting. Faced with me, he was silent so long that I prepared for the worst. Then he said, 'Well, dear, you're really quite funny and your make-up's all right and your dresses are pretty. In fact, you're rather good.' Both of us looked surprised.

It was pleasant to have that little speech to remember—and to know that, when I was sacked a few weeks later, it was not for poor acting. The disaster occurred during the third week of the tour. We were at Ripon where, as at Aldershot, it seemed impossible to find any cheap accommodation and most of us had to stay at an expensive hotel. Here the manager refused to give us supper after we got back from work at night; dinner was at seven and if we were out (as we had to be) that was just our bad luck. And he only reckoned to give us a cold, sparse lunch. He did, finally, agree that the lunch should be a hot one, provided we were in not later than one-thirty. After that, no lunch would be served.

We were by then rehearsing *Peg o' My Heart* and our youngish, recently-arrived director liked to work until two-thirty before breaking for the day. However, he was himself staying at the hotel so we presumed he would break at one and rehearse again in the afternoon. I was playing a maid and by five to one I had gone through my very small part. He told me I could leave. As he was showing no sign of ending the rehearsal, our leading lady, Evelyn Hope, decided to remind him of the deadline for lunch.

She was a tall, dark, handsome young woman with a very calm manner. Possibly her calmness annoyed him for he cut her short rudely, saying he would rehearse as long as he liked and might not break before three o'clock. Evelyn said she could not face a long drive to a camp and two performances just on a very small afternoon tea, but the young man remained adamant. He said that if she left his rehearsal to have lunch he would report her to the Navy and Army Canteen Board and would report anyone who left with her.

I reminded him he had given me permission to leave; he instantly withdrew it. This seemed to me unreasonable, also I felt someone should support Evelyn, who was now getting ready to go. The company who, before rehearsal, had talked glibly about walking out *en masse* at one o'clock, were now as meek as lambs. So I followed Evelyn out. We doubted if we really would be complained of, as the director was normally a pleasant man and he particularly admired Evelyn's work.

But complain he did, though afterwards he was apologetic and more worried than we were. Evelyn was a valuable leading lady and we both felt sure she would be given a chance to state her case which seemed to us a reasonable one. But the Navy and Army Canteen Board was obviously not interested in hearing it, for the next day she and I received telegrams, signed Basil Dean, saying: 'Understand you have not been rehearsing properly. Your engagement terminated at the end of your trial month.'

Indignation raged. The company held a meeting, talked of going on strike, signing petitions . . . In the end, it did nothing whatever. But the poor young director did. He wrote to London saying he had never expected our dismissal and asking for its withdrawal. This being curtly refused, he wrote to say that if we left, he would too—which he ended up doing. The three of us departed on warmest terms with each other and entertaining the coldest feelings for the Navy and Army Canteen Board.

During the correspondence it became clear that, though Basil Dean had signed the telegram, the matter was really in the hands of the playful official who had engaged me, so I wrote to him putting my side of the case. But I had evidently turned out to be not the kind of not-good-girl who provoked him to playfulness, for he sent me a stern letter about my lack of 'morale' which, I gather, was just about enough to lose the war. I replied scathingly that as the Navy and Army Canteen Board took no interest in its companies' welfare and sent them to places where there was no accommodation they could afford, I should find it an economy to leave—and it was true I was out of pocket, what with hotel expenses and the dresses I'd had to provide. The following year, I wrote to Basil Dean asking if I could come and see him 'up the back stairs as your colleague would have me shot on sight'. My letter must have amused him for he replied that, if I would write again in a month, he could probably reinstate me. But by then I had got another job and we did not meet again until thirteen years later, when he bought my first play, *Autumn Crocus,* thus ushering in five years of highly profitable ructions.

The only touch of light comedy for the Light Comedy Company while at Ripon was when the hall porter at the hotel stalked into the lounge at tea-time and announced, loudly and pompously, 'Ladies and gentlemen of the Navy and Army Canteen Board, your convenience is at the door.'

Before returning to London I spent a few days in Blackpool, where the family was taking a holiday. They were all together, my uncles, my aunts, Nan's two children, and I hoped I could recapture the atmosphere of my early holidays. But I (not they) had changed and I felt faintly aloof. I remember walking along the Blackpool front with my aunts thinking 'If they only knew all I have been through'. They were more than anxious to, and they pressed for news about romances and admirers and Nan said there was something about my letters I had written home on my twenty-first birthday which made her feel I must be in love. Impressed by this surprising bit of intuition, I unwisely disclosed that I was in love with a married man. The result was unfortunate. Nan said a girl's purity was like a limb, one never knew how much one would miss it until one had lost it; and Auntie Bertha said it would break her heart if any married man ever got hold of me. I'd been given no chance to lose my purity, my married man was determined not to be got hold of, and I was more interested in my own broken heart than the possibility that Auntie Bertha's might be broken. So, much as I loved my dear aunts, I refrained from further confidences.

It was now late autumn so there was no chance of getting into a touring company before Christmas; but I still had some savings. Also I had at last inherited the three hundred pounds in Consols which had been put in Chancery during my early childhood. It was all that remained of a much larger sum, most of which had been embezzled by a trustee. (He was my father's brother-in-law; as Ivy Compton-Burnett remarked, people don't know about families.) The three hundred pounds went into Chancery three hundred pounds and came out three hundred pounds; Chancery having presumably taken the compound interest for many years as a payment for the onerous job of safeguarding the money. I took the Consols and my savings to the first bank I came to in Baker Street. This was the National Bank of Ireland, of which I have affectionate memories. The manager, an elderly man with a beard, took a kindly interest in me and was always distressed whenever I asked him to sell some of my Consols because I was in need of ready money. When I was down to the last fifty pounds worth, he suggested I should accept a job in the bank—a noble gesture seeing that he had never succeeded in persuading me to make out a paying-in slip.

Happily I had not, in 1917, any vision of the days when my inheritance would be exhausted, and I left the bank with the Consols intact and my first cheque book, feeling I was now a woman of means. (The income from my Consols amounted to about half a crown a week.)

I had plenty of good friends at the Club that autumn and had never enjoyed life there more. I had a cubicle on the second floor; there were seven others with it, all enclosed in what had once been a very big room. We called our group 'The Village' and prided ourselves on having no dogsbodies—girls who snored or used strong-smelling soap or complained if we talked after midnight. There was a good deal of eating in the small hours. I remember complaining of hunger and being instantly hit on the head by half a Veda loaf from an adjacent cubicle. (Lovely sticky brown Veda bread, which would keep fresh over a week without any bread tin.)

I visited agents regularly though they told me this was pointless until spring tours were being planned. I had never been out of work more than a few weeks before and I was soon obsessed by a feeling of guilt. So I was glad to accept a walk-on in the Christmas season of *When Knights Were Bold* at the Kingsway Theatre. The pay was only a pound a week but that would cover the cost of my food. I played a page and turned my hair up as well as I could, but was told to let it hang down below my waist because that looked more medi-aeval. There were no tights to fit me, so I had to wear green stockings held up by visible suspenders which looked very unmediaeval indeed.

I dressed with five other girls who were all experienced actresses and were only walking on because, like me, they were hard-up. We decided we would do a really good job, and add to the excitement of the fight scene by our changes of expression. After the first matinée we were sent for and told we must cut out expression. The stage manager told us to study the behaviour of the regular walk-ons, who toured with Mr Bromley Challoner. They would never dream of distracting attention from him. We had already noticed this. They stood with wooden faces staring at the audience and then, at the end of the fight, broke into loud cheering which was turned on and off as if by some invisible tap. We had to do exactly the same. I gave in my notice when I got the chance to play in a trial week of a music-hall sketch but we only got one booking.

It must have been about this time that Lee Ephraim made one of his many attempts to get me work, in a sketch with one of his clients, Lily Langtry, at the Coliseum. He took me to a Sunday evening rehearsal, put me in a box at the back of the theatre and told me not to make any sound unless he called to me. He felt a maid was needed to show Mrs Langtry in at the beginning of the sketch and he planned to tell her so at the end of the rehearsal, and then introduce me. The sketch began and Mrs Langtry sailed on resplendent in deep blue velvet. It was an odd little play in which two women talked politely to each other, while their secret souls crouched beside them and said what they really felt. At the end Mr Ephraim made his suggestion. It was badly received but Mrs Langtry finally said that, if he felt so strongly about it, her own maid could come on and announce her; that would save an extra salary. She then left the stage and soon all but one of the stage lights were put out. There were no lights whatever in the auditorium.

I expected Mr Ephraim to come and collect me. Nothing happened. I considered calling out but, apart from the fact that I had promised not to disclose myself, there was no one to call to. The stage was deserted and now so dimly lit that it was only just less dark than the auditorium. After what must have been quite twenty minutes I decided I had better try to make my own way out of the front of the theatre, so I opened the door of the box and groped my way along a really pitch black passage, but after stumbling down a couple of steps I decided to go back to the box—on my hands and knees. It would be better to spend the night there rather than risk breaking my neck trying to get down to the foyer—which, anyway, would probably be locked up as late as this. Once back in the box I gazed despairingly at that dim square on the stage. Would it be any use calling out? I had a horror of shouting into that enormous empty theatre. Still... What should I call? I had just decided on 'Help!' when I saw a figure move across the stage and then heard Mr Ephraim call my name. He said he'd almost forgotten me.

When he at last reached me in the box (and how he managed to I've no idea) he said the unusual circumstances made him feel romantic. They did me, too, but not with Mr Ephraim, so I said, 'Surely you know I wouldn't be here, in such circumstances, if I didn't feel sure I could trust you?'

'Well, I guess that puts a man on his honour,' said Mr Ephraim nobly, if a trifle plaintively, and then managed to pilot me safely out by the expenditure of many matches. In a way, it seems a pity. To get oneself seduced in a pitch black and totally deserted Coliseum would have had a certain *cachet*.

In the spring I was smitten with a completely undangerous, unpainful but utterly infuriating complaint which, throughout my life, has added to my worries at times when I have been feeling particularly low: a small bald patch appeared on my head. The hairdresser who discovered it said it was due to war nerves, to which I hardly felt I had a rightful claim, sold me a pot of ointment and said all would be well. A few days later I astonished myself by landing a job at five pounds a week. I had recently become friendly with a small, plump, pretty Club member named Nadine March who was engaged to go to the Portsmouth Repertory Theatre as juvenile lead. She decided she did not want to go, and secured me an interview with the manager of the theatre, Peter Davey, when next he came to London. He not only engaged me, but pressed an advance of ten pounds on me to help with my 'wardrobe'. (Advertisements for repertory actresses almost always included 'good wardrobe essential'.) All was bliss—except that I feared I was going bald. My spot had already grown from the size of a sixpence to that of a shilling—rather a large shilling.

Nadine then took me to her distinguished woman doctor, Dr Ettie Sayers, who said I was suffering from alopecia nervosium, which meant nervous fox-mange (God knows, foxes have cause to feel nervous) and she would guarantee to have my missing hair growing again before I went to Portsmouth in three weeks' time, if I would come to her every day. I knew she charged a guinea a visit (a very high fee for those days) so this seemed impossible for me, but she said we could discuss the cost when I was cured. She then settled me in an armchair and waved a stick at me. Blue sparks came out of me in all directions. Then she concentrated the stick on my bald patch. For days I believed the electricity was in the stick and was astonished when she showed me that a ruler would do just as well; the current was mysteriously pumped into me by the seemingly innocent arm-chair I sat in. I never understood any of it, but in three weeks I had a fine crop of new hair growing on my spot. I reckoned I owed Dr Sayers eighteen guineas, but she presented a bill for one guinea and said there was no hurry for that. She also told me I was repressing my nerves and if, for instance, I hurt myself by bumping into something, it would be as well if I turned and kicked it.

Nadine and I were then establishing a close friendship which lasted until her far too early death in 1944. She had a little more money than I had and was extremely generous; again and again she would take me out to large meals at an ancient chop-house near Piccadilly Circus. We would work these off by walking back to the Club 'through the purlieus', as Nadine called it. This meant we must go exclusively by back streets and mews, and was one of the best ways of getting to know an older London. Our chop-house has long since been pulled down, as have many of the 'purlieus' through which we walked by moonlight, full of steak.

One early adventure Nadine and I shared was far from

pleasant: we were both of us poisoned by arsenic, in common with fourteen other Club members. One morning every girl who drank coffee for breakfast was mysteriously smitten. I was lucky enough to have had breakfast in bed, but some girls were ignominiously sick in Whitehall on their way to war-work.

I had never known any sickness like it and I guessed I had been poisoned as soon as I heard how many girls were ill. We lay in our rooms and cubicles wanly asking for news of each other. In the afternoon a doctor called on us and asked me if I had any enemies and, though he confessed he had no idea what was the matter with me, ordered me to take a dose of castor oil. I refused, mainly for Christian Science reasons. (This was before I backslid to medical treatment for my bald spot.) Besides, I felt no confidence in that doctor. There was then talk of forcing me to take castor oil but, before this could happen, the girl called Vincent who only seemed to erupt into my life at important moments, walked into my cubicle and put a hot-water bottle on my stomach.

She then said firmly, 'You will not take castor oil and you will now stop being sick and you will shortly drink a very hot cup of tea I shall bring you.' She was correct in all these statements and I was better days before any of my fellow sufferers who all of them meekly accepted castor oil. As always, after her sudden appearances, Vincent quietly disappeared from my life.

It was soon known we had been poisoned by arsenic, but how or why was never discovered. There was a theory it had been the work of a German spy, but one cannot feel that the young coffee-drinkers of a woman's club would be worthy of his arsenic. I suspect it was due to some kitchen accident but, if so, it proved untraceable as the club cateress, determined to avoid any further catastrophe, made a terrific clearance in the kitchens, throwing out everything she felt might conceivably have contained arsenic. Anyway, we all lived to tell the tale, though one girl nearly died.

The poisoning incident was over before I started for my job in Portsmouth. I had rooms in an old terrace house overlooking the sea and particularly liked my upstairs sitting-room with its big bow window. I remember sitting in that window reading D. H. Lawrence's banned novel, *The Rainbow*, which surprisingly, I had been able to borrow from a little nearby library. I had admired Lawrence since reading his poems in the *English Review* while still at school.

I took to my gypsy-like landlady on sight (she proved to be good at horoscopes) and she was much impressed by the permit to buy cream Dr Sayers had given me; it was supposed to soothe my poor war-torn nerves and ward off fox-mange. Things promised well. I had all my clothes ready for the first production, an old farce called *The New Clown*, and was able to go to the first rehearsal word perfect.

And then the snags began. The part that had been sent to me was that of a society girl who dressed up as a circus girl. Our producer now informed me he was using an earlier version of the play in which I was *really* a circus girl, and the society girl was to be played by someone else. No, there was no new script for me. I must just cut out the lines that didn't apply (including the whole of one act). None of the lines remaining to me were now in character for a real circus girl. And all the clothes I had brought with me were unsuitable. I found I should have to make myself a gingham dress during rehearsals. (Mercifully, my elaborate circus dress was supplied by the management.) I could see the producer was not impressed with me. However, Peter Davey and his wife invited me to tea and seemed to have high hopes for me. (*They* hadn't seen me rehearse.)

By the opening night I was more nervous than ever before. But I had one thing to be thankful for: the large white horse on which I was supposed to make an entrance wearing a ballet skirt had failed to materialise. There remained, however, one long scene I had to play sitting on a donkey, which had not attended rehearsals. Much was expected of this scene and when the curtain rose, with me perched on the donkey's back, there was a murmur of admiration from the audience. All went well for about three speeches. Then the donkey took me off into the wings. I saw nothing for it but to slip off the donkey and play the scene on my own feet. When the curtain fell there were bitter laments from the producer and I was told that, in future, I must stay on the donkey whatever happened. If it took me off-stage, he would drive it back.

At the next performance (we were playing twice nightly) it again walked off. The producer pushed its nose; I pulled its ears. The chief comedian, on stage, dangled a carrot—but, of course, at the wrong end of the donkey. It remained adamant. Finally, I turned round and sat facing its tail, playing the rest of the scene with only my head—and the donkey's behind—emerging from the wings.

Afterwards, the producer insisted I had wrecked the scene, though I pointed out that I'd, at least, obeyed his instructions and stayed on the donkey. During the entire week of twelve evening performances and two matinées, my mount and I did not give one satisfactory performance—except, of course, to those members of the cast who stood in the wings enjoying every moment. One nice girl, whom I had told about my hair trouble (free of Dr Ettie's magic wand, it had broken out again), chose a night when I was having particular hell with the donkey to whisper loudly—and untruthfully—'Look out, your fox-mange is showing.'

Our next play was a forty-year-old farce named *Betsy* in which I had a small, peaceful part independent of livestock. And half-way through the week I was cheered to get a letter from Phyllis saying she had got herself engaged by Peter Davey. She joined us almost at once and came to share my rooms, which she soon decided were dirty. I knew they weren't exactly well-scrubbed but they didn't smell, there were no insects, and I was attached to the sea view and to the jolly landlady and her horoscopes. However, Phyllis went out and firmly found us something more hygienic. The floors might be cleaner, but there was no sea view and the landlady said that if we each of us expected a hot bath every day, we would have to share the bath water. I hankered for dirt, horoscopes and my own personal bath water. We should have moved again had I not received a letter from Peter Davey saying my engagement would end in a month.

Phyllis feared her engagement must have meant my dismissal.

We hurried to the theatre intent on finding Peter Davey, only to learn that he had gone into a nursing home and the man who produced the plays was now in charge. He told me I had to go simply because there would soon be no more parts for me. Phyllis had nothing to do with it and he'd no idea why she'd been engaged as there would be no parts for her either. Phyllis was a character actress, I was a juvenile; what *he* wanted was a full-size leading lady. He went on to say that, unsuitable though we were, Phyllis and I would have to play the leading parts in his next production, *Facing the Music*, and very bad we should undoubtedly be.

With a long part to learn quickly I had no time to worry; also I hoped Mr Davey, who had liked me, would come back and re-engage me. I was to play a young wife. Phyllis was 'Miss Fotheringay, an actress' and she was going to be very, very glamorous. (I don't think she had cared for being described as a character actress.) Her first concern was her hat. After wearing her county velours Homburg for the whole of the Camp tour, she was suffering from hat starvation and ready to break out. She supplied herself with wire and gold lace and turned out a staggering creation. It had no brim, just a triangular crown quite fifteen inches high, and at each of its three top corners there was a plume of emerald green feathers. With this she wore a black and silver evening dress she happened to have and she carried a very tall stick surmounted by a large emerald green bow.

When, at the Sunday dress rehearsal, she appeared in this outfit, the producer said, 'But you can't wear that dress. The scene takes place in the morning.'

'In farce', said Phyllis, 'one disregards the probabilities.'

She had been undermining the poor man all week. Having decided to leave the company when I left it, she had acquired a devil-may-care arrogance that seemed to have an almost hypnotic effect on him. He struggled at times, but there was little he could do; he could not take the part away from her because there was no one else to play it. Also, he obviously liked her and realised she was a good actress. His last stand was made at the dress rehearsal of our next play, *The Strange*

Adventures of Miss Brown, in which she played the schoolgirl heroine. She made her first entrance in apple-green georgette.

'No, no, Miss Morris,' he protested. 'You should be in white, like the other girls.'

'In farce,' said Phyllis, 'one dresses simply to give the audience pleasure.'

In the next act she had to come downstairs in a nightgown, having just got out of bed. She certainly wore the nightgown, but came in through the french window. This was an accident, but Phyllis had no intention of admitting it.

'In farce,' she said, 'one makes the most *effective* entrance.'

The producer turned away with a low moan.

This was our last play at Portsmouth. I played a schoolgirl with a cold and was really rather good. After the final performance Peter Davey, back from his nursing home, congratulated me and asked me who I was. I told him.

He looked puzzled and asked if he had engaged me.

I told him he had not only engaged me, but also dismissed me.

He said it was the first he had heard of it—'I've been ill, you know.'—then drifted away, shaking his head. I imagined he must have been coerced into signing the letter of dismissal, and I wondered if I should ask to be reinstated. But by then I was ready to go, I had never been in an engagement I disliked so much.

When Phyllis and I were finally leaving the stage-door she noticed I was waggling one foot in the air, and asked what I was doing.

I said, 'I'm shaking the dust of this theatre off my feet.'

She said she would, too; and under the astonished eyes of the stage-door keeper we shook our feet very thoroughly.

XII

The Foothills of Sex

At this time Phyllis was again involved in married man trouble, a different married man from the one who had, the previous year, caused her to suffer 'physically'. She had met her new love while touring the Camps; he was a South African major, stationed at Borden and, like my Canadian, a man of unnecessarily high principles. Phyllis now planned a campaign to undermine those frustrating principles.

We embarked on what we called 'The Siege of Borden'. We stayed in a hostel, close to the camp, wore stage wedding rings and said we were soldiers' wives—not that anyone cared. The company playing at the Camp theatre was one Phyllis had been in. So we called on her particular friends while they were getting ready for the show and asked if I could stay in their dressing-room while she did some telephoning. Only when the theatre was about to close for the night did Phyllis return with her Major to say she was going out to supper with him and they would first escort me back to the hostel. It turned out that this was her Major's idea; she herself had simply forgotten my existence.

He was a tall, dark man, more than old enough to be Phyllis's father, with a long, mournful face suggestive of a poetic horse —if one can visualise a horse with a drooping moustache. He both looked and sounded a nice man and a good man, and somehow I didn't fancy Phyl's chances of getting herself seduced—which I understood to be her objective. I went to sleep wondering if her bed would still be unoccupied the next morning.

She woke me soon after midnight, very obviously unseduced. It was hopeless, she said—and she had put in three hours' hard work while I waited at the theatre. 'I did everything,' she told me. 'I even tore my dress open.'

I looked at her with interest. She was wearing one of her most 'county' outfits—a navy serge dress, pleated from hem to neck, with a high collar band. The only opening was on one shoulder.

'*How* did you tear it open?' I asked.

With a dramatic gesture she tore at her shoulder. Three press-hooks popped open revealing two inches of collar-bone. Nobly resisting this stupendous temptation, the Major had courteously refastened the press-hooks. Still, he had promised to see her off at the station next morning.

We got there early and found an empty compartment. Phyllis closed the door, stood at the window, and was furious whenever she had to move to let someone in. Time passed, only a few moments were left—and then he appeared, on horseback! I can still see him, riding down the slope to the station, at a very stately pace. I felt at least he might have galloped.

Phyllis shouted and waved madly. The Major took his time about parking his horse, but at last he arrived at our compartment. Phyllis, by then half out of the window, proceeded to talk with complete lack of inhibition. The whistle blew, doors slammed. Phyllis leaned even further out to embrace her Major. He shied, though he continued to look benevolent. She stayed at the window long after the train started. Only when it gathered speed did she totter to her seat, where she sat in dazed silence for a good five minutes. She then murmured to the world at large: 'Didn't he look glorious on that horse?'

Back in London she said she felt much better, because she now 'knew where she was'. Very shortly she got the chance to rejoin a Camp Theatre tour. I had no such luck and it seemed unlikely I should get a job before the autumn tours began; and we were still only in May. I decided that, as well as looking for work, I would try to write some stories and would therefore allow myself the extravagance of a room instead of a cubicle. I managed to get one of the cheapest rooms in the Club, around eighteen shillings a week inclusive of breakfast. It was on the top floor and had a dormer window with a deep window-seat, so high up that one could only reach it by climbing up on the table. But once there, one had a marvellous view west across the Marylebone Workhouse roof. (It was a standing joke at the Club that our two views were the Workhouse and Madame Tussaud's.) Up on that window-seat I could undoubtedly write masterpieces. But I needed cushions; and I would make a bedspread, a tablecloth and covers for the pillows. I still had most of the three hundred pounds in Consols I had inherited, so I sold some of them.

I decided to go to Heal and Son, in Tottenham Court Road. Why, I wonder? Perhaps because much of the Club furniture came from there and I suppose someone told me Heal's was particularly modern. I hankered for modernity and I particularly fancied black and primrose. But the impressive young lady in Heal's more than impressive shop said that would be very ordinary. I must have off-black, which looked slightly rusty, and mustard not primrose. The material was a thick cotton. And I must have two cushions in rose-pink muslin and two in saxe-blue satin. And I must have a pillow covered in hand-woven sage-green linen to 'pull the whole thing together'. I jibbed at the sage-green linen. It was dull and it was expensive. But she was firm. Without the sage-green the scheme would not work. I gave in.

As I walked away from my helpful assistant, laden with my purchases, I saw in the distance the open door of an office, inside which a red-haired man sat working at a desk. Nothing told me that, five years later, I should be inside that office asking the red-haired man for a job, or that he and his shop would be of the utmost importance in my life. Indeed, only when I eventually entered the office did I remember I had ever looked through its door before.

Once up in my attic bedroom I soon realised I could only use the off-black and mustard materials. The black became a bedspread and a tablecloth; the mustard stuff became pillow covers.

I did without cushions and the blue satin eventually made the bodice of an evening dress; the rose-pink muslin and the sage-green 'puller together' were sold, for a fraction of their cost, to some misguided Club friend. My refurbished bedroom was much admired, but not by me; mustard remains one of my least-favourite shades. And I was depressed at having wasted so much money when I saw no prospect of work. Also my trip to Borden with the love-lorn Phyllis had made me particularly conscious of my own love-lorn state. It was now eleven months since my Canadian had bowed out of my life by saying '*Au revoir*' on the telephone. I particularly remember one Saturday afternoon when I was feeling very low indeed.

I went up to the roof, leaned on the iron balustrade, and thought about life, and quite soon started to think about death. It would be peaceful to be dead. Suppose one jumped off the roof? I took a penny from my handbag (one seldom moved about the Club without clutching one's handbag), dropped it and counted the seconds until it hit the ground. Six seconds. Would a body fall quicker than a penny? (This is something I have never been able to work out.) Anyway, give or take a second or two, six seconds would take me into eternity. I considered it very seriously—so seriously that I became alarmed and rushed down to the safety of my room. I felt pretty sure I had had a genuine impulse towards suicide.

On my dressing-table stood a vase with three roses. (I doubt if there was ever a time when I was too poor to spend money on flowers.) I looked at those roses and absolutely challenged God to send my Canadian back before they faded. I say 'God' but I'm sure I wasn't praying. I never did believe in the efficacy of prayer. But I did believe one could sometimes force things to happen by sheer will power. Prayer carries a built-in 'If it be Thy will' clause; forcing doesn't. Indeed, I mentally added: '*Whatever* the consequences.' And I had an instantaneous flash of certainty that I had done the trick.

The certainty vanished, but I felt much less depressed. I went downstairs and joined friends for a reasonably good half-crown Club dinner (first retrieving my penny from the garden). And I completely forgot the incident until Monday morning, when I went to my pigeon-hole and found a letter from my Canadian.

It was a short, almost formal letter actually asking if I remembered him and saying he would like to have news of me. And perhaps we could meet when next he came to London. (He was still stationed at Folkestone.) He signed it with his full name and rank—he was now a sergeant-major. He enclosed a small snapshot, to remind me what he looked like.

Those roses were still unfaded. (I may say that I have during my life again and again tried this trick of forcing fate, but never again pulled it off.)

I advised myself to keep my answer friendly and unemotional and to keep the length down. I did—to four pages. I then relaxed and waited blissfully for an answer. I presumed I should get one by return. I had to wait ten days. Then he said he'd had Spanish 'flu, which I didn't believe. I took it that his stopping and starting technique was operating again. However, he rang up on the Sunday to say he was in London and would I meet him at Charing Cross Station. I took a taxi. Happiness such as mine could not be wasted on a bus.

I have an account of that day, written in a red, leather-bound notebook in which I only described very important occasions. I say, 'I can't write all I feel'—but I must have been doing my best, having turned out forty pages.

We had lunch at the Trocadero and sat there until the waiters were laying the tables for dinner. Then we went to Hyde Park—'that afternoon, all green and gold', and then we went to the New Gallery Cinema in Regent Street. This seemed to me a waste of time, when we could have gone on talking, and may have contributed to my still existing dislike for that great artist, Charlie Chaplin.

Not even at the pictures did we so much as hold hands and yet the Red Leather Notebook mentions his repeated declarations of love, and that he suggested taking a flat and keeping me in it. This is reported in dialogue and, on careful study, I can't say it amounts to a definite offer.

It was still daylight when we came out of the pictures. He said he would ring up next morning and arrange to take me to South Harrow, where he was playing in a cricket match. He then went off to stay with relations.

As usual, I took my thoughts up to the Club roof. A hard-up Club member had recently sold me, for one shilling, a little book of Ballades and Rondeaus that contained a poem by George Moore beginning: 'The lilacs are in bloom, All is that ever was.' It was too late for lilac, but a faint scent of hay was wafted over from the dried grass in Regent's Park and, for me, certainly rather more was than ever had been.

Next morning I settled in the lounge and luxuriously awaited my telephone call. By lunch time I had given up hope of the cricket match, but felt sure he would ring up to explain before he returned to Folkestone that night. No telephone call. No letter. After three days I wrote in fury and received an affectionate answer, but no explanation. Correspondence, more and more affectionate, continued for a couple of weeks and then I was asked to spend a weekend at Folkestone. Rooms would be taken for me. It would be a completely respectable weekend; I was to *trust* him. A Club friend remarked that she had never seen a girl starting off for a respectable weekend taking so much trouble with her underclothes.

Ah, but there were see-through fashions in those days, too— but what was seen, through georgette blouses, were elaborate camisole tops. I favoured filet lace and apple green shoulder-straps, and considered the usual pink ribbons and rosebuds conventional.

Just before my train reached Folkestone it occurred to me that he might not be there to meet me. But he was. We shook hands very formally and he then escorted me to a waiting taxi, in which he informed me he had engaged my rooms for a week, taken a room in the same house for himself so that he would not have to return to camp early every evening, and told the landlady I was his fiancée. I instantly felt self-conscious and even more so when I found that the landlady, though pleasant, had none of the warmth of theatrical landladies; nor were her rooms anything like theatrical digs. They had a cool, clean, unlived in atmosphere.

There was a large high-tea waiting, but I said I wished to unpack first. My Canadian carried my suitcase upstairs, then closed the door and said: 'Well, are you at last going to let me kiss you?'

This was it. Not a kiss at childish parties. Not a stage kiss;

but the first real kiss of my life. (And, God help me, I was already twenty-two.) I indicated willingness and waited.

It must have been a fairly long kiss, because I did so much thinking while it lasted. I certainly wasn't thrilled; I had experienced more when he took my arm to see me across the road. And the steady pressure was hard on one's front teeth. Still, I didn't *mind* it and was prepared to give it every chance. But, unfortunately, I remembered having heard that a man never respected a girl who didn't end a kiss before he did. I backed hastily.

He looked distinctly surprised, then said he would leave me to unpack. I took so long over it that the landlady came up to hurry me, saying she wanted to go out for the evening. At tea there were large, chilly tinned peaches, a luxury in war-time, but never liked by me. I feel sure I failed to express appreciation.

After clearing away, the landlady returned to say she and her husband would be out until ten o'clock and we should have the house to ourselves. Her manner might be less than warm, but she was obviously giving the go-ahead to war-time lovers.

We then embarked on a good three hours of what I later described to Phyllis as 'heavy love-making'; I doubt if the term 'heavy petting' had yet been invented. Unfortunately, most of this came as a complete shock to me. Thanks to ever-blessed Dr Marie Stopes I was fully informed about the sexual act, but about what one might call the foothills of sex I knew nothing. Were such goings-on permissible? Was my Canadian coarse, abnormal—even insane? Or was he right in saying that, between people who loved each other, nothing was wrong? There were a few peaceful interludes when love was merely discussed but, on the whole, it was a hot, heavy evening. And as regards kissing, damn near suffocating.

Shortly before ten o'clock he closed the curtains, put on the lights and carried me to the mantel, so that I could look at myself in the glass. I think I was supposed to look awakened. I thought I looked blowsy. Hastily I put up my hair, retrieved my shoes and tidied up generally, before the landlady tapped on the door and said she was going to get us supper. I didn't want supper, but I could see the advantages of a meal; one couldn't be kissed while eating.

Actually I was recovering fast and we laughed a lot over supper. And I agreed that he could come to my room to say goodnight, on being assured that I could trust him. This proved to be true—just.

Next morning he had to return to camp, leaving me to spend the day on my own. I walked on the Leas and explored the old town below. I found it romantic and wanted to write a poem about it, but no ideas came. Heavens, had some coarsening process already set in? However, I was happy to see my Canadian when he returned in time for tea, after which we embarked on another evening of heavy love-making, and I came by one authentic thrill. This nearly frightened me out of my wits, but seemed to give him much pleasure, though he then said it would be best if he didn't come to my room to say goodnight. I was both relieved and disappointed.

On Sunday morning I was again left on my own. I again tried, and failed, to write a poem. And I felt a little ill, almost like feeling sick, but not quite. I decided I was suffering from 'spiritual sickness'. Still, I was again glad to see my Canadian when he returned in the early afternoon.

It was then I made the mistake of showing him the one attractive thing in the room: an old solitaire board with clear, green glass marbles. He had never seen one before, and, when I taught him to play, he became fascinated and played for a good two hours, only stopping when the usual large high-tea came in. By then I was bored and irritable. Well, at least tea would lead to conversation—and that, unfortunately, led to disaster.

He said he had decided to return to camp every night because there had been trouble about men bringing women into town and spending the night with them, and he didn't want anyone to think he was doing this. I was outraged he should compare me with such women. He pointed out he was doing just the opposite, but I remained indignant. And then, out of the blue, he said: 'Look, we're not getting on very well, are we? Would you like to go back to London? After all, I haven't done you any harm.'

No harm? And me spiritually sick and unable to make up poetry? I made a queenly gesture towards the sofa and said: 'And what about all that?' He said that was nothing, adding, 'Don't go if you don't want to but . . . Anyway, let's drop it for now and go for a walk.'

I didn't want to go for a walk. I wanted to be implored to stay on in Folkestone. But walk we did, for a long, weary while and I was furious when he had to salute officers, all of whom looked like worms compared to him. (He had some financial reason for remaining a sergeant-major which I never understood.) He baulked my attempts to talk about ourselves, either discussed life impersonally or spoke of his plans for after the war (which didn't seem to include me) and remained smilingly good-tempered, courteously bending his head to hear everything I said.

When we got back he played solitaire until supper came in. It was still undecided if I was going back to London. I forced the issue by asking what should be said to the landlady. He said, 'Then you *are* going? Well, that's decided. I'll settle up with the landlady and tell her I have to be away on Escort Duty.'

I climbed down and said I didn't want to go back. He remained adamant. It was *decided*. I then reminded him that, again and again, he had told me he would love me for the rest of his life. He said, to the best of his belief, that was true, but love was a very small part of his life and he could get on without it, had done so in fact for many years—and he advised me to do the same, anyway as far as he was concerned. He spoke kindly, sensibly and almost impersonally. Unfortunately, I found him more attractive in this mood than when he was making love.

We ended the evening when he decided on it, and parted without one kiss. I lay awake that entire night, in the middle of which I tiptoed to his bedroom door. He was snoring most unfeelingly so I tiptoed back again. I told him about this in the morning and he said cheerfully, 'Well, you wouldn't have got in, anyway. The door was locked.'

He was in a hurry to get back to camp. I asked him to kiss me goodbye. He said that wasn't fair, and when I pulled his head down, I might have been kissing a piece of wood. He then walked out of the room, the house and, I imagined, my life. (How wrong can you be?)

I found Phyllis unexpectedly at the Club, on leave from her Camp tour. She said I looked ghastly, insisted I should go to bed, and then sat beside me nobly listening. She finally gave me her considered opinion that nothing seriously abnormal had happened to me during the heavy love-making. She had *heard* of such things. But I don't think she fully approved, whereas she would have approved of complete seduction. She was a great girl for inciting herself and others towards seduction. (But she was still a virgin when she married, over three years later.)

By the evening 'spiritual sickness' had worn off and I was able to write poems almost as fast as I could get the words down. The worst started off with the immortal lines:

> Love lies dead at Folkestone,
> And perhaps it's just as well.

When I read this to Phyllis she laughed, and I had to admit that it sounded funnier than it felt. Actually, we found quite a lot to laugh at, but this didn't prevent me from feeling deeply miserable and, to add to my mental miseries, I found I had acquired quite a liking for heavy love-making and could have done with some more of it.

I think many girls of my generation had to face certain unique problems connected with sex. Bar notable exceptions, we were the first girls to adopt what we considered an enlightened, emancipated attitude, but this was unsupported by very necessary knowledge; also we had inherited a backlog of taboos. One way and another, some of us must have been a menace both to ourselves and to the men in whom we were interested. And though I was soon writing letters to Folkestone insisting that I was to blame for everything, I only meant that I had lost my temper, been unreasonable, etc. Not one thought did I give to my unfortunate Canadian's sex problems during that disastrous weekend.

All my letters remained unanswered. I began a play about a young actress and a ruthless Canadian (I now felt mine hadn't been ruthless enough). I don't remember looking for work. And then, out of the blue, a job I hadn't even tried for was offered to me.

The Club sometimes gave theatrical entertainments. I had acted in one of these during the winter, playing a music-hall artist (in my check suit, white fox fur and high white boots), singing a song and making quite a success. An elderly character actress, named Marie Ault, had seen me. She was now to head one of the Lena Ashwell Concert Parties which played to the troops in France. I was sent for and at once engaged, on Miss Ault's recommendation. I didn't even have to see Miss Ashwell, who was away. I was to be part of a company doing one-act plays and we should leave England in little over a month.

Short of playing a good part in the West End no job could have pleased me more. The salary was small but I should get my complete board and lodging and be given a warm YMCA coat under which I could wear what I liked. I should play a variety of parts. And, above all, I should be going to France in wartime—I who had never been abroad. And I got a distinct kick out of remembering how often my Canadian had alarmed me by saying *he* might have to go to France. Now *I* was the one to go into danger; not perhaps great danger, based at Dieppe, but no doubt there would be plenty of air raids.

I sent him full details. Surely he would see me before I left? No answer—and I was too busy to feel particularly stricken. I planned, shopped, sewed, having been warned I should need evening clothes for dinners in officers' messes and occasional dances. The thought of all those officers was intriguing and I was told that many girls who went to France in Concert Parties came back engaged. I began to be very sorry for my Sergeant-Major, so liable to lose me to an officer. Had he not said he would love me for ever? Was not his unforgiving behaviour really intended for my good? If we really loved each other I was prepared to refuse proposals from generals downwards. But

I must, before leaving England, make sure how he felt. I remembered the Siege of Borden. The Siege of Folkestone should now take place.

Phyllis was not available to support me, but Gwendo was back in my life and spending her weekends helping with my sewing. She took the poorest view of my chances at Folkestone, never having ceased to maintain that a door must be open or shut. But she had promised a little niece a week's holiday by the sea and had nothing against Folkestone. She and the child went on ahead to find rooms and I joined them at the weekend.

These rooms were theatrical rooms with the type of landlady I had no hesitation in confiding in. She was highly sympathetic and even offered to go to the camp and rout my Sergeant-Major out for me. As she was very obviously eight and a half months pregnant, I couldn't feel that any sergeant-major would enjoy being routed out by her, so I went out and telephoned. He said he would come along the next evening at seven o'clock.

I returned to our rooms in triumph. Gwendo was still dubious, but the small niece was excited—I think she felt she was sharing in a great romance. After supper we went for a walk and then sat, until long after dark, watching a troopship leaving far below, a dark mass on the dark water while, above, searchlights cut patterns in the sky. Thinking of the men going to the trenches, I, for the first time, felt guilty at having been so little affected by the war. I was glad to feel that I should soon be having some share, if small and belated, in it.

The next evening the landlady went out; so did Gwendo and the niece, all undertaking not to return before ten-thirty. I settled down to wait in the twilight and I was still waiting when it was pitch dark. Then Gwendo and her niece returned and I called them in.

'No Sergeant-Major?' wailed the niece.

'I was so afraid not,' said Gwendo—and forbore from any further reference to doors being shut or open.

During the night I planned that I, not our pregnant landlady, would go up to the camp. But as I combed my hair in the morning I noticed a new bald spot. I had found a London hairdresser who was a specialist in curing alopecia, had a number of treatments from him and had been pronounced cured. But he warned me that I might have further outbreaks. In my opinion this new spot was the direct result of worry. Worry must now stop. I could imagine dying for love (witness my near-jump off the Club roof), but I could *not* imagine going bald for love. So I returned to London by the next train and rushed to my hairdresser. Luckily for me, our departure for France had been postponed until the end of September and I had time for more treatments, which included practically boiling my unfortunate head.

Rehearsals now began and I met the company. As well as Marie Ault and myself, there were two leading ladies, Susan Claughton and Elfie Leigh-Hunt; a leading man, and a young character actor. I liked everyone. And as I was the only really young woman it seemed likely I should get plenty of parts, but the first one I got nearly spelt disaster. The play was Gertrude Jennings' *Between the Soup and the Savoury*, which takes place in a kitchen during the serving of an elaborate dinner upstairs. I expected to be the pathetic little kitchen-maid, but Susan Claughton fancied that part and I was given the haughty parlour-maid. Susan was tall, fair and elegant and when she tried to make herself plain for the part she simply looked years older. I, barely up to her shoulder, looked every inch a musical comedy soubrette. And I had a great many entrances and exits carrying trays of food, which was not there for rehearsals.

Before going to France we were to give one performance of this play at a camp in Winchester, when Lena Ashwell would come down and see us. Things went better than I expected and we all returned to our hostel looking forward to meeting Miss Ashwell, but she had gone back to London without a word to any of us—except to Marie Ault, who had been told that we were all bad and I was much the worst; indeed, I was so bad that she had at first felt she couldn't let me go to France. However, she had decided I could go if I took on the stage management, packing clothes for every performance and generally making myself useful. I was to go and see her as soon as we got back to London.

The interview took place at her office in South Molton Street. She sat the other side of a desk, white-haired, efficient, and suggesting to me a head-mistress (and never had I liked head-mistresses). But she was reasonably kind and she admitted that I had been badly miscast. She also said that the company was wrongly constituted; there were two leading ladies, one elderly character actress and one young character actress (me). There was no ingénue (I guessed she meant no *pretty* girl) and she must send one to join us. She could only afford this if I did the stage management for which she had planned to employ a man. I didn't feel I should be too good at a man's job, but I said I'd try.

I particularly remember saying I hadn't before made a failure in a part—and instantly realising this wasn't true. Miss Ash-well, in a superior voice said, 'What a pity! No one who hasn't made a failure ever makes a great success.' I thought this a highly sententious remark—and I still do.

Anyway, I had hung on to my job, and that was the day when I picked up my uniform. This was a long, mole-coloured coat with blue facings and a large YMCA badge, and a black hat much machine-stitched and trimmed with blue. It could be worn turned up or down and wasn't too bad. The coat was ugly.

After that, we were soon due to start. I packed the clothes I was taking in suitcases, and all the possessions I was leaving behind in a large trunk to be stored at the Club, and at last I was ready to leave the attic bedroom which had seen me through an emotional summer. (In these present days, when I hear of girls starting their sex lives in their middle-teens, I think they're lucky not to be troubled by the soul-searchings that still held me back when I was so much older than they are. And yet . . . don't they find such a matter-of-fact acceptance of sex a bit *dull*?) Then, on a misty night in early October 1918, I sailed for France in the good ship *Vera*.

XIII

Dieppe 1918 and the Battlefields

But she was *not* a good ship. She was a notorious demon; we learned later that members of her crew were frequently sea-sick. All the members of our party knew themselves to be good sailors—some of them had crossed the Atlantic. I was far more frightened of sickness than I was of enemy submarines, especially as we were to be eight hours at sea. As civilians we only rated the longest Channel crossing.

But to start with we might have been on a mill pond and, when we had located our cabin and berths, I went up to the top deck. I was entirely alone there, surrounded by a thick mist. Of course I at once made up a poem, trying to get the sound of the ship's engines into the rhythm: 'Night on the waters, beloved, beloved. Throb of the engines and sob of the sea.' Almost always when I had perpetrated a poem I felt like a hen which had achieved an egg, and I went back to our cabin feeling cheerful.

It was a cabin intended for seven but it had to house eleven; four American girls had taken up residence on the floor. I stepped over them with some difficulty and undressed, in my berth, with even more difficulty. I then tried to sleep, but they were very, very talkative Americans. Also I was hungry and wished I had bought some chocolate. Then the *Vera* began to show her form. I could not have believed that a boat was capable of such acrobatics; I fully expected her to turn a somersault. In no time at all, ten out of the eleven women in that cabin were very, very seasick. The eleventh was me; I went on hankering for chocolate.

The turmoil lasted until we landed, in the grim light of a sunless morning. I found myself unpopular. It was sheer uppishness not to have been sea-sick, and most unfeeling of me to want breakfast. We then started a day of long railway journeys and even longer waits between trains. One clear memory comes back to me. Late at night I found myself the only woman in a compartment full of Frenchmen. I recalled being told that Frenchmen made love in extraordinary ways, starting by kissing a woman 'all over'. Peering at those dimly lit faces, I didn't fancy the idea at all.

It must have been around midnight when we reached Dieppe and went to the Chariot d'Or where we were to stay until a house was found for us. Most of the hotel was in darkness. Susan and I shared a bedroom. It was large and comfortable, but its only window opened on to a seemingly unventilated passage. We wondered if our health would suffer. Late as it was I dutifully used my hair lotion and got some in one eye. The agony lasted for several minutes during which I remember thinking: 'I *can't* go blind in a foreign country.'

Next morning we learned that there was such a bad influenza epidemic that no concerts were, for the moment, being given to the troops. There was nothing for us to do except explore the town on foot; we were almost always followed by children who, having noticed our YMCA uniforms, called after us: 'Christians!' and didn't make it sound like a compliment.

The hotel was run by pleasant people, but due to wartime shortages they were unable to give us enough to eat. Lunch consisted of two slices of thin meat, scarcely any vegetables and no puddings. Dinner was the same except that the glory of *Petit Suisse* cheese and French bread was added. Apart from this, bread was not served and there was no butter. We tried augmenting our meals, but there was little to be bought—no slabs of chocolate. So we were much relieved when a house was found for us and a YMCA official assured us we should be properly fed.

It was a narrow house in a narrow street leading to the sea, which was visible if we leaned out of our windows. On the ground floor there was a small drawing-room with silk-brocaded walls, gilt furniture and an old upright piano. An archway led to the dining-room. Upstairs there were three floors on each of which were two small bedrooms, two tiny dressing-rooms and a lavatory.

Nowhere was there a bathroom, but the dressing-rooms had running cold water and a gas-ring on which one heated water in an enamel jug. Once one got used to washing in what was known as penny-numbers (why?), this wasn't too bad; anyway, it was better than the public baths where one had a bath in a clammy sheet and, on looking under the sheet, found the condition of the bath most repellent.

Susan and I shared the top floor where the walls were covered with printed linen. We each of us had a writing-desk and an oak bed that ran on runners which I repeatedly fell over. I loved my room, particularly during the mild autumn when I could have the heavy windows open. The fact that they folded right back inwards, rather than outwards, made one much more conscious of the sky which seemed to come right into the room.

On the opposite side of the narrow street was an under-taker's yard, where a boy worked on coffins. I never found this depressing, because the yard was more of a garden, the pale wood was a pleasant colour and the boy sang softly at his work. It all seemed part of those mellow French autumn afternoons. Having rehearsed during the morning amidst the sitting-room's gilt chairs, we often had the afternoons to ourselves.

Susan and I were good friends from the outset, but never intimate friends. She was unhappy about some love affair (I knew this from hints dropped by Miss Ault), but she never told me her troubles and I never told her mine, which anyway no longer loomed large. At the Club I had confided in many people, but I had already begun to feel this was ener-vating. Nobody in this company was going to know anything about my private affairs.

I stuck to this resolution, which was perhaps why I got on so well with everyone in the company. This was important, as we were all so cooped up in the little house. Not that our two men were allowed to sleep there. The YMCA insisted that they should remain at the hotel and that two YMCA secretaries should have the first-floor bedrooms. Miss Ault protested valiantly. It was insulting that we couldn't be trusted to have our men in the house; also we suspected the girls were there to spy on us. But we had to have them. And it seemed they disliked it as much as we did. They looked scared when spoken to and they always dashed to their bedrooms after supper and locked their doors.

We were now being reasonably well fed. Our housekeeper (known as 'Mamselle' and helped by a pretty maid called Juliette) went to the market for vegetables, and later acquired the knack of making filling puddings. Meat, and all our groceries, came from the YMCA. One week there was a note apologising for the lack of a joint. As a consolation, presumably, there were twelve bottles of HP sauce. Usually enclosed was a large tin of small cheese biscuits which were much appreciated. But one day I wore a blouse with a gaping halter collar at which our two men took shots with the cheese biscuits. After that the cheese biscuits came no more. It seemed our YMCA housemates had reported us for 'throwing food about during wartime'.

The YMCA did not supply butter and, very occasionally, Susan and I would buy ourselves a quarter of a pound for half a crown. Miss Ault considered this 'wickedly extravagant', but she almost always asked if she could have just a little 'to see how it tastes'. I regret to say this infuriated me. Once a week I treated myself to an egg, price one shilling. Our little maid, Juliette, always brought this in on a salver, announcing proudly: 'Mademoiselle, the egg!'

The embargo on concerts persisted and the women of our company were asked if they would help with canteen work. This meant that each of us joined a different group of regular canteen workers (known as the Y-Emmas) and drove to one of the outlying camps. Here, in a dimly-lit hut where groups of Tommies sat at tables all around the walls, we stood behind a counter, manipulated tea and cocoa urns, and sold what little there was to sell. Only occasionally were there cigarettes and then the supplies always ran out. It was distressing to see the disappointment when the men had to go away without them.

Now and then there were deliveries of small things like tooth-paste, and then everyone crowded up to *look* at them even if they couldn't afford them. The real standbys were tea and cocoa, and cocoa was first favourite.

My first Y-Emma explained to me that the men could have their tin mugs half-filled for a penny, three-quarters filled for three-ha'pence and filled to the top for twopence. I decided to give a three-quarters mug for a penny and a full mug for three-ha'pence. It was astounding how quickly the good news got round; a large queue formed at my cocoa urn. One of the Y-Emmas rumbled me and I then said that it was extremely difficult to stop an urn at exactly half-a-mugful. Soon after this a glorious thing happened. My urn tap got stuck and cocoa continued to pour out. Practically every man in the room had his mug filled free before that tap was at last turned off. At all the camps I worked in I continued to give good measure, but I never again struck such a public-spirited tap.

I think most of the Y-Emmas disliked us heartily. Perhaps this was because they were voluntary workers who even paid for their keep, while we were not only kept but also paid a salary. But it seemed to me they had the knack of disliking people and were almost on terms of enmity with the Tommies, towards whom they maintained a 'don't let them get away with anything' attitude. Meanness over a cup of cocoa seemed to me shocking.

Still, I enjoyed canteen work. It was the first time I realised there is pleasure in selling and I took pride in totting up my takings. Even when I wasn't dispensing cocoa I got more customers than the regular ladies. Perhaps the men were glad to be served by someone who smiled.

It was usually very late when we got back from canteen work yet, after supper, Susan and I would often take a walk along the Dieppe sea front past the deserted, boarded-up luxury hotels. We would walk to the far end and then on to the end of a stone mole running out to sea. We hardly ever spoke. I just thought about life—which wasn't coming up to my expecta-tions. After a month or more, we hadn't been to one dance, one mess dinner or met one officer.

We were still doing canteen work when the Armistice was declared. Historically, this was on November 11th, but (I never discovered why) the news hit Dieppe on the night of November 8th. I was on my own at a small, far-out hut known as the Bakery. It was dimly lit, by lamplight only, and very smoky. Most of the Tommies seemed to be middle-aged. They grouped themselves around the counter and showed me pictures of their wives and children. (Being on my own meant that they got their cocoa mugs filled full for a penny.) All during the evening there were rumours of impending peace, but we didn't let ourselves dare believe it. Then, suddenly, we heard the sirens, and the men were called out of the hut, leaving me alone with the Padré. A moment or two later we heard cheering and then an announcement: 'Armistice declared at two o'clock today.' Outside the hut there was wild cheering and shouting; I suggested we should go outside, but the Padré was much against this. Perhaps he feared I might get assaulted, but when I insisted on going out all I saw was one elderly Tommy on his knees deep in mud, thanking God. Cheering was coming from far and near, but I couldn't see the cheerers and as we stood there in the cold air, under the stars, I was stabbed by the thought that the end of the war would mean that my Canadian would return to Canada.

The YMCA drove me home; when we reached Dieppe the streets were packed with cheering crowds and, uninhibited by the Padré, I felt I could do some cheering myself. It was an anti-climax to get back to the rue de Cigogne and find the concert party stolidly settling down to supper. I persuaded them to come out to the streets with me. We made bully-beef sandwiches and ate them on the way. Some Belgians were forming a procession and we tried to form a British one, but we lacked a Union Jack and our efforts to sing 'God Save the King' were swamped by the 'Marseillaise', which we ended by singing ourselves, 'God Save the King' hardly being a festive song.

Eventually we got home and sang popular songs round the piano, until an official from the YMCA called on us and said: 'Rather let us sing hymns.' When at last I got to bed I made an entry in the Red Leather Notebook (the first since my forty-page outbreak in early July; I must have been cutting down on introspection). I wrote until my candle was flickering out, feeling I was describing an historic night—so it was deflating to find next day that the Dieppe Armistice had been a false one; we were told not to mention it in letters to England.

The real Armistice, on November 11th, was anti-climactic. We were invited to a dance at the Chariot d'Or and Susan and I accepted. We were told we should be called for and eventually a young officer arrived, but only to tell us that our prospective hosts did not consider they were in a fit state to dance with us. They offered profuse apologies and a bottle of *Grand Marnier*. 'They sent me,' the young officer explained, 'because I am the only teetotaller.'

Susan and I sat up till late drinking the *Grand Marnier*. I fancy it was the nearest I ever in my life came to being drunk. And if what I felt in the morning was a *Grand Marnier* hangover, it was in the nature of an Awful Warning.

Soon after that the embargo on concerts was lifted and we started work, driving out almost every evening to one of the many camps, and then firmly performing three short plays. One play I remember was called *Dick's Sister*. In it a young woman, played by me, arrives to meet her brother at his flat and gets there ahead of him. I had a soliloquy explaining the situation which concluded with the statement: 'Well, here I am, with no Dick.' These words, at our first performance, were received with a gale of laughter, followed by stamping of feet and whistling. At later performances we felt it wise to substitute: 'Well, here I am but my brother has not yet arrived.'

If we played at a hut for Tommies only, we were afterwards entertained by the Padré, who almost invariably fed us on stewed dried apricots and rice pudding. But at larger concerts we were usually given dinner in the officers' mess. This invariably began with sardines on toast, but often rose to champagne. I found our hosts difficult to talk to and even more difficult to dance with after dinner. The dancing was no doubt my fault. I had done hardly any ballroom dancing and though I was under the impression that I could fox-trot, my impression was wrong because a fiendish little step called 'the twinkle' had come in. It entailed changing the balance of one's feet at moments never anticipated by me and I was always being stepped on, or stepping on, embarrassed and apologetic. It came to an end one odd evening at a fancy dress dance.

This took place at one of the large hotels facing the sea. It was opened for the occasion, which was rather a grand one. I had a chintz dress which, with a mob-cap, did duty for Little Miss Muffet. I got plenty of partners and seemed to be dancing rather better than usual but, as the evening wore on, I began to feel ill, rather as if I were starting one of my colds but without any cold, and I could still enjoy dancing—which was surprising as my legs felt shaky. Eventually I had a partner who remained with me for the rest of the evening and said I was the best dancer he had struck. Certainly I had stopped missing steps and was twinkling away without giving it a thought. For that matter, I wasn't giving anything a thought. I had suddenly picked up the art of following steps physically because I was no longer functioning mentally. I was starting influenza—the first and only time I have ever had it. I only hope I didn't hand it on to my nice partner, whom I never met again.

The next morning not only was I prostrate, but all the women of the concert party were. We lay in our respective rooms and were fed by the little maid, Juliette, who came in every few hours and announced: 'Bouillon, mademoiselle'. Her tone of voice was always exactly the same and so was the bouillon and both got on our nerves. Poor girl, she climbed innumerable stairs and I fear we weren't very grateful—particularly on her first visit of each day when she always reported how many people had died locally of 'flu the previous day. The English doctor, who called every morning, was even more depressing. When I eventually told him I was feeling better he shook his head gloomily and remarked, 'I'm afraid that's often the way: better in the morning, dead at night.' Presumably he was advising me to go carefully, but one cannot feel it was tops in bedside manner.

We were still shaky when we started work again, also suffering from post-'flu depression. And I was further depressed when, around mid-December, we heard that Lena Ashwell was sending out a new girl to join us. Miss Ault made no secret of the fact that Miss Ashwell wished this girl to play as many parts as possible and wished me to concentrate on stage-management. (I was finding this work hell, particularly the packing of all the stage props and costumes, and could not be relied on to include everything that was needed.) It so happened that the girl who was coming lived at the Three Arts Club and, though I didn't know her, I could describe her. She was unusually pretty, said to be extremely well-off, and had recently made a hit while playing Peter Pan on tour. I feared I should never get any new good parts and might even lose some I already had. It was some small comfort that the whole company were prepared to resent the newcomer. And she didn't help matters by arriving in a handsome fur coat.

I will call the new girl Peter, which was the name she liked to be called, in honour of having played Peter Pan. (She had brought her costume with her and intended to treat the Army to scenes from the play.) I have seen more beautiful girls, but I have never seen a prettier one. She was small, with light brown bobbed hair and a face like a particularly intelligent kitten. And she had enormous vitality, not to mention self-assurance which instantly made itself felt. As there was no room in our house she was to stay at the hotel. She did so, for one night. Then, having inspected our house, she visited YMCA headquarters and insisted on joining us: those two YMCA girls would have to move out. To our surprise, they protested; they said they had come to find life with us 'so amusing'. They even offered to share one small room. They did so, and Peter settled herself into the best bedroom in the house.

The company disliked her heartily and so did I—for about forty eight hours. Then she discovered me packing stage costumes and said, in a brisk voice, 'Not very good at packing, are you?' and waded into the job herself. The company considered this bossy. All that mattered to me was that someone else was doing that dreary packing. (Later I was to find that all her own clothes were meticulously packed in tissue paper. When showing me this she remarked: 'You see, I'm a born old maid.'

1919. 'All alone, all by myself
Growing old and quite on the shelf.' Age twenty-three

The Man of Principle

Basil Dean, when I first knew him, in 1917

Gwen Ffrangcon-Davies: as Etain in *The Immortal Hour*

Gwen Ffrangcon-Davies: as Betty in *The New Morality*

Nadine March

Madge Compton

About to start for the Three Arts Club Fancy Dress Ball. Members of the Gang: Peggy Calthrop as Trilby, Eleanor Street as Water Nymph, Madge Compton and 'Norse' at taxi window. The author 'showing her knickers

Lord Leverhulme, 1923

Ambrose Heal, Heal & Son, Tottenham Court Road

The Old Shop with the New

'And already I was twenty-five'

She often said this and I really think she meant it. Her age then was the same as mine: twenty-two.)

None of my parts were offered to her and, had they been, I'm pretty sure she wouldn't have accepted them, on her own account as well as mine; she was choosy about what she played. Her acting was always an energetic single turn, not relating to anyone else's; still, it gave the evening a lift. But her greatest success was at parties. Men fell over themselves to talk to her and dance with her; indeed, the falling over was almost literal when she danced, because she would not even attempt to follow her partners. Discussing this with me, she said, 'Why should I? I like to make up my own steps.' But men still queued up to dance with her.

I don't remember feeling envious, perhaps because I was becoming popular myself. My small success dated from an evening when, at a particularly dull mess dinner, I accepted an invitation to dine with a man alone. Then we all received an invitation to dine with a group of staff officers whom we hadn't yet met. They usually ignored concert parties, were considered extremely grand and lived in a beautiful house some miles along the coast. The dinner was to be followed by a dance at the Chariot d'Or—and the invitation was for the night of my *diner-à-deux*. Miss Ault suggested that I should tell my dinner partner she wouldn't allow me to be out with him after ten o'clock and he must, by then, deliver me to the Chariot d'Or.

I was called for at the same time as the rest of the party were called for by several Staff Officers, who looked to me very glamorous. My man now looked the reverse but I had to go with him, leaving Miss Ault to explain that I would come on later to the dance. I then found myself taken to a small, sordid-looking hotel near the docks and, worse still, we were shown upstairs into a private room. That is, it was private by virtue of only having one table laid; the others were piled on top of each other; no one could have called it a seductive love nest.

The dinner was deplorable and still being served at nine-thirty when I told my young man (who had needed quite a bit of quelling) I must go. With very bad grace, he took me to the Chariot d'Or, where I left him flat.

In the foyer I was intercepted by a group of staff officers who said, 'So this is the girl who wouldn't dine with us.' Already I had acquired prestige. But what really raised my stock high was a ludicrous incident after I had danced a couple of dances. I had been sitting out in the foyer and, as I walked back towards the dance floor, the man I was going to dance with said: 'I think I ought to tell you that you've had some kind of accident to your dress, at the back.' We were near a mirror. I looked in it and saw that on the seat of my pale grey georgette dress there was a dark, damp patch well over a foot in diameter. I doubt if ever in my life I have felt as embarrassed as I did for the next half minute. Then someone cried 'She's been sitting in a pool of rain.' I had indeed; rain was still dripping steadily, from a glass roof, on to the wooden chair I had just vacated.

I was hurried to a stove. My pleated dress was lifted up at the back and spread out to the heat, while in front of me on the floor sat half a dozen young officers who said they would keep me company. Never before had I been such a social success.

And it was that evening that I found my perfect dancing partner. Among our staff officer hosts was one in Intelligence (green tabs instead of red) nicknamed 'Hush, Hush'. He was of medium height—more than tall enough for me—slightly built, unobtrusively nice-looking, with a very quiet voice. He held his partners with the lightest of hand-clasps, giving little indication of the highly intricate steps he intended to perform. Susan and Peter found him sheer hell to dance with, but I had no difficulty at all. It wasn't a case of two hearts beating as one, for we took little interest in each other when not dancing. Indeed, we barely talked at all as, when the others were sitting out, he put classical records on the gramophone and we danced to Chopin, Debussy, Bach. I derived extraordinary pleasure from it, a pleasure that seemed curiously mindless and timeless. I had become a good ballroom dancer, but never experienced anything similar with any other partner.

Our staff officer friends gave us many parties at their handsome house on our free evenings. The men who escorted us home were always entertained in our dimly-lit kitchen where we concocted a wonderful drink out of Horlicks and cocoa mixed—known as Horco. But we got through so much that the YMCA stopped supplies.

Two of these favoured friends fell in love with Peter. One of them proposed (she just told him she was a born old maid) and I've no doubt the other one would have, if he hadn't been married. She and I went with them to midnight mass in the Dieppe Cathedral on Christmas Eve and there was a moment when I thought they would come to blows. If they had, I should have felt it quite suitable for their surroundings, because I was shocked at all the loud conversations and banging of chairs. Mass was taking place at the altar, but the main body of the cathedral was as restless as a railway station.

The entire company started the New Year with one determined resolution: we wanted to go up the line, see the battlefields, give performances to some of the troops still stationed there. We were told this was out of the question. The YMCA wouldn't help us (probably couldn't), our staff officer friends were willing but powerless. But when we found out that what we needed was to be asked for by a general, they managed to supply a general. And by lucky chance he was a general who longed to dance and didn't know how. We worked hard on him and in between dances we implored him. Within a few days there was an official request for our services, and the Army undertook to supply all transport.

The trip began early in February, when a jolly corporal and a Tommy called for us and we drove off in a large covered lorry. There was only room for two of us at the front; the rest had to travel at the back where one could only see the country when one had passed it, and the exhaust fumes were bad. We were warned not to let the back tarpaulin down as two nurses who had done that had been fatally gassed. At first we all wanted to travel at the front so we took it in turns; but there was no windscreen and most of us found the cold too much. The Dieppe winter had been cold enough but we had been warned that the battlefields would be much colder. However, it wasn't particularly cold when we reached Amiens, where we were to spend the night in a hotel. Peter and I explored the town in the gathering dusk and lit candles in the cathedral, where we were most determinedly followed by two young officers who said they hadn't seen an English girl for months. We were sympathetic but not to the extent of letting them get affectionate almost on the altar steps.

The next morning the sun was shining, but it had become bitterly cold and, soon after we started out, we ran into country where there had been a heavy fall of snow. From then until we were back in Dieppe, three days later, we were in an utterly white world.

What amazed me about the battlefields was their sheer emptiness. I had expected ruins, splintered trees, at least some form of vegetation. All I could see for miles and miles and miles was snow, in which one could barely trace the lines of trenches. But soon we found a way of telling where there had been a village: the roads there were paved or cobbled. And sometimes there was a little notice saying: 'This was . . .' and then the name of the village. And sometimes there were crosses to indicate graves, but they barely emerged from the snow.

That first day we drove down the hill to Albert, where the ruined church still stood against a brilliant sky. (All that day the sun shone brightly, giving the snowy landscape an appalling beauty.) We got out to look at the church and found that here there were still a few ruined houses, though nothing was left above the ground storey. Two old men stood watching us, and our driver told us that everywhere the peasants were already coming back, mainly living in the cellars.

We spent the night at Caudrey in a once beautiful chateau where we were the guests of some nurses. The house was still whole, but the walls were badly cracked. Most of the furniture was gone, but there were still many mirrors and gilded brackets which looked strange as a background for the Army furniture. Susan and I shared a large bedroom at the top of the house where the window was unshuttable. The cold was intense. We put on all the clothes we had brought with us—day clothes as well as night clothes and even put the floor mats on our beds, but we still could not get warm.

The next morning we reached Cambrai where we gave two performances. The afternoon performance was at a small Army hut where our dressing-room was doorless and one had to walk carefully to avoid the icicles hanging from the ceiling. For one of our sketches Peter and I were supposed to change into full evening dress and Miss Ault thought we ought to: 'Miss Ashwell would expect you to sacrifice comfort in order to give our brave boys a little extra pleasure.' Peter said tartly that if she caught her death of pneumonia she would never again be able to give any brave boys any pleasure at all, and put on an extra sweater. So did I.

The evening performance was in a huge hall packed with men, many of whom coughed almost continuously which made it hard for us to be heard. But at least we knew that the coughs were due to painful necessity, not boredom; the enthusiasm was tremendous. We treated them to our scenes from *Peter Pan*, in which I played Wendy. Peter played with what I can only describe as staccato *espièglerie*, and so much movement that one expected her to fly without benefit of overhead wires. She looked exquisite, though perhaps more like Tom Kitten than Peter Pan. Anyway, it always went very well, as a curtain raiser. Our *pièce de résistance* was Gertrude Jennings' *The Rest Cure* in which I prompted and made the noises off—which included singing *Killarney* in the piercing voice of a street singer, and whistling like a parrot. I was strong on *Killarney*, but unreliable as a whistler and I often got some Tommy to stand beside me and do the whistling when I held up my hand. At Cambrai, when I gave the signal, I was deafened by a whole orchestra of parrots: my Tommy had lined up a half a dozen mates to assist him.

We gave five performances before starting the return journey, when we took a different route. The battlefields were still under snow; I can still see the vast waste of whiteness, dotted by tiny crosses and the great cross on the Butt of Warlencourt. And I remember eating sandwiches in the ruins of the cathedral at Péronne and thinking that there was no longer any feeling of sanctity there, such as was round every cross indicating a war grave. Would it be that day we travelled on the road to Bapaume, so exactly like Nevinson's war painting of it? And one last vivid memory is of the battlefields by moonlight when we stopped and Peter and I got down into a trench and looked into a dug-out. When we climbed back to the road we danced together, which astounds me now, considering the effect the battlefields had on me. But that effect was retroactive. At the time, I felt little more than a superficial emotion and considerable pride at having achieved such an experience.

I began to feel more deeply as we ran out of the snow and were in normally populated country again. I found myself depressed; it was as if I had descended from grandeur to triviality. I doubt if I thought this out then, but I did when we were back in Dieppe and living our usual lives. I continually thought about the battlefields, continued to be depressed, and finally realised that the depression was partly guilt, guilt because the war had meant so little to me. I had never even considered doing war-work (for that matter, few of my friends had). Surely I ought to have done? If I were back at the beginning of the war, feeling as I now did . . .

But while I was still in this mood I had an extraordinary dream. I saw a figure coming towards me with a bayonet, and I too had a bayonet. A voice said, 'It is kill or be killed' and I raised my bayonet, and then flung it down, thinking, 'Then of course I must die'. The figure—it had no identity—came on and on and the bayonet went right through me. I felt no pain but I knew I was dead. Then I woke up, and I never again felt I ought to have done war-work; I knew I ought to have been an active pacifist. After that, I stopped feeling depressed.

Our time in Dieppe was coming to an end. Susan and Elfie and one man were going back to England. The rest of us were moving on to Le Havre. Susan and I took a farewell walk around Dieppe, finally climbing the hill to the YMCA and looking back towards the sea. The hill ran down, then a hill ran up, so that the sea itself seemed to be running steeply uphill. Years later I saw exactly the same effect in a painting by Derain and was instantly back saying goodbye to Dieppe.

But my last memory of all is of an encounter with a rat. For months Mamselle and Juliette had told us terrible tales of rats. They were said to inhabit the castle at the end of our back garden and to have eaten a German prisoner. German prisoners having been removed, the rats were said to be invading the rue de Cigogne. I saw one dead in a trap, thrown into the gutter and, though I felt more pity than revulsion, I was as scared as the rest of the company at the idea of meeting a rat. On one of our last nights, after we had all gone to bed, I came down for something, lighting myself by my candle. In the staircase wall was a little window which could only be opened or closed by a cord stretched across the stairs and secured on a hook. Coming downstairs one had to pass under this cord. On this particular night, as I stood at the top of the stairs holding my candlestick, I saw a large rat travelling along this cord, very slowly, very carefully, doing a real tightrope walk. It stopped. We looked at each other. Then it went on as slowly and carefully as before and took itself out of the window. I suddenly knew that I *liked* rats. Some forty years later I used to feed them in our Essex orchard (to the indignation of neighbours). One snowy midnight I got back from a day in London and remembered they hadn't had their usual evening meal. They came out to meet me, such well-fed glossy rats, and as I stood there in the moonlight I had a dreamlike, composite memory, both of the battlefields by moonlight and the candle-lit Dieppe rat.

XIV

Life at Le Havre

At Le Havre we stayed in a large house on a busy highway. It had none of the charm of the little Dieppe house but was more comfortable. There was, for instance, a handsome bathroom with a geyser. We shared the house with the resident Le Havre concert party, who were much grander than we were. They had their own theatre-like hall in which they did far more ambitious plays than we had ever attempted. The head of the party was Herbert Lomas, whom I had often seen with Miss Horniman's Company in Manchester and greatly admired.

I doubt if we were needed at Le Havre, but we gave a few performances with our depleted company, which was further depleted when Peter decided to go home; she said so many of her men friends were on leave. (No doubt she told them she was a born old maid; she was still unmarried when we last met in her fifties.) Then Miss Ault and our one man went and there only remained myself and two men who had joined us before we left Dieppe. One was a tall, fair young man called Derek Zoya who brought down the heavens on his head by shaving in our dining-room. ('And he used one of our *teacups*!') I couldn't feel strongly about this and I found him kind and interesting; he was the first highbrow I'd ever met. The other man was a mature baritone and it was my job to walk on stage and announce: 'Mr Vincent Print, late of the Carl Rosa Opera Company, will now sing *The Trumpeter* and *The Bandolero*.' I then had to accompany him which was agony for me, and probably worse agony for him.

At Le Havre Mr Print disclosed that he could act as well as sing, and he and I did a one-act play called *The Last Waltz*. I was a society widow and Mr Print was an Australian millionaire who had loved the widow in his impoverished youth, then gone to Australia to make his fortune. The two meet again during the last waltz at a London ball. Derek Zoya composed and played the waltz which was used as background music and made a beautiful job of it.

I should never have been given this part if Susan or Elfie had been around to play it, but I felt fairly confident, especially when I found a becoming deep-blue evening dress among our theatrical costumes and cut a foot or so off it. On the way to our first performance, the driver told us we should be playing to an audience entirely composed of Australians.

Panic struck. Australians were the most difficult of audiences. If bored, they walked out; if annoyed, they were capable of throwing things. They rarely understood English humour and were adept at finding double-meanings in seemingly respectable lines. ('I shall tell mother what you did to the swans' convulsed them; we heard afterwards that, in Australia 'swans' meant prostitutes.) Above all they were touchy and apt to suspect they were being played down to. Our play was wildly unsuitable for them, high society comedy and sentiment; but, far worse than that, it was packed with lines about Australia, many of them highly critical. Mr Print and I doubted if we should end the evening alive.

However we started well; they actually seemed to like us. Then we came to the first hurdle. Mr Print had to say, describing his early struggles in Australia: 'The sheep wouldn't live and the rabbits wouldn't die.' He was stopped by an enormous laugh. Bravely he continued: 'If you dug for gold you found water and if you dug for water you found nothing.' This was received not only with laughter, but got a round of applause. Later criticisms of Australia got whistles of delight. A romantic interlude obviously gave great pleasure, especially as a few nice double-meanings were unearthed. The happy ending brought the curtain down to cheers. We were a wild success.

So successful, in fact, that we received numerous requests for the play, which had never been the case with any of our other plays. And it wasn't only Australians that we pleased. To me, there is still sadness in this memory for I seriously believe that was one of the few parts I ever played really well. I had an unrecognised talent for high comedy which I was never again given the chance to prove. For high comedy was then the prerogative of beautiful leading ladies. Such parts were not given to rather large-headed shrimps.

However, I was as yet untroubled by any such self-assessment. I enjoyed giving pleasure to the Australians and was grateful for the pleasure they gave me; almost all of my social engagements were with Australians. There were plenty of American troops in Le Havre but also plenty of American girls, so English girls were not sought after. Nor do I remember meeting many Englishmen. It was the Australians who gave the best dances, several nights a week, at large huts some distance from Le Havre. The only problem was getting there; transport was scarce and no one below the rank of colonel seemed to be able to arrange it. I was lucky enough to secure my own personal Australian colonel, but one had to pay for the transport with at least six dances every night, and he was a short, stout, elderly man whose dancing and conversation were equally unexciting. But he was exceedingly kind and never amorous. In fact, during the two months I spent at Le Havre only one man got as far as trying to kiss me; and when I said, 'Please don't', he didn't. We afterwards became particularly friendly and he then told me how grateful he was to me for saying 'No!' He said his wife would have been, too.

The charm of those Australian dances began when, on evenings when we gave no concerts, I was driven out to them in the sunset (having spent much time buying flowers to wear). If the Colonel let me down, someone would arrive dashingly in an Army lorry. One got a glimpse of the countryside in spring. Then one arrived in a hut decorated as if for Christmas, and was given an old-fashioned dance programme. Queues formed and one's programme was filled for the evening. There was always a good little orchestra, and music had become Americanised. Gone were the musical comedy tunes of Dieppe gramophones. They were replaced by something called 'Jazz' which, at first, I disliked heartily. But it grew on one and soon all other dance music seemed tame, except for the mournful

'Missouri Waltz' which was enormously popular. That tune always brings back those Australian dances but, even more so, does 'How're you going to keep them down on the farm?', now so nostalgic that it has lost its gaiety.

One other memory of Le Havre: someone told me there were woods at Honfleur which were filled with wild daffodils. I went in search of them—none too optimistically, remembering all the times in my Manchester childhood my mother and I had hunted in vain for them. But it was true, they were there, not just a few but acres of them under the budding trees. I sat there among them, thinking of my mother, wishing I could share them with her and knowing that this was the place of all others in which she would like to be remembered.

My return to England was due in early May. Sometime in April I was sent for by Penelope Wheeler, who was head of the Lena Ashwell Concert Parties in France. She asked me if I would like to go on to Cologne, for the summer at a higher salary. I was tempted, but felt I ought to get back to England and look for normal stage work. 'Before you are forgotten by managements,' said Penelope Wheeler, sympathetically. (It would have been no bad thing if a few managements *had* forgotten me.) I then got permission to stay an extra day for the Anzac Day Ball, and left the office feeling as warm towards Penelope Wheeler as I had felt cold towards Lena Ashwell.

The Anzac Day Ball was to be a great occasion, in a large hall in Le Havre with a full American band. I was looking forward to it—and to the whole day. I lunched with my Colonel and was the sole woman guest among five hundred men. I was then escorted to a boxing match. I had enjoyed romantic novels about prize fighting and was under the impression I should enjoy boxing. I was wrong. Fairly soon I closed my eyes against the blood and wished that I could also have closed my ears against the blood-thirsty noises made by the Australian spectators; so might lions have been exhorted to eat Christians.

After a while I heard, in a quiet moment, a loud whisper. Since lunch the Colonel and I had been joined by a French girl who was sitting on the other side of him. 'Colonel', she now said, 'your friend is not 'appy. Ask 'er if she is in need of the little 'ouse.' The Colonel said, 'What? *I* can't ask her that. *You* ask her.' A moment later the French girl was beside me. 'Come', she said firmly. 'I show you the little 'ouse. Not far to walk.' Well, it would mean getting away from the boxing.

The little 'ouse, conspicuously placed in the middle of a field, proved to be an inadequately screened commode; no place to dally in. Anyway, the French girl was kindly waiting. So I had to rejoin her and face lots more bloody boxing. I couldn't go home until the Colonel arranged my transport. The wrestling that followed later was uglier than the boxing, but less gory.

I enjoyed the evening no more than I had enjoyed the afternoon. The atmosphere of the Great Ball was unlike that of so many pleasant Australian dances. The orchestra was too strident, some of my best friends seemed tired and bad-tempered, and I quarrelled with my kind elderly Colonel. It was a sad end to my happy months in Le Havre, and my depression lasted through my journey back to London next day. In the taxi on my way to the Club, I decided my time in France had got me nowhere. It certainly hadn't helped my stage career. And of the dozens of men I had met, not one had really attracted me. Did that mean I was still in love with my Canadian? It did not. I had been *willing* to be attracted. A tuneless little tune began in my mind, to the words: 'All alone, all by myself. Growing old and quite on the shelf.' Anzac Day had been my twenty-third birthday.

No one I knew at all well was staying at the Club, but I chattered to a few acquaintances and spent some time looking at papers and magazines. Fashions had changed. Pleats were out; tight narrow dresses were in, described as 'Chemise Dresses'. I must do something about that. But first I must get my hair bobbed. I should have followed this fashion earlier had I not felt that, while I still had alopecia, I must hang on to all the hair I had. I was now cured (until my next outbreak eight years later) and felt only the slightest pang at sacrificing about two feet of heavy hair. After that I took great pleasure in shaking my head and feeling my Marcel-waved hair flowing free. Indeed, hair-bobbing did wonders for my spirits.

Phyllis got back from some tour intending to take a short

country holiday and I was happy to go with her. Ever since
I had known her she had talked about Birch Grove in Sussex,
which was part of her childhood. I found it hard to believe
that any such fairyland existed, but it did. There was a handful
of houses alleged to be a village, with one shop that sold practically nothing. There were pine woods, larch woods, bluebell
woods, a tiny common enchantingly named Stumblewood, and
two estates so tactfully cared for that they gave the impression
of being natural countryside. One of these had three lakes,
ancient Rackham-like trees, and grassy slopes dotted with wind-
flowers. The other was a maze-like wood; narrow paths, at first
bordered by shimmering birch trees, led down and down to the
heart of it, where a stream ran, over-hung by giant beeches,
one of which could be climbed. Some of its branches stretched
right across the stream and one could sit there, looking down
into the clear water.

After showing me the neighbourhood with pride, Phyllis
started work on a book for children, so I took my walks alone,
accompanied by a notebook in which to write poems. I found
not being in love uninspiring until I managed to make use of it
in a poem called 'The Inn of the Empty Heart'—in which 'the
beds are hard but there's nothing to pay'. I then became more
cheerful in a long poem beginning:

> I long for the small, quiet intimate things,
> For life in a red-roofed town,
> For the High Street taking its midday doze
> With the sunblinds all drawn down.
> Hearing the house wake up each morn,
> The rat-tat-tat of the post,
> The smell of coffee in pale, wide cups,
> The good, crisp crunch of toast.

That toast was undoubtedly homage to Rupert Brooke's 'rough
male kiss of blankets', which I both laughed at and loved.

I got back to London, minus Phyllis, not long before the official
ending of the war. I had heard a great deal about Armistice
Night in London, was sorry to have missed it, and was

determined to see life on Peace Night, preferably in Trafalgar Square; but I didn't feel I could go there alone and no one at the Club wanted to join me. At last two girls agreed to.

I suggested we should take a taxi to Trafalgar Square, but my two friends decided we should take one to Oxford Circus and then walk down Regent Street. Soon after we got out of the taxi, I realised that the idea of junketing in Trafalgar Square did not appeal to my companions. They hoped we should meet officers who would take us out to dinner. And the chances seemed good. Both girls were tall, beautiful and very well dressed; and, though I could not compete with them for looks, I thought my new chemise dress was becoming. I had made it out of tubular stockingette so had only needed to cut holes for the neck and arms, and turn up the hem. The colour was a light, but vivid, green.

Soon we saw three young officers coming towards us. They got to within a few feet and then stopped dead. We did, too. I noticed that the middle young man was gazing fixedly at me. Well, my tubular dress *was* attractive. Then the young man, still staring, said 'My God, it's a caterpillar.' His friends led him away. They were a little less drunk than he was.

We ended by having to pay for our own dinner, but the evening had one good result: one of my companions knew a man who was backing a touring musical comedy, *Telling the Tale*, and she got me into it.

I was to sing two numbers and do a tap dance. The woman who was presenting the show, Gladys Archbutt (a name frequently corrupted into Archbitch), said she could teach me the tap dance during rehearsals. She was wrong.

My first number, specialy composed for the tour and said to be a worldbeater, was called *The Return of the Knut*—'a saucy, flippant blighter, but by Gad what a fighter.' For this, as a French maid, I wore a very short, black silk dress with a white frilly apron and an outsize officer's hat—only by wearing it on one side could I see, out of one eye, where I was going. Behind me I had the support of twelve chorus girls dressed as Parisian ladies. After two verses and two choruses, I was supposed to bring the house down by drilling the girls and finally growling: 'Wait for it, damn you!' Houses remained unmoved and provincial theatre managers were apt to insist that 'damn' was replaced by 'dash'.

My second number was called 'Jazz' and it was followed by that tap dance I had never been able to learn. No doubt it was nervousness over this that caused me to develop a neurosis about starting singing. I kept feeling I must swallow just once more before beginning. Our musical director was a kind man who understood my trouble. He would give me a little ad-lib phrase, then look at me hopefully. Seeing me swallowing he would repeat the phrase, and he would do this three or even four times. Then, in desperation, he would start the number. I would give one gigantic gulp and manage to catch him up half-way through the verse. I had to lead the chorus by singing: 'So don't delay, start right away.' My finest hour came on the night when I accidentally said: 'Stite rart away.' The orchestra enjoyed this, if I didn't.

My so-called tap dance was truly awful, but it was followed by some musical comedy steps which I did rather better; they entailed a certain amount of violent movement. But they were only rewarded by a few perfunctory hand-claps. One day the juvenile lead of the company, a charming middle-aged lady of much experience, said to me: 'Look, dear, when you bow to the audience after your dance, put your hand on your heart, bow from the waist and *breathe* heavily. They'll think "at least that kid's worked hard" and it'll do a lot for your applause.' It did indeed. After that, my plucky exhaustion gave the impression I had risked a heart attack in the line of duty.

I suffered agonies of nerves over my songs and dances—I remember sitting on the grass outside Salisbury Cathedral and wondering, seriously, if I would not prefer to be peacefully dead, rather than face the evening's performance. But, as usual, I enjoyed touring and I very much liked the company, particularly the chorus girls. I wrote some character sketches of them; I thought well enough of these to have them typed later on, and I sent them to various periodicals, but I never had any luck. (Until twelve years later. The week after *Autumn Crocus* was produced the editor of the *Sunday Graphic* persuaded me to unearth them and paid me handsomely. He also published another sketch about the people I had fallen in love with up to the age of thirteen. I was surprised to see this announced, in advertisements on the front of London buses, as '*My Love Affairs* by the new girl playwright.')

As things turned out, it was my friendship with the chorus girls which caused me to leave the company. I usually had a small dressing-room to myself, but at Bath no small room was available and I was put into a large room with two of the girls. I liked sharing with them, they liked having me, BUT! . . . It was a bitter offence against protocol. They resented it on my behalf—and so did the principals. I must COMPLAIN—or else for ever lose face. It so happened that Miss Archbutt joined the company that week. I spoke to her, very civilly, about my dressing-room; she responded, very rudely, that if I didn't like her arrangements I could make others. So I instantly gave her the customary two weeks' notice. Actually, the notice to end the tour was put up that Saturday night. This was something of a disaster for me as several of my chorus friends had coaxed me into selling them clothes to be paid for by instalments; with the tour ending nobody paid me anything.

It was late to look for another autumn tour. And a girl at the Club asked me if I would like to join her as a teacher of ballroom dancing. She had a room and fifty pounds capital. If I could bring another fifty pounds I could share with her. I liked the idea very much as I had greatly missed all the dancing I had done in France. I said I would go back to Manchester and ask my uncles to help me.

I had not been to the house in Ashton-on-Mersey since 1915, soon after the family had moved in. The fresh wallpapers and paint were now dimmer, the furnishings more faded; also I now noticed for the first time the odd contrast between my aunt's over-pretty Edwardian furniture and my uncles' heavy Victorian mahogany. Tiny drawing-room occasional tables clustered round overstuffed armchairs. The little armchair given to me when I was nine was still there, looking not only like a child's armchair, but also like an armchair's child. It still fitted me perfectly and I was glad to hear that it was already too small for my cousin Esmé, now in her middle 'teens. She was at boarding school at her own request and to my uncles' satisfaction; since the days when she had eaten the plaster arms and legs of her dolls she had always been a trifle exhausting— though pleasant with it. My boy cousin, Ronnie, was charming and already much respected; though one could not then have foreseen what a highly successful businessman he would become.

The boom in ballroom dancing had by now hit Manchester, so my uncles were willing to supply the necessary fifty pounds. I at once wrote to my friend and said I would be back with the money in a few days. By return I got a devastating reply. The whole scheme was off. I dissolved into tears and retired to my bedroom where my worried aunt got out of me that I had now used up my three hundred pounds inheritance, and had nothing to live on while I looked for another job. What was to become of me?

My aunt told me she would talk to my uncles, which she did as soon as they got back from business; then came up to tell me they would give me three pounds a week whenever I was out of work. I went down to thank them and they treated me as if I had recovered from a long illness. They assured me they could spare the money; business was good. All they asked was that I should write to them more often and try to come home whenever I could. They would always pay my fare and would give me a pound a week pocket-money while I was at home. And wouldn't I now stay on for a few weeks?

But I doubt if I stayed more than a few days. I was never bored with any of them. But I was absolutely determined to get back to my own life. They didn't press me and it was not until my next visit that I fully realised how very much they missed me and wanted to keep me with them.

I went back to London in high spirits, found Phyllis at the Club and broke the glad news of my allowance. I had always resented the fact that she could count on one and I couldn't. True, she now got *five* pounds a week and continued to get it when she worked. But my three pounds was affluence when compared with nothing. I had told my uncles I would try to get West End work. Phyllis said she would do the same. No more tours. From now on we were holding out for London.

XV

'Searching for Lambs' at Midnight

It was something of an anti-climax when, within days, Phyllis accepted a job to tour the Army camps again and persuaded me to join her. The attraction was that W. G. Fay—Billy Fay— once a well-known actor at the Abbey Theatre, Dublin, would be directing. Phyllis knew him well and had a great affection for him, which I was soon to share. He was a leprechaun-like little man who was said to have seen leprechauns and if leprechauns are to be seen, Billy Fay was certainly the man most likely to see them.

The tour was only to last two months, and there was little hope of getting any London work during December and January. Also I was glad to be able to tell my uncles how soon they could discontinue my allowance; it would renew their faith in my ability to earn a living. The West End would have to wait just a little longer.

We were to do two plays, a drama called *Under Cover* and a farce. I had a good, short-part in *Under Cover*. In the farce I only had to understudy, so could work at my writing. There was another would-be writer in the company, Frank Vosper, then only nineteen. He had begun a novel about life in a public school and I was both impressed and shocked because it referred to bed-wetting.

Billy Fay was the kindest of directors and seemed pleased with me at rehearsals. For once, it was Phyl who ran into difficulty. She played a tough American who, when caught smuggling, took refuge in pretended deafness. The high spot of the scene came when, in order to test her, a gun was fired unexpectedly. She was supposed not to so much as flicker an eyelid. In order to get her used to the noise, Mr Fay had the gun fired a few days before the dress rehearsal. Phyllis nearly shot out of her seat. Much laughter—and of course it would be all right when she'd heard the gun several times. It was not all right; it got worse—until she was jumping before the gun was fired. She tried again the next day, and the next; again and again she jerked her head violently. There was no way of cutting the incident and it began to seem that she couldn't play the part. Then she heard about ear-dummers, rubber plugs which are often used by people who sleep badly. With these in her ears she remained solid as a rock when the gun was fired. The only trouble was that she now couldn't hear her cues. She had to watch the mouths of the people who spoke them and leap in the minute the mouth was still.

On the first night I was less nervous than usual, I liked myself in the part and particularly liked the clothes I was wearing; a pale grey dress and a picturesque black velvet hat. Billy Fay had persuaded me to use the lowest register of my voice (how often I had been told to do this when I trained at the Academy) and Frank Vosper had said he found it thrilling. For once I was going to be good.

All went well until, when being questioned by a brutal American policeman, I had to answer: 'I lost a lot of money playing cards.' This was a dead serious line and I said it dead seriously, in my 'thrilling' voice. I was astounded when it was received by the audience with loud laughter. I had barely recovered from this when I had to say: 'Don't take me to prison.' I said this with my whole soul—and the audience now positively rocked with laughter. Soon after this the curtain mercifully descended on the first act—the only one I was in.

Everyone was most sympathetic and no one could tell me what I'd done wrong—in fact, Mr Fay assured me I *hadn't* done anything wrong. I'd played the scene exactly as he wished, sincerely and not over-dramatically. But could I try being a little less dramatic? I did, at the next performance, and the laughs were just as loud. Mr Fay finally decided the laughs

didn't matter. He got the feeling that they were sympathetic
laughs and that the audience liked me.

It was Frank Vosper who eventually diagnosed the trouble—
correctly, I feel sure. He said that in my pale grey dress and
picturesque black hat I looked so small, young and innocent the
audience thought of me as a little girl. It was *funny* that I had
lost money at cards. As for sending me to prison—the idea was
preposterous. I saw what Frank meant; it would be like hand-
cuffing a puppy. Perhaps if I wore a hat that was smart, not
picturesque, and used a harder voice . . . I tried both and the
laughs were even heartier; presumably I was now taken to be
a *saucy* little girl—and good luck to me. So I alternated hats
and manner according to my mood and it was generally decided
that a couple of goods laughs did the first act a power of good.

Phyl and I became very fond of Frank Vosper and spent
much of our time with him. At Ripon, where there was no
hostel, the three of us shared rooms overlooking the market
place. We had an upstairs sitting-room and, on evenings when
I was not acting, I sat there alone, trying to write. I still think
of that room as an ideal one to write in. There was old-
fashioned furniture and a round table with a red plush tablecloth, on which stood a paraffin lamp which gave a gentle
light. And I liked the thought of being in Ripon, with its
Wakeman who blew his horn at sunset and its motto: 'Unless
the Lord keep the city; the Wakeman waketh but in vain.'
I sat down at that round table full of hope and began a novel
called *The Primrose Path*. A carefree, happy-go-lucky novel . . .
But I wasn't a happy-go-lucky writer. Doubts began to rush at
me. Was the tone of voice right? How was I going to get in
the heroine's past history? By the time Phyllis and Frank got
back from the camp theatre, I was hopelessly stuck.

Frank, while trying to comfort me, said he was sure I would
eventually make a great success of my life *or* find a philosophy.
This didn't help me as, from the way things were turning out,
the philosophy seemed the more likely, and I didn't fancy it.

We were at Ripon for New Year's Eve and, after supper,
we joined the townsfolk who were dancing in the square.
Next day, Frank sat at our window and made an admirable

pen-and-ink sketch of the square which he presented to me. The inscription read: 'In memory of a glorious night.' Dear Frank, I have never believed that, when he drowned in the Atlantic while on a voyage home from America, he committed suicide. Had he wanted to, he would have done it far more comfortably. It must have been some kind of accident. I still shudder at the thought of his split-second realisation that he was plunging down into the Atlantic. It's a comfort to remember that when we danced the New Year in at Ripon he still had seventeen years ahead of him and much success both as an actor and playwright.

Towards the end of the tour Phyllis sold her book for children outright to John Lane for twenty pounds. It was called *Peter's Pencil* and was about a magic pencil that drew, as a child draws, and what it drew came to life. She did her own illustrations. The book was published, got good notices—and sold barely at all. Some six or seven years later, when I was in charge of a children's book department, I bought up remaindered copies and sold dozens of them. In the nineteen-sixties it was republished and again sold barely at all. All it needed was promotion.

When the tour ended I willingly went home to my uncles for a month. One reason for my willingness was that, now I could count on an allowance, I was in no desperate hurry to get a job. Another reason was that I had recently heard from my Canadian again. He was out of the Army and, having put the Atlantic safely between us, he would 'like to correspond'. I answered, though guardedly, and he then wrote saying he was starting to get a divorce, with a view to my joining him. Well, I'd never fallen in love with anyone else and I certainly missed being in love with someone. In no time at all, those lilacs were in bloom again. His letters, registered and sealed with gold sealing wax, were now coming at the rate of two a week. In view of the fact that I might eventually go to Canada, I felt inclined to spend some time being kind to my kind family.

From the first there was a feeling of welcome and holiday. My uncles invited friends I had known as a child to come for 'musical evenings'. We even had little dances, though only

Uncle Eddie danced (very experimentally). I was taken to
theatres. And of course, my Auntie Bertha and Uncle Bertie
came over to take me for drives. The B's were the same as
ever, interested in their golf and their car (the ancient de Dion
and the Renault had been succeeded by a Clement-Talbot).
Uncle Bertie was slower than ever and even more absent-
minded. Auntie Bertha still frequently cursed him and he responded with 'Woman, have done!' And they were, as ever,
devotedly happy with each other.

It was from Auntie Bertha that I learned how much my uncles
missed me. Uncle Eddie had once said to her: 'I'm afraid we've
lost Dodie.' And Uncle Harold had said: 'Madge's children
aren't like Dodie was.' Well, of course they weren't. I had been
brought to live with my uncles when I was eighteen months
old. They had been twenty years younger then, happy to share
in my upbringing and let me share their interests, their jokes,
the noisy arguments. It was inconceivable that my young cousins
could now take my place. Ronnie thought the uncles were the
most admirable of men but to him they were 'the uncles', not
'the boys', as they always had been to me, and he treated them
with quiet respect.

I soon found that Ronnie, at twelve years old, was already
a very good companion. Once a week we went to the pictures
together, Ronnie firmly paying for my seat (my aunt supplied
the money for this, but I never let him know I knew). In the
course of regular visits he had got to know the manager and
proudly introduced me to him as 'my cousin, the actress'. The
manager then became very matey. On the way home Ronnie
suddenly sighed deeply and said: 'Oh, Dodie, love, I wish you
weren't on the stage.' When I asked him why, he said: 'I'm
afraid you've got such a frail chance.' An astute boy, Ronnie.

Early in my visit I told my aunt about my Canadian; I could
hardly avoid doing so once those registered, gold-sealed letters
began being forwarded by the Club. She listened sympathetically and said that, if I really wanted to marry him, she hoped
he would get his divorce, though she was against my going to
Canada. (So was I, for that matter.) She then assumed a blank
expression which I had known since my childhood. It was her

withdrawal-of-approval face. She said: 'Has he ever given you anything?' Now I came to think of it, he hadn't. Surely there must have been *something*? But there hadn't been so much as a box of chocolates or a bunch of flowers. I told my aunt the circumstances hadn't permitted it, there'd been no time and, anyway he hadn't much money. She said: 'You can take it from me, if a man *really* loves a girl he gives her presents, whatever the circumstances.'

My dear Nan undoubtedly had something there. For though I didn't, later, do too badly out of men who were, more or less, in love with me, the only man who *really* loved me started giving me presents he could ill afford soon after we met. ('Reader, I married him.')

Towards the end of my visit my uncles made one last effort, earnest but un-nagging, to keep me with them. I could work at my writing or take a secretarial course, which my uncles would pay for. I noticed that Uncle Harold did not say I could join him in amateur theatricals. No doubt he was too good an actor not to know that I was a bad actress. (The only time he had seen me act was when he had made a special journey to see *Ye Gods*. He had said it wasn't fair to judge me as he found the whole production so crude. The standards of good Manchester amateurs were much higher than those of second-rate touring productions.)

I thanked 'the boys' most gratefully, but did not let them persuade me; already I was longing to be back in London. And I can't say I felt particularly guilty. Uncle Harold had his amateur theatricals, Uncle Eddie had his club for cards and bowls. This club was a bit of a nuisance to Uncle Harold who, unless rehearsing, liked to spend the evenings in arguing— and no one but Uncle Eddie could stand up to him.

So my allowance started again and I returned to the Club, where I got the cheapest room to be had (seventeen shillings and sixpence a week) and a particularly nice one. It was on the fourth floor, a narrow, cell-like strip of one of the old attics. There was a high, raftered roof and a heavy oak beam which suggested a country barn. I threw a green ribbon over the beam and tied its two ends to a rush basket into which I tossed gloves, stockings, letters—anything I hadn't time (or room) to put away. The ribboned basket looked festive, as well as helping me to keep the room tidy. I loved that room, all the more because it was only a few feet from the tiny staircase leading to the roof—which, all that summer, I used as an outdoor annex to my room.

My first job was to equip myself with some clothes; I had little suitable for summer, thanks to those defaulting chorus girls. My savings amounted to nearly twenty pounds which I hoped would be ample. But prices were sky-high. A few years earlier I had bought charming suits from little Soho shops for three guineas. Now I had to pay nine guineas for a less-good suit. But I got an almost new summer coat from a dress-agency and I could make my own summer frocks out of a wonderful material called cotton georgette. It hung well and never creased. (Whatever happened to cotton georgette?) I had a pale mauve dress which I wore with a transparent, grey, horsehair hat trimmed with a wreath of mauve stocks. This hat (cost ten shillings) was so beautiful that my friend, Nadine March, borrowed it to be photographed in. I took this as a compliment, for Nadine was now a slim, elegant young woman with her own flat and beginning to get West End work.

Thus equipped, I started the hunt for work. I visited all the agents I knew and told them I was now standing out for London. They wrote 'West End Only' in their books. I then hinted that something *very* good on tour might tempt me. No temptation was offered but they would remember me. And one had to leave it at that. One could not keep on calling on the average agent. There was, however, one agency where one could call every day if one liked. It was famous and long-established, and said to handle many stars.

This agency was Blackmore's, in Garrick Street. There was an outer office, always full of people, which was presided over by a Mr Nicholls, who had a facial resemblance to Napoleon and behaved like that too. Every now and then he would usher someone in to Mr Blackmore's office. There seemed no rhyme or reason about this; it wasn't a question of having an appointment, it was just according to Mr. Nicholls's fancy. Again and again I had asked him if I could see Mr Blackmore. Mr Nicholls would then say, 'Wait a while, dear. We'll see." Nothing had ever happened after that—and I had been going there for years. However, this particular year, Mr Nicholls suddenly pounced on me, led me to Mr Blackmore's office and hurried me in.

I saw several men talking around a desk and looked towards them winningly. But Mr Nicholls kept a firm hold of my arm, took me straight through the room, through another door, and then out onto the staircase. There he said 'Another time, dear' and left me flat. I could only imagine that all the people I had seen go into Mr Blackmore's office had been thus hurried off the premises. And I was very, very angry.

I wrote a stern letter to Mr Blackmore asking if he knew how Mr Nicholls behaved to clients and was it with Mr Blackmore's approval? And I ended by saying 'If this letter offends you, your agency cannot become of less use to me than it has been up to now.' I got an answer by return, hand-written by Mr Blackmore himself. It gave me an appointment and I was to bring the postcard with me. With what delight did I flourish it at Mr Nicholls—keeping firm hold of it though, in case he snatched it and tore it to shreds. Actually, he gave me a pleasant smile and at once showed me into the inner office.

Mr Blackmore was alone. I remember him as a small man, with white hair and a gentle manner. He opened a very large book and, after questioning me, made a long entry about me. He then looked up, smiled sweetly and said, 'And now, dear, what is it you want me to do for you?'

Slightly surprised, I said, 'Well, get me some work.'

'But *what* work?' He went on to explain that he had to have some special objective. If I told him, say, that I wanted to play Principal Girl in the Cardiff pantomime next Christmas, he would do his best to get it for me.

I said I had no experience in Pantomime, also Christmas was a long way off.

'Got to make plans well ahead,' said Mr Blackmore. 'That's the way I work. Can't you think of *anything* you want?'

I said, 'Wendy, in *Peter Pan.*'

'Ah!' Eagerly he wrote that down, then said, 'Of course I'm not *sure* I can get it for you. As a matter of fact, I can't quite place your type.' He studied the entry he had made about me and asked more questions. I had sung, I had danced, I had played straight parts? Suddenly his expression cleared, 'I've got it,' he said triumphantly. 'You're a Singing Chambermaid.'

Mr Blackmore then courteously showed me out on to the stairs, his last words being, 'Don't get too annoyed with poor Mr Nicholls. He *has* to act the way he does.' I guessed that Singing Chambermaids must have belonged to melodramas, in the days before my theatregoing began. Certainly Mr Blackmore never sent for me to play one—nor to play Wendy.

As well as visiting agents I called at stage doors, offices attached to theatres . . . any place where I might hear of new productions before they were announced. I wrote dozens and dozens of letters—to managements, directors, even authors. I secured a few interviews but nothing ever came of them.

All the same, I look back on that summer as one I should particularly like to live again. I had a circle of friends who gradually formed what we came to call 'The Gang'. There was Madge Compton, once married to the famous comedian, George Graves, whom she divorced; Peggy Calthrop, Eleanor Street, a girl known as Dan, another known as Norse; Doreen— married to a rubber planter but managing to spend much of her life at the Club. Phyllis only ranked as a semi-member as she never stayed long at the Club and had now taken a cottage at Birch Grove.

The Gang's great charm was that it would sympathise but never pry—not that there was much to pry about as we never ceased confiding in each other, particularly about our love interests. There was great excitement when my Canadian sent me two large photographs of himself. I could have wished he had not written on them 'To my dear little pal', but there was no doubt that he looked distinguished in civilian clothes. The Gang, however, declined to de-mob him and continued to refer to him as 'Sergeant-Major'. They had a ribald song which began, 'Round the corner, Under a tree, Sergeant-Major, He said to me . . .' And they treated me to this very, very often.

Sergeant-Major had also sent me his gold signet ring. At last, a present! But I could only wear it on my thumb and even then it was apt to fly off if I moved my hand unguardedly. Also someone hastened to find out that it was only nine-carat gold.

But I vaguely expected to be married some day and now my main problem was how to live on three pounds a week. If I had all my meals at the Club it would cost six shillings a day. This, added to seventeen shillings and sixpence for my room, would leave me with sixpence a week for all other expenses—including stamps, telephones, bus fares, toothpaste, soap, cosmetics, repairs to shoes and my great standby, chocolate. I gave up tea, though friends often gave me a cup in their slop bowl (known as Act-of-God tea). And instead of having the half-crown dinner, I tried to wait until 'Night Cupboard' (a hatch in the wall of the dining-room) opened at half-past-nine and then had two sandwiches and a cup of cocoa. This regime left me with eighteen shillings and sixpence spending money. But if the whole Gang was having dinner, one wanted it too . . . and so on. I pined for the days when I could trot round to the National Bank in Baker Street and draw on my vanished inheritance.

Still, I went to a fair number of theatres, in the Gallery (one shilling) and on my own; the Gang did not favour Galleries. Most evenings were spent in the Green Room; when we moved in, 'foreign bodies' were apt to sigh heavily and move out. Sometimes we played games but, as a rule, we sewed and talked; and occasionally we invited in some non-Gang member to play or sing to us. I liked it best when Gwen Ffrangcon-Davies sang. She had belonged to the Club for some years, but I only met her around this time, when she had already acquired some celebrity. This was the year she played Etain in *The Immortal Hour* at the Old Vic; she got me a seat. I thought she was exquisite and loved the music.

Gwen brought back memories of my schooldays at St Paul's, singing classes with Gustav Holst, the Church Festival at Thaxted, and I realised how starved I had been for anything approaching good music. I had always loved folk songs and

Gwen sang them admirably, very simply and unaffectedly, accompanying herself with Cecil Sharp settings. I must say that the Gang, so often noisy and ribald, appreciated her fully and would listen for as long as she would sing.

Sometimes she would take me to concerts and once she invited me to join in a bus ride to Hendon, so that she could sing in an old churchyard at sunset. I feared this might prove embarrassing, but it certainly didn't. There wasn't another soul in sight and the setting was perfect for folk songs. She ended by singing my particular favourite, 'Searching for Lambs'.

What did I read in those days? Quite a lot of Georgian poetry (and I went to poetry readings at the Poetry Bookshop, in a barn-like, candle-lit building; admission threepence). And never was I too poor to have a library subscription. The Times Book Club was both cheap and good. It was then in Oxford Street and, every few days, I would walk there down Marylebone High Street, which still retained a hint of the atmosphere of a village High Street. I always looked in the windows of Gayler and Pope, an old-fashioned drapers where the bills and cash still whirled about in wooden balls on their overhead railway. The Gang called this shop 'La Maison Gailère' and believed it was often better, as well as cheaper, than Oxford Street shops.

Arrived at the Times Book Club I would investigate the newest books on display in the shop, and then go up to the library and ask for them—and get them. Among others, I read D. H. Lawrence, Compton Mackenzie, Galsworthy, Arnold Bennett and the early Michael Arlen. I particularly liked Arlen's first little book *The London Venture*, which contained a phrase I memorised (for ever). This was: 'Seductions are successful through women fearing to look fools if they refused to be seduced.' This had special meaning for me by the late autumn of 1920 when, with a new acquaintance, I so narrowly avoided seduction that the degree of avoidance might be said to be purely technical. As I had now got over my dislike of 'heavy love-making', I'd had nothing against this, but by the time I came back to the Club, at nearly midnight, I had begun to feel what I thought of as 'soiled'—so much so that, when I found Gwen Ffrangcon-Davies alone in the Green Room, I instantly asked her to sing me 'Searching for Lambs', in the hope it would un-soil me. She asked not one question, just sat down at the piano and sang beautifully. The net result was that I felt more soiled than ever.

But a month or so before this happened I had made a decision which, by improving my appearance, not only led to that near-seduction but also to rather more beneficial results. One early autumn morning I got up to find the kind of day that tempted me to walk right round the Outer Circle of Regent's Park. 'Tempted' is the right word because the three-mile walk was hard on shoe-leather; I had no solid walking-shoes. The weather was sparkling, stimulating, and just chilly enough to suggest the end of summer. I found myself planning the kind of clothes I would have for the winter—if only I had some money. There was usually a touch of originality about the way I dressed. And by the time I was half-way round the Park I had created a superb winter outfit and was enjoying a great success in it. Then I came down to earth and began wondering how I could best refurbish last winter's clothes.

And suddenly I knew I wasn't going to do any refurbishing. I was going to have that outfit. Somehow I must give myself both a mental lift and a new personality. Otherwise I should go on scraping through on three pounds a week until my uncles finally withdrew it. They weren't grumbling, but they were certainly astonished that I had been out of work so many months and they were wondering if I ought not to accept a tour. Accept? They didn't know I'd already been to various agents and told them I would, now, tour. Not one sniff of an offer had I had. But in my new outfit I should be a different person. I was *sure*.

I totted up the cost. I should need forty pounds—a fantastic sum, but necessary. For I was not going to make these clothes myself or even employ a dressmaker. I was going to a Russian tailor in Marylebone High Street. I always stopped to look in his window and he had once come out and talked to me.

I knew his prices, reasonable for a tailor, but I should need every penny of that forty pounds. How, how, how was I to get it? And then the words 'forty pounds' rang a bell. Nan, my aunt, had told me that when she had sent for a dealer in order to sell some unwanted furniture, he had told her he would pay forty pounds for my mother's piano.

XVI

'French Leave'

I didn't want to sell the piano. I was fond of it for its own sake as well as for my mother's. But I had to have that forty pounds. I wrote at once to my aunt who replied that she needed my piano for Ronnie to practise on and she herself would buy it for forty pounds. I was glad it was to remain in the family.

I had already alerted my Russian tailor. His name was Faikosch and he was small, fair, middle-aged and gently mannered. He admired my designs, which were unlike anything he had ever made, and was excited about the whole project. Instead of hard, tailored revers I wanted high, round necks and stoles: a small fur-edged stole for the suit and a large, shawl-like stole for the coat, to be used in cold weather. Both suit and coat were to be of pale grey face-cloth and Mr Faikosch had already found a beautiful one, and a pure silk satin lining. He did the work quickly and admirably; in all the years I went to him (when I could afford to) and introduced many customers to him, only once was he a day late with promised work. On this occasion he said with pathetic apology: 'It was the weekend. Sometimes, at the weekend, things happen in tailors' shops.' I have been wondering ever since, *what* things?

Once equipped with coat and suit I hunted for one of the fashionable knitted silk jumpers and found a scarlet one into which bands of old-gold tinsel had been knitted. This cost five guineas and the hat that went with it cost three guineas; fantastic prices for me. The hat was really a cap, made of gold tinsel and knitted chenille in various shades of red, and edged with moleskin. Like my pale grey summer hat, it was one of the hats of my lifetime—of which I only remember one other, bought by me nearly ten years later, in Bolzano.

I then got a pale grey rain-cape, a red umbrella and a red handbag. In those days few women took any trouble over accessories. A handbag was a handbag was a handbag and, even if of heavy black leather, would be used with brown tweeds or white muslin.

I gave a dress rehearsal of my new clothes to my most dress-conscious friend, Nadine March. She took them very seriously and finally pronounced: 'That is real dressing; you could go anywhere.' Then she invited me to lunch with an important manager. It was her he proved important to, not me; but he was very nice to me and I had never before been in such an expensive restaurant; it was my first visit to the Ivy. If not yet in the West End Theatre, I at least felt I'd had a meal in it.

My new suit had its next outing on a bright morning when I went to an interview at the newly-opened Everyman Theatre, Hampstead, with which I fell in love on sight. I entered through a small foyer, decorated in yellow and orange. This was deserted, the box-office not yet being open. I tried a swing door and looked into the little theatre (converted from a drill hall). This was deserted too. I then found some stairs and, at the top of them, doors marked 'Wardrobe. Private', 'Board Room. Private' and 'Secretary. Enquiries'. I knocked on 'Secretary', got no answer, tried the door and found it locked. Continuing on my way upstairs, I found a door marked 'Fireman. Private' and another door marked 'Director. Strictly Private'. Obviously the Director was absolutely tops as regards privacy, but I *had* come to see him, so I tentatively knocked on the door. I was told to come in.

At a quick glance I took in yellow walls, orange curtains at two tall, sky-filled windows and some very black furniture, which included a table on which stood models of stage-settings, and a large desk at which sat a small man. This was Norman Macdermott, then aged thirty, who had recently arrived in London out of the blue (actually from Liverpool) and with practically no money, no experience and no influence, had provided himself with a Repertory theatre out of seemingly thin air.

He was slight, dark-haired, pale-skinned and had a longish nose; his eyes were a striking dark blue. His manner was so gently ingratiating that one could describe it as wheedling— and, my God, how he must have wheedled to get backing for his theatre. I came to know him well, over a period of years, and I am convinced that he was a remarkable and underestimated man.

Mr Macdermott rose and came to meet me, which no manager had ever done before. He then settled me by the fire— never before had I seen one in a manager's office—and apologised because his secretary, out on an errand, had not left him any particulars about me. Would I give them to him in full? Would I not? I launched into my life history and he was interested to hear that I had seen so much of Miss Horniman's Repertory Company in its earliest days in Manchester. Later we talked of the London theatre and I was surprised to find how little he knew of it. Here was a man with a theatre to play with, plays to cast, and he knew little of most London players beyond their names. I poured out information; never had I had such a successful interview. And he admired my clothes, examined my red handbag which had a small white elephant attached to it. (You pulled the elephant when opening the bag.) The whole atmosphere was delightfully informal; I felt I was talking to a friend, not a manager. The only snag was that he had no work to offer me and didn't expect to have any. In fact, he seemed a little doubtful if the theatre would be able to go on.

It had not made a propitious start. Its first production, a translation from the Spanish, had received poor notices. I gathered it hadn't been quite *ready*. (Later, someone who had been there on the first night told me that the scenery, apparently, was being finished very noisily during the performance, at the end of which Mr Macdermott had come on stage to apologise, 'in a carpenter's overall, carrying a hammer, and looking like Jesus Christ.')

However, I could hardly believe that a theatre on which so

much had been spent would come to a sudden end, and already a new production was in hand. I was being told about it when the secretary rang through to say she was back. Obviously it was time for me to leave, which I did very reluctantly. As well as wanting to go on talking, I disliked leaving the bright room and, indeed, the whole theatre. On the way down I vowed to myself that I would come back; I would play there. And went out feeling so exhilarated that I walked all the way across Hampstead Heath to Finchley Road, thereby getting soaking wet feet as my grey suede shoes had holes in them. My forty pounds hadn't run to a new pair.

A few weeks later I went to the new Everyman production, *Romeo and Juliet*. There weren't many people there; again the notices hadn't been good. But, apart from the fact that I didn't think Juliet's balcony should have been represented by a porthole, I liked the production and still hankered to play at the theatre. However, I had by then landed a job. I got it through an agent I had never visited before; I think I saw his name on a door and just walked in. He was polite but not, I thought, impressed—this was before I had my new clothes. So I was surprised when he sent for me 'to meet a manager'.

It was a pouring wet day; I hesitated to risk my new outfit, but 'to meet a manager' . . . And I had my red umbrella and my rain-cape. I dressed up. Visiting cards went inside my grey suede shoes. If you stepped lightly and weren't out too long they would keep the damp out.

From the moment I entered the agent's rather dingy office I created a sensation. My cape was admired, then my suit, and particularly my red handbag—'And she's got a red umbrella.' Was I absolutely determined not to leave the West End?

This was one agent I hadn't bothered to tell of my willingness to tour and I didn't rush to tell him now. What had he in mind? I was then ushered in to see the manager and introduced as 'the young lady who has spent six months in France.' 'Looks like it, too,' said the manager, making a dive for that handbag. '*Very* pretty!' He meant the bag, not me. 'And you really can speak fluent French—fluent enough to play an entirely French part?'

I had realised in France just how unfluent my French was, but I could certainly play a part written in French. I reassured the manager and he at once offered me a five months' tour in a comedy called *French Leave*. I would play an old French woman and understudy the leading lady. I said I was a little young to play an old woman. He said that didn't matter as my one scene would be played in the dark. I was about to refuse the job with hauteur when he said the salary would be six pounds a week.

Six pounds! Never had I been offered so much. And it was nearly a year since I had been offered anything. I accepted and a contract was made out then and there.

So soon had my new clothes done the trick! Well, they had helped, no doubt, but it was my ability to speak French that counted. Touring actresses who can speak English with a French accent are two-a-penny, but touring actresses who can sustain a part in French are rare. And I was to find that to sustain that particular part was far from easy.

The play was still running in London so I went to see it. The part I was to play was that of an old crone who came on in a dressing gown and nightcap, carrying a dim candle, and proceeded to speak torrential French, punctuated by a few shouted interruptions, for what I reckoned was about three minutes. I barely heard a word she said because the audience was laughing so much, but she had to keep on talking. That part was going to need some learning. I wrote and asked for it and was told that parts weren't yet available. Rehearsals weren't due to start for several weeks.

It was during this interim period that I felt the need to hear 'Searching for Lambs' sung at midnight. I soon stopped feeling 'soiled' and found it quite a comfort to know that full seduction was available on demand. I should have found it anything but a comfort had I known that I had begun an association which was to lead to the culminating disaster of my youth. But I'll cross that chasm when I come to it.

Rehearsals for *French Leave* began in late November, in a Soho pub. I at once saw that the company all had their parts. Where was mine? The stage manager explained that there wasn't exactly a part for me; I just had to talk some French. But *what* French? What did the woman playing the part in London say? Well, she'd been asked to write something down for me, but didn't feel she could—she just said whatever came into her head. The chance of three minutes of idiomatic French coming into my head was nil. I began to see my six pounds a week vanishing into thin air.

Mercifully, there was a young actor in the company, Dino Galvani, who really could speak French. And he said that if I would write the part in English he would translate it. Even to write it in English was pretty difficult as all the old lady really needed to say was 'What are you doing in my kitchen at midnight?' and 'My daughter has gone to Paris', and it was hard to make this last three minutes. However, Dino Galvani and I turned out a fair amount and decided that, if I ran out of words before the leading comedian decided the audience had had enough of the scene, I would simply say in French: 'But I've already told you.' And then tell him all over again. I ended the scene by retiring upstairs shrieking 'Ah, ces Anglais, ces Anglais!' which always brought the house down as it was something the audience could understand.

I was made to use a falsetto voice and play 'Madame Denaux' as a very, very old lady. By the time I had got busy with red lake wrinkles I looked at least ninety. It must have been hard to believe that I had a beautiful daughter in her twenties (but then, of course, my daughter *wasn't* my daughter, but the wife of an English officer *pretending* to be my daughter). To round things off, the leading lady, who played the 'daughter', was possibly old enough to be my mother.

We were due to open at Aldershot just after Christmas. During the last week of rehearsals I went to the Everyman Theatre one evening to see a new production—and hoping, also, to see Mr Macdermott and tell him I had a job. I sent up my name and was invited to come up during an interval. Again I found the atmosphere delightful, but poor Mr Macdermott was far from cheerful. He was now almost certain the theatre would have to close. And he mentioned, quite casually, that he probably only had five years to live—and there was so much he wanted to do. I was harrowed and hastily tore the white elephant off my handbag and gave it to him for luck (though it seemed a bit trivial to ward off a death-sentence). A few weeks later he wrote to me to say the elephant had done the trick: a new backer had turned up! (And I'm thankful to report that the death-sentence also proved to be a false alarm.)

I was determined to live alone on the *French Leave* tour and try to write. But the day after we opened (quite satis-factorily; I shrieked in French for a good three minutes and got a fine round of applause) the business manager of the com-pany, Reginald Fry, arrived to ask if my landlady would take him in as he didn't like his rooms. He carried a leg of lamb, rather as if it were a bouquet, and hoped I would help him eat it. After that, we often shared a sitting-room and meals. He was a charming man, in his middle thirties but seeming quite boyishly young, in spite of his grey hair. He had the repu-tation of being a martinet with the companies he was in charge of and he could be tough with resident theatre managers but, unless he felt toughness was called for, his manner was playful.

A few days after we started sharing rooms Reggie informed me that he was very susceptible (I had noticed it) and had been, ever since he was eleven: 'Never leave a boy alone in the house with the housemaid.' Since then he had had many romances including one that took place under water. (Someone had told him that cold water was death to the sexual urge. 'If so', said Reggie, 'why are there so many frogs?') But now he combined a rare talent for verbal dalliance with an iron deter-mination to remain faithful to his wife. He was devoted to her, also to four motor-bicycles which he called his mistresses. He had his favourite of these with him on tour and one day sent his wife a postcard saying 'Please send some cheap vaseline for my mistress'.

I became an accomplished pillion-rider, but I found this a bit nerve-racking, especially as I doubted if he would have noticed if I had fallen off. I preferred him in after-supper sessions when we sat up till the small hours, usually on the hearthrug to get close to the fire. As well as demonstrating both susceptibility and devotion to his wife, he told me many interesting things about the theatre. One of his maxims was that, when casting, if you have to choose between two actresses of equal talent, beauty and suitability, and one is a blonde and one a brunette, it is always wise to choose the blonde: 'She will light up your stage better.' This is, of course, arguable but I remembered it when I came to have a hand in casting plays.

Alas, after a month or so, Reggie left to manage a more important company and I did not meet him again for over ten years, when he presented a tour of my first play *Autumn Crocus*; I'm thankful to say he made a good deal of money out of it.

Left on my own, I tried to work hard at writing. In the autumn I had begun a novel called *As It Happened*. I now went on with this but found myself worried about my style—not without cause, judging by the still-surviving work. I turned to journal writing in a shiny black notebook I found inspiring. I see that I was reading Dorothy Richardson and could neither love her nor leave her; I got into the state of *dreaming* books written in her style. I was becoming conscious of such things as point of view, subjective or objective tone of narrative, the intrusive author. . . . (Worrying about such matters held me back from finishing a novel for a quarter of a century—and then it was in the form of a journal.)

At Windsor I record that I have twice walked along the three-mile avenue in the Great Park and climbed to the bronze statue of George III. 'All along the avenue woodmen were working on the elms, trying to doctor them up for a while longer. Some have already gone and been replaced by thin little saplings. One great tree had just been cut down and its roots were being dug out. Townspeople were out gathering wood, in their arms and in prams, children helping. There is something pleasantly feudal about gathering wood in the King's park. There was a clamour of birds all congregating on one recently felled tree, perhaps an indignation meeting because a favourite elm had been cut down . . . I clambered up and sat on one of the great stones at the base of the statue. Looking up I saw one gigantic hoof of the bronze horse in mid-air above me. I began to fancy it would descend . . . I watched the sunlight travel slowly along the avenue and finally turn Windsor Castle into a golden fairy castle. Now it is shrouded in mist.'

I record that I have got all my thoughts into order and almost grasped a philosophy. 'I hid a halfpenny in one of the crevices in the base of the statue, so that I can come back after years and find it. By then I shall realise how far I was (and probably still shall be) from achieving a philosophy.'

There are stray gleams of humour in the journal. Our leading lady was an attractive, red-haired woman ('dyed, dear—and I always give pussy a dab'). She had recently spent some very sporting months in Ireland and was determined not to get them out of her system. Everything reminded her of Ireland; country with hedges, country without hedges, woods, pastures, gorse and even grass. On train journeys she would gaze out of the window and cry, 'Look, wild duck! No, snipe! No, woodcock!' The only time I caught sight of the bird it was a crow. But hunting was her great passion. In Ireland she had ridden a mare with a red ribbon on her tail. While at Windsor she persuaded Aubrey Fitzgerald to take her riding in the Great Park. He reported that first her hat fell off, then her hair fell off and finally she fell off. Before I heard this, I asked her how she had enjoyed her ride. She said, 'Not very much. I had a fussy horse.'

But I liked her and we got on well; indeed I got on well with the whole company. The younger men treated my dressing-room almost like a club. I think one reason for this was that I was made-up to look so very old that they came to think of me as a sympathetic great-grandmother. And I was almost always there, available, whereas the only other woman in the company—the leading lady—was almost always on-stage. *I* was only on-stage for three minutes, though I was supposed to go down to the wings for a couple of minutes to help with off-stage farmyard noises. I was said to do a good hen. If I failed to turn up, the assistant stage manager could get on without me, but would say later, 'No soprano hen tonight?'

The journal must have been siphoning off all my creative energy; there are fifty pages recording small events. In Maidstone I find the theatre full of fleas. And I also find that I can hear every word spoken in the next dressing-room and am astounded by the almost continuous bad language used by men who never say so much as 'damn' in front of me. 'And the quietest, most sheeplike man swears the worst—monotonously, without conviction. Do *all* men swear like this? Do charming men who make love like poets let forth a volley of oaths the instant they are alone with other men? Is it expected of them? I don't think I could feel the same towards a man I loved, if I heard him use some of the words that have issued from the next-door dressing-room.'

And at Norwich, in the late spring, I appear to have fallen in love with trees. Apparently, I had never before realised that all trees have flowers—lilac, laburnum, hawthorn, chestnut, oaks, elms, limes, sycamores . . . were they really all coming out together, as I say they were? I had particularly nice rooms in St Paul's Square, a small sitting-room, sunlit by day and lamp-lit for supper; and every morning I walked in wide, residential roads where I saw all those trees. I almost worked myself into a state of belief in tree-elementals.

Only once did I feel the need for the Red Leather Note-book, that recipient for emotional outbursts, at a time when those gold-sealed registered letters from Canada had failed to turn up for seven weeks. I had come to take them for granted, but when they didn't come I missed them. There had been one longish break before, the reason for which was eventually said to be that 'a bridge had broken down'. The latest lapse was to be explained by 'floods'. I now find it hard to believe that these two catastrophes completely cut Canada off from the outside world.

The tour ended in early June and, as with other tours, I severed connection with pleasant people I had shared life with for many months. Apart from Reggie Fry I met only one member of the company again; that was over ten years later. When my second play, *Service*, was in rehearsal at Wyndham's Theatre in 1932 a message was brought to me that someone who had acted with me in *French Leave* was enquiring for me. I hurried to the stage door and found the young man who had played a small part and been the assistant stage manager. My first thought was regret that my play, in spite of having thirty parts, was already fully cast. But this was not a question of an actor job-hunting; my friend was in work. He said, 'I just wanted to find out if you really were our Madame Denaux—to make sure you really were you. Remember the days when we did those off-stage farmyard noises together?' I remembered.

XVII

Towards the Everyman

I had saved sixty pounds. Back in London I drew this out of the Post Office Savings Bank and a member of the Gang provided an escort when I took the money to the National Bank. She said she had never before seen so much and was proud to be escorting it. My old friend, the bank manager, was delighted to see my account in working order again.

My uncles had assured me that, if I hadn't got work before my savings ran out, they would certainly help me again. But I felt sure there would be no need. If I spent only three pounds a week, sixty pounds would last me five whole months.

Well, perhaps I would spend a little more than three pounds a week. I took a fairly good room on the first floor, sorry to be so far from the roof, but glad to be able to reach the Green Room, down the back stairs, in half-a-minute flat. And the room had other advantages. It looked onto the mews at the back of the Club and it was unusually sheltered; I could keep the large, sashed-window wide open even during a rain storm without a spot of rain coming in. I don't think I ever closed that window even in winter when I sometimes, before falling asleep, gazed out at a grey, opaque, London fog, wondering why it so obligingly stayed out in the mews. I had my bed right across the window and could use the window-sill as a bedside table. And on the other side of me was a most unusual, ancient gas-heater about three foot high and with a gas-ring on the top. It was most convenient to be able to boil a kettle without getting out of bed.

Of course I had no idea, in June, that I was fated to remain in this room for over a year; but fortunately I made it comfortable from the beginning. There was space for my theatrical basket, disguised with orange draperies, and over this was a bookshelf, made of three-ply, blacked with hat-paint and hung by green ribbons. On this I kept my Georgian Poets and other poetry from the Poetry Bookshop . . . Harold Monroe, Frances Cornford . . . and rhyme sheets with Lovat Fraser decorations were fixed to my wall by stamp paper. On the table I (fairly) proudly displayed the two photographs of my Canadian.

The room gradually came to seem a womb-like home which was just as well, in view of what it had to see me through. But when I moved in I was still in the confident high spirits which stemmed from sixty pounds in the bank . . . well, not quite sixty pounds now, after several weeks out of work and a certain amount spent on clothes. I made myself one particularly beautiful dress, of amber organdie, with which I wore a heavy string of clear amber that had once been my grandmother's.

Once equipped for the summer I wrote to Norman Macdermott at the Everyman Theatre, asking if I could come and see him again. I got no answer—which seemed to me outrageous; had not my white elephant practically saved the theatre from bankruptcy? But I did want to play at that theatre, so after waiting a couple of weeks, I went to the current production —wearing my striking organdie dress and left myself about in the foyer . . . As I hoped, Mr Macdermott flitted through and caught sight of me. Why hadn't I been to see him? Because I hadn't been asked. Well, he had certainly told his secretary to make an appointment.

(Frankly, I didn't believe this. But when, eventually I did get work at the Everyman—though only on the front side of the curtain—I routed my letter out and asked the secretary, by then my good friend, the meaning of her shorthand squiggle on it. She admitted it meant 'make appointment'. I felt retrogressively apologetic to Mr Macdermott.)

I was invited up to that pleasant office, I was given a free cup of coffee, I was shown my white elephant—still in the pen tray—but there was no job for me. However, not long after, I was rung up and asked if I would like to 'walk-on' in Shaw's *The Showing up of Blanco Posnet* which, with Schnitzler's *A*

Farewell Supper, was transferring from the Everyman to the Queen's Theatre. The pay would only be a pound a week, but I thought of the job as a thin edge of a wedge into the Everyman Company, and I jumped at it.

Blanco Posnet was to be directed by Edith Craig (Ellen Terry's daughter). She was a stocky, white-haired woman, no doubt estimable, but I took agin her from the first rehearsal and not only because she took agin me; I disliked her manners in general. Before the rehearsal began she called all the 'walking ladies' around her and said she would hand out some lines. She threw me one first. 'You', she said, 'say "Did you hear what he called us?"' I had seen the Everyman production and knew that American accents had not been used. So I said the line in good English. 'Not a bit like it,' said Miss Craig, with the utmost rudeness and told another girl to try the line. She then said, still rudely, 'Well, you can keep it for the moment' and then handed out more lines. None of them came my way.

At the first dress rehearsal she gave a very cursory glance at the other extras, most of whom looked very pink and white, and then pounced on me. 'That's a musical comedy make-up. Use 5 and 9.' Sticks of greasepaint numbers 5 and 9 form the conventional make-up for brunettes but I thought the beige 5 gave a lifeless impression and I used a darker foundation, nothing to do with musical comedy. Miss Craig added, 'And put your fringe back under your sunbonnet.'

Of course I changed my make-up for the next rehearsal and also retired my fringe, which I had only kept because I believed it to be right for the period. I rather liked the effect when it was back under the bonnet, as I have a good widow's peak. Miss Craig gave this one look and then said: 'Pull your bonnet down over your eyebrows.' I really don't think she could have liked my face.

Both plays were well-received by the critics though there were some adverse comments on Mr Macdermott's setting for Schnitzler's *A Farewell Supper*. This was one of my first glimpses of what I thought of as *avant-garde* scenery and I admired it enormously—though I admit it did not suggest a supper room in Old Vienna, being simply a tall, snow-white box. Looking back on it, I find myself reminded of a refrigerator with all its shelves removed.

Alas, the public stayed away and it was hard to keep the show open for the month the theatre had been engaged for. I was sorry as I had enjoyed the engagement. I particularly liked our long narrow dressing-room at the top of the Queen's Theatre. I used to lean on the window-sill, looking down on lamplit Wardour Street and watching the sky turn to a steely blue beyond St Anne's, Soho, with its clock set in something that always reminded me of a beer barrel. Cats congregated in the churchyard, under the rustling trees. Some seventeen years later, during the rehearsals of *Dear Octopus*, I climbed to that dressing-room and looked out on St Anne's, comparing 'then and now' with considerable satisfaction. Not that the 'now', with Dame Marie Tempest in the company, was entirely devoid of troubles.

Apart from the pound a week I got at the Queen's Theatre, the only other money I earned that summer was four guineas for a day's work as an extra in a film starring Lady Diana Manners. Dressed as a lady at the court of Charles II, I spent a great many hot hours in a garden somewhere. By the late afternoon we hadn't had a glimpse of Lady Diana, but we were promised she positively would appear, and when the sun was sinking she, accompanied by Mr Stuart Blackton, passed between the ranks of extras, most of whom were by now prostrate on the grass. This must have presented a problem to Lady Diana: if she ignored us she would look snooty, if she smiled from side to side she would look like royalty. She got over the difficulty by talking with great animation to Mr Blackton, but smiling if she caught anyone's eye. Anyway, she looked exquisitely beautiful.

That well-paid day in Lady Diana's film and two days years earlier, less well-paid, were my only experiences of film work though I had showered my photographs on studios and obtained a few interviews. One casting director told me frankly that I wasn't photogenic, because the modelling of my face wasn't flat enough. He pointed out that I looked younger in real life than in my photographs. I think I looked younger than I actually was because I was small and vivacious but, in that summer of 1921, I realised old age was creeping up on me, and I remember the exact moment of realisation. I was in the Club garden, having come back from work-hunting on a hot day, and I took powder and a mirror out of my handbag and studied my face. The bright sunlight showed me what I took to be a hair near my mouth. Then I saw it was no hair but a thread-like line. I thought, 'That's the first age-line—and you haven't got *anywhere* yet.' And already I was twenty-five.

Incidentally, the age of twenty-five had a special significance for me. My first Club friend, Pixie Shackleton, had said that, if a girl reached the age of twenty-five without marrying, she had the right to have an affair. I firmly believed this; indeed, I had come to think of it as almost a duty. What was I doing about it?

Well, since returning to London, I had at least made sure that I could still count on seduction. But though there had been several exotic occasions, I can't say that the demand had been really pressing.

Still, I was happy that summer, because the Gang was such good company. Every one of us was out of work. It was around this time that Dame Madge Kendal kindly gave an address to the Club and mentioned that what was wrong with young actresses now was that they wouldn't work. As she spoke to an audience of young actresses gasping for the chance to, I wonder she didn't get lynched. Another distinguished visitor about this time, and one who made a better impression, was the first Lord Leverhulme.

He came to see an exhibition of paintings done by Club members. These were displayed in the lounge, and seven of the artists just happened to be sitting there while he walked round. I—and this *was* accidental—happened to be talking to one of them. A flashlight photograph was taken which appeared in some paper and the girls were described as artists. A few days later, the Club secretary received a letter from Lord Leverhulme inviting the eight artists to dinner with him. I was in the photograph so I was included. I asked the Club secretary to explain that I was an actress and Lord Leverhulme replied an actress would be very welcome. So I went. It was the first of many visits.

I remember the Hampstead house as a rambling mansion where various dimly-lit, antique-filled rooms led out of each other. We wandered around for some time before Lord Leverhulme and his sister, Miss Lever, came to receive us. Then we went in to dinner. Two sides of a very long table were filled and I think all the guests were women. Lord Leverhulme and his sister were the deafest people I ever met. They each had a box-shaped hearing-aid on the table in front of them which, when in action, emitted blue sparks. Lord Leverhulme pointed this box at every guest in turn and that guest had to answer, very loudly, while all the other guests remained dead silent. This could be nerve-racking, particularly when he made some joke which one couldn't see. He was also fond of accusing ladies of having—again—refused to marry him. There seemed no way of replying to this except by smiling coyly, shaking a finger at him and saying, 'Now, now—you *know* you haven't asked me.' He seemed quite satisfied with this.

After dinner we were taken to the picture gallery and a few men, relations or business associates, appeared. We were shown round the pictures and then we danced; there was a small orchestra. Lord Leverhulme (who always wore full Court dress with knee breeches) danced with every lady in turn. And to every one of us he said, 'Please tell me when the music stops. I can't hear it at all.' He did not so much dance as walk, very sedately, turning round as he did so, and slowly getting around the room. I found he could just hear me if I spoke loudly and right into his ear—which I was able to do as we were much the same height.

After a few dances it was made plain to us that the evening was over, and Lord Leverhulme then asked us if we would all write to him and say what we thought of his house. Taxis were then sent for. I shared one with an artist called Evelyn Herring, a beautiful girl who was later to have a great effect on my life. As we drove back, we passed the Everyman Theatre and it occurred to me that some of Lord Leverhulme's immense fortune would be a godsend to it. Could I do something about this?

When I wrote to him I began by praising his house and saying how happy his pictures must be to belong to someone who loved them so much (I think he did love them.) I then said I knew he was a very generous man and there was a cause in which I should like to interest him, but I couldn't bring myself to mention it in a letter which ought only to contain thanks for a happy evening.

I got an answer by return, handwritten. (His letters to me were always handwritten, but in varying hands and none of them were his own.) He said he was particularly pleased with what I said about his pictures, as many people accused him of knowing nothing about them. And he would be very glad to hear about the cause I was interested in. So I wrote a long letter about the Everyman and had it typed by a professional typist. Lord Leverhulme replied that he had found my letter most interesting, but he had never helped a theatrical enterprise without losing his money. Would I, however, come to dinner again and bring all the same young ladies?

At this dinner I was put next to him. Only when we were dancing did he refer to my letter. Did I not agree with him that, if he backed the Everyman, there would be a risk of his losing his money? I said, 'Not a risk. I'd say it would be more of a certainty. But couldn't that be worthwhile?' He was so astonished that he stopped dancing. Never, he said, had anyone before advised him to lose money. I pointed out that he *gave* plenty of money, to charities. He said, 'Well, it's an interesting point of view. You must let me think it over. And you must come to dinner again very soon, with all your friends. Let's try to make these dinners a monthly affair.'

Except for hoping to help the Everyman I didn't hanker for any more dinners, particularly as the taxi fares were expensive. I should have felt differently could I have brought the Gang; we thrived on mass outings. One such was to the Three Arts Club Fancy Dress Ball that year at Covent Garden. I have a flashlight photograph, taken by some journalist, showing 'Members of the Three Arts Club about to leave for their Ball'. There are two antiquated taxis, their drivers benignly smiling, and ten girls, five of whom were Gang members: Peggy

Calthrop as Trilby; Eleanor Street as a very fully clad water nymph; Madge Compton and 'Norse'—only their heads visible, at a taxi window—and, dead centre, sitting on a taxi step, I am showing a great deal of leg, with a garter under one knee. I was wearing orange velvet shorts, a yellow organdie blouse with a giant frill, a green bandeau trimmed with peacock-blue feathers, and the coat made by Mr Faikosh, now past its heyday but the lining still looks rich. All the other Gang members were better looking than I was, but I must say I catch the eye: I don't know if this is due to my grin or my legs.

Actually, that Ball proved a disappointment. 'Norse' had announced she meant to pick up a rubber-planter who, having married her, would give her a large allowance to live on at the Club, return to Malaya and leave her in peace. She didn't find him and, indeed, few of us even found any partners. We had imagined it would be the kind of wild party where everyone would dance with everyone. We were wrong; the women held on to their men. Still, at the end of the Ball we sat in a circle on the floor and declined to leave. We were warned by the police that we should be carried out and a particularly large policeman started with me. Grinning affectionately he deposited me on the pavement—where I found, to my delight, that some member of the Gang had got hold of an elderly business man who was prepared to give us all breakfast. But where? Someone said you could get bacon and eggs at cab shelters, which we eventually did. We all called the business man 'Father'. When he got us back to the Club as dawn was breaking we all thanked him, shook him warmly by the hand, and said 'Goodnight, Father', before scuttling up the steps. He was left on the pavement murmuring, 'All those breakfasts and not one kiss'.

Soon after that the Gang had another mass outing: to Phyllis Morris's wedding at Brighton. For some time I had been seeing little of Phyllis; she had published another book for children, temporarily lost interest in the stage and was mainly living at home. But we wrote to each other fairly frequently and, of course, I knew when she became engaged. Her fiancé was a doctor (but he only accepted locum tenens work),

a skilled photographer whose work appeared in many magazines, a gifted poet, and a writer on folklore and natural history.
In all he was a highly distinguished man; but he was thirty
years older than Phyllis.

She arrived at the Club, with a good deal of money from
her ever-generous father, to complete her trousseau and buy
her wedding dress and going-away outfit. But with Phyllis-like
originality she wanted to reverse the order of these: she would
be married in the going-away outfit and wear the wedding dress
at the ball her mother was giving on the night of the wedding.
So the going-away outfit became known as the wedding-suit,
made by my Mr Faikosch of bright russet cloth and topped by a
dashing hat, high with russet feathers. (Phyl's passion for hats
was a Club joke, but they were sometimes beautiful and always
worn with great *élan*.) The wedding-cum-ball-dress presented
difficulties. Phyllis declined to wear virginal white—though she
had every right to—and wanted gold. And at no shop could
she find a gold wedding dress. In the end Peggy Calthrop—
out of work like the rest of us—made it most exquisitely, of
orange georgette and gold lace. There was a glittering gold
veil which Phyl was determined to trim with miniature oranges.
One shop assistant looked horrified at this, 'Orange *blossom*,
madam, not *oranges*—not on a wedding veil!' We eventually
settled for gold and orange berries which looked very well.

We were all invited to stay at Phyl's home, The Garden
House, Hove, for the wedding and the ball which followed it—
at which the bride and bridegroom appeared during the formal
supper. Phyl was radiant in her shimmering gold dress. The
bridegroom, though no Adonis, had an admirable figure and a
touch of elegance. He made a speech mainly about folklore and
mentioned that his wife believed in fairies. They then left for
the honeymoon which, in line with all the oddness of the wedding
arrangements, was to be spent in a near-by Brighton flat which
had been lent to them.

We were sad to feel that Phyllis might be lost to us; she
was to live in Hurstpierpoint, Sussex, and didn't expect to come
to London often. But my own main worry was my lack of work.
My sixty pounds had run out and I was again living on three

pounds a week from my uncles, which was far from easy. I still hoped to work at the Everyman Theatre but, though I went to all the productions, generally managed to see Mr Macdermott, had met and liked Mrs Macdermott, no hope of a job had been held out to me.

A week before Christmas I went to the Catholic church in Spanish Place. I had no leanings towards Catholicism, but ever since my visits to Catholic churches when on tour in *Mr Wu*, I had occasionally lit a candle to St Anthony, on the off chance that he would find me a job. And that day, as I watched my candle flickering in the dim church, an idea came to me that had nothing to do with job-finding. I suddenly knew I must go home for Christmas, and at the back of my mind was a conviction that I should not, after this, go home again for a long time.

Strangely, seeing how important the visit had seemed (and it was to become more important with the passage of years), I remember little about it. I know I told Uncle Harold about the Everyman Theatre and we talked about the great days of Miss Horniman's Company; but he was losing his interest in the theatre and no longer played with amateurs: 'Time I stood down and gave younger men a chance.' But the truth was that he preferred to spend the evenings in his armchair, puffing at a pipe which was sometimes empty and glad to see the whisky tray come in at ten o'clock. I gathered that none of my uncles were doing quite so well at business, but they raised no objection to continuing my three pounds a week allowance.

I left on New Year's Eve having been invited by Gwen Ffrangcon-Davies to break my return journey at Birmingham and hear her sing in Rutland Boughton's *Bethlehem*. She was now leading lady at the Birmingham Repertory Theatre, a marvellous change of fortune. The previous Christmas she had been so hard-up that she had spent the entire holiday working feverishly on six hats, ordered by Christabel Russell, who was then becoming known as a fashionable dressmaker. But she was better known as the victor in the famous Russell divorce case, a case which had led many young women, including me, to fear that spermatozoa could practically leap at you out of thin air. Gwen had put one hat made by herself in the Club exhibition of Christmas presents. Mrs Russell had placed an order for six—if Gwen could meet her deadline. Gwen, working till the small hours, had met it. But, alas, the hat Christabel Russell had seen had been a very smart black one, trimmed with lacquered red leaves. Gwen had interpreted the order to mean any hats she felt like designing. Only one hat was a copy of the black hat. The others were turbans, embroidered, be-beaded and be-tasselled; decorative but arty. Mrs Russell repudiated the whole five, leaving Gwen out of pocket for the cost of the materials.

I saw her working on the hats, but was away in *French Leave* before the blow fell. How she supported herself through the winter I can't imagine. But when I came back in the summer she was engaged to play in *The Immortal Hour* in Birmingham. This was a very different production from the one I had seen at the Old Vic and she made a spectacular success in it, wearing a black wig with ropes of hair reaching to her knees and a wonderful green-blue dress. (Not that I saw this production until it reached London, the following year.) She remained in Birmingham, playing many important parts. At last her career was set fair.

I was enchanted with her singing in *Bethlehem* and I loved the music; it was a perfect way to spend New Year's Eve. But afterwards I wished I'd spent it in Manchester and somehow made more of my visit. For I was not to go again for nine years, and by then both Uncle Arthur and Uncle Eddie were dead.

XVIII

Seduction on Demand

When I got back to the Club I found a telephone message: would I ring up the Everyman Theatre? I hadn't recently been in touch with Norman Macdermott—I hadn't told him of my attempt to interest Lord Leverhulme as I feared nothing would come of it. Surely this message, arriving out of the blue, must mean a job?

It did, but not an acting job. I was asked to run the bookstall in the theatre foyer and occasionally do a little office work in the afternoons. The pay could only be a pound a week. But my uncles would not stop my allowance if I earned so little, so I should be a pound to the good. And I should be in the theatre—surely some opportunity to act would turn up. And I liked the idea of running the bookstall, reading all the plays on it, chatting to customers and seeing all the productions.

Actually, running the bookstall wasn't as simple as I expected, because I had to do the ordering as well as the selling and that, at the beginning, was difficult. During the previous year the Everyman Theatre Ltd had gone bankrupt; evidently my white elephant had fallen down on its job—or perhaps its allegiance was to Norman Macdermott personally, because he was now running the theatre on his own, and with more success. Some creditors of the Limited Company couldn't see why he didn't pay them which, even had he been able to, wouldn't have been legal. Among such creditors were W & G Foyle from whom many of the bookstall books had been obtained, on sale or return and without Foyle's help we could not have carried on. I was told to go and see Mr William Foyle and be both explanatory and persuasive.

I saw him in his office high above the bookshop in Charing

Cross Road and, after some very difficult minutes, found him reasonable. He finally said I seemed 'a little brighter than the last young lady' and he would go on supplying us. I went back to the Everyman triumphant.

My takings at the bookstall usually amounted to about three pounds a week which, as we got a thirty-three-and-a-third discount on the books, meant that my pound a week was covered. Also available in the foyer were very good coffee and lemonade, made by Mr Macdermott's secretary, Barbara Kent. Miss Kent (it was some while before I called her Barbara) was a small, slim young woman who gave the impression of being older than she was because she had a much-needed authoritative manner. She was pretty, with superb red hair and the pink complexion that often goes with such hair; but her pince-nez and her way of dressing—a cross between a typical secretary and a school-mistress—disguised this. She was unfailingly kind to me and never complained that I was of little use to her during the many hours I spent in her office; I got to the theatre at two-thirty and seldom left before eleven at night and, except when I was in the foyer, I sat at a double-desk facing Barbara and frequently distracted her with my chatter. I offered to type, with one finger, but she was particular about the appearance of her letters. I did learn to do some filing, I filled orange chocolate boxes with good chocolates, and I had one job which lasted a long time. This was to return dozens of plays that had been submitted to the theatre. I would willingly have read these, but I was told they had been read. All I had to do was to pack them and enclose a handwritten note saying, tactfully, that the theatre was not at present considering new plays and the manuscript was being returned 'for safety'. The title of only one play remains with me: *Domatilla, a Tragedy in Five Acts.* I still wonder who Domatilla was.

Another job I could do, though none too well and I disliked it, was to make tea for Barbara, myself, Mr Macdermott and various lady helpers. For this I had to descend to the basement where an enormous room ran the full length of the theatre above it. On either side of this, dressing-rooms had been made, divided by a wide corridor. At one end was a small

Green Room where two spiral staircases led up to the stage. But no one ever sat in this room; all the social life of the theatre revolved around the two fireplaces at the other end of the basement. One of these was used by the stage carpenter, stage hands, etc. The other was for the company who made great use of it when not on stage or dressing.

I believe that fireplace was one of the chief reasons why people liked acting at the Everyman, but it was rotten for tea-making. The great black kettle was never boiling when one wanted it—whereas the great black kettle on the stage-hands' fire seemed to be invariably boiling. I used this once and the water came out pitch black, so I just had to wait for the official kettle to boil and then carry a heavy tray up a vast number of stairs. I didn't look forward to tea-making and invariably prefaced it by a groaning rendition of 'I must go down for the tea again', sung to the tune of 'I must go down to the sea'. I often sang in the office and Barbara raised no objection. Indeed, she sometimes sang herself, particularly a Negro spiritual, *Nobody Knows the Troubles I Seen* and I would join in loudly for 'Nobody knows but Jesus'. Barbara usually took to this when things were going wrong, for the office, for the theatre or for both—which they quite often were, but never to the detriment of my spirits.

At first I saw little of Norman Macdermott who was usually directing, or in his office working, or interviewing people. Apart from Barbara, I mainly consorted with the stage management, George Carr and his two assistants, Edith Harley and Henzie Raeburn. I often had an evening meal with some or all of this trio. Henzie, whom I had known on my first, short-lived Camp tour, had become very lively. It was she who satirically christened Mr Macdermott 'The D.D.' standing for 'The Dear Director'. She also said he was a witch at getting backing out of people and the phrase was all the more suitable because he wore an unusual black felt hat. George Carr, an admirable stage manager, was a small man with a squeaky voice which made almost everything he said sound funny. Some of his expressions have lingered with me ever since. Once, when someone spoke of two women said to be lesbians, he said, 'But not really. They just throw cream puffs at each other.'

On one occasion I was surfacing to Hampstead in the Tube lift at the same time as George, who happened to have John Goss with him. I had known John, that most admirable singer, for some time, through Gwen Ffrangcon-Davies. He, like George, was a small man. Neither of them greeted me, but they looked at me in a very odd way, or rather they looked at the small parcel I was carrying. Then George said to John, in his squeakiest voice, 'What's she got in that parcel?' And John said, 'Let's find out.' They then advanced on me, holding up their hands as if they were begging dogs, and proceeded to scrabble at my parcel while making shrill, yapping noises punctuated by occasional barks. They had paper and string off by the time the lift gates opened. The other occupants, huddled together, gave us one last alarmed look and hastily shot out.

Soon after I began running the bookstall, I was called up into the Dear Director's office to give him advice on the casting of a new production; he still had only a sketchy knowledge of London actors. A surprising number of players were sent for on my recommendation and I began to see myself as an *éminence grise*. However, this didn't last long because so many players were used again and again, so much so that the theatre came very near to housing a permanent company. This was the time of the Shaw revivals which were to do so much both for the Everyman's reputation and for its box-office. In the Tubes green and orange posters showing a mask of Shaw looking remarkably like the Devil, helped to draw audiences in. I was about to say 'from near and far', but 'from far' would be truer for the Hampstead people neglected their theatre disgracefully. I do, however, remember one regular Hampstead customer who came to each production in the cheaper seats, which were a little hard. She always brought a cushion with her and when she saw me looking at it she said, 'You see, I have a weak heart.'

The Shaw productions got good notices and yet I do not think they received the critical acclaim they deserved. As a child I had seen Shaw played by Miss Horniman's Company and also amateur productions that were fully up to professional standards. I had seen some of the original productions in London. And over the years since I have, of course, seen many others. And I still think the Everyman presentations were the best of all. In 1922 it was too early to treat them as period pieces and the players wore 1922 clothes, though whenever possible, with strong touches of characterisation. The settings were, for those days, ultra-modern: simple, box-like interiors very clean in colouring and very little cluttered by detail, or even furniture. As a background to Shaw they were quite unrealistic —and would have been unrealistic even for a modern play. But their starkness had the effect of throwing the players and, at a deeper level the characters they played, into sharp relief, giving them a timeless quality and liberating them from any period. The plays were wildly funny—and yet the characters were never guyed, as I often feel they are in present-day productions. Alas, I can no longer enjoy Shaw, the hero of my youth, but I feel that I might again if he could be treated as unrealistically as Shakespeare is.

The Shaw plays were very well directed, though this might be denied by many who acted in them. Actors judge directors by reputation, though even with a famous director they often wonder if he is as good as they expected him to be. When a director is unknown, as Norman Macdermott was, they start by being quite sure he is hopeless and, if the play turns out to be well-directed, they are apt to say they directed themselves. This can be true as regards individual performances; there are actors who can produce the effects they want without any help. But an ensemble does not become a satisfactory one unless pulled together by direction. I have watched many directors at work and I am quite sure that Norman Macdermott was a good one, astonishingly good for someone who had so little experience. He was also a gifted impresario and a talented scenic designer. But none of this prevented him from, at times, being a maddening man and, frequently, his own worst enemy. I was soon to have evidence of this.

Not long after I had settled down at the Everyman I was again asked to dine with Lord Leverhulme, along with the other Club members who usually attended these parties. I then told Norman Macdermott of my attempt to interest Lord Lever-hulme in the Everyman. I was thanked for my efforts, but told my chances were slim. Still, I was given the evening off to go to the party. After it, I returned to the theatre much excited. Lord Leverhulme had said he would like to come to the current production (it was *Fanny's First Play*) and I was to book the whole of the front row for him on a night he specified. This was done and the party arrived. He and Miss Lever carried their hearing aids, but I gathered in the first interval that they weren't hearing much. However, they seemed pleased with the outing and, within a couple of days, the whole company—up to twenty-four—was invited to dinner on a Sunday evening.

At this dinner party Mrs Macdermott and the actress who played Darling Dora sat next to Lord Leverhulme and never during the evening did I get a chance to talk to him, but every-thing went well and he spoke of coming to the theatre again soon. Next day Norman Macdermott wrote a thank-you letter and included some such phrase as 'we shall be most grateful for your help and interest.' Lord Leverhulme replied that, though he didn't know how he could help, he would certainly continue to take an interest. Norman Macdermott then said he was going to ask for fifty thousand pounds.

I said this would be fatal. The old gentleman was now obvi-ously interested in the theatre. He needed time to get fond of it. As it was almost on his doorstep, he was likely to come often, might come to think of it as *his* theatre. He knew from me it needed money. He might offer it eventually. But if rushed at now, he would almost certainly sheer off. I concluded, 'Please wait, if only for a little while.'

Mr Macdermott overruled this by saying the theatre could not wait. It needed fifty thousand pounds *at once* if it was to keep going. (This surprised me, as it was then doing well.) Besides, Lord Leverhulme had written that he didn't know how he could help which must mean that he wanted to be told. And told he was going to be immediately.

Told he was and he answered by return of post with a curt refusal and never came near the Everyman again. Nor did he ever invite me to his house again, which was something of a relief, though I did genuinely like the old man. And the theatre kept going all right, without the fifty thousand pounds.

My next effort to help the Everyman was more successful, if on a smaller scale. One evening when I was standing by my book-stall I was approached by two quietly-dressed, quietly-spoken ladies who proved to be mother and daughter. The mother held out the orange-jacketted theatre programme and indicated a paragraph which was to the effect that orders could be accepted for clothes, specially designed by Mr Macdermott, which could be made up in the theatre studios. I knew Mr Macdermott designed scenery and furniture, I did not know he designed women's clothes. But perhaps Mrs Macdermott did? Anyway, I asked what the ladies had in mind. The elder lady said they would like dresses similar to the one I was wearing.

I had recently taken to dresses with very tight bodices and very full skirts, partly inspired by the Lovat Fraser dresses in *The Beggars' Opera.* Gang-member Peggy, still out of work, made up my material for one pound a dress. I had two which I considered suited the decor of the Everyman foyer. One was green cloth, the short sleeves, neck and hem bound with silver braid. The other was orange curtain velvet, bound with gold braid. (I had discovered that curtain velvet was cheaper, creased less and was dyed in better colours than real velvet.) That night I was wearing the orange velvet. The ladies, having admired it, asked if it had been designed in the theatre.

Well, I worked in the theatre so I felt I could say Yes. And I was all for securing any work which might help the Everyman. Still, I was doubtful if Mr Macdermott, extremely busy, would be keen to arrange for inexpensive little dresses—the total cost of my orange one was under two pounds. I was thinking about this and chatting tactfully when the elder lady said gently she would like to spend about two hundred pounds.

Never had I heard of anyone spending so much money on clothes all at one time. Either the ladies were very rich, or they were eccentric time-wasters. Anyway, I said I would discuss the matter with Mr Macdermott and meet them in the next interval.

Mr Macdermott was even more dubious than I was; still

he saw the ladies, reported that he thought them genuine and that he had arranged for them to see his wife next day. Mrs Macdermott made several suggestions which were well received and promised to let the ladies know when they could be fitted. She then came up to the office cheerfully excited, her only troubles being that she had no materials, no dressmaker, no tailor and this was a rush job. It had turned out that the elder lady was married to a Lancashire cotton merchant, due to visit America, taking his wife and daughter with him.

I offered my Mr Faikosch, I offered my friend Peggy (warning her to charge much more than a pound a dress). They both came up to scratch magnificently, conducting fittings at the theatre in the most businesslike way. Mrs Macdermott bought a great many expensive materials (none of them were curtain velvet) and roped in other helpers. Mr Macdermott did a design of coloured triangles, which was to be appliquéd on to something— I don't know what because, around this time, the whole matter was whisked away from me; possibly I had been a little bossy. I never saw any of the finished clothes. The whole order came to much more than two hundred pounds and the customers become loyal friends of Mr Macdermott and financial supporters of the Everyman. I sometimes wondered if they remained wistful for just one dress of orange curtain velvet.

The weeks flashed past. Every day I took a bus to Warren Street Tube station and then the Tube to Hampstead. If I was kept at the theatre too late to catch the last bus home from Warren Street, Barbara stood me a taxi out of the petty cash. In bed at last, I boiled a kettle on the gas-ring on one side of my bed and made cocoa, using cocoa-and-milk powder in a cup I kept on the window-sill on the other side of me. In the morning I made more cocoa in the same cup, without even rinsing it, and went to sleep again. I was almost always tired, but extremely happy.

However, I had something of a setback after I had been at the theatre about two months. Uncle Harold wrote to say that he did not think I ought to go on working such long hours for only a pound a week and, what was more, he and my other uncles did not feel they could go on paying my allowance indefinitely. Had I any real hope of getting *acting* work at the Everyman?

The only sniff of a stage appearance that had come my way was a suggestion that I might like to walk-on as a boy in a one-act play with an Eastern setting, the production of which was being paid for by its author. I discovered I should have to brown myself all over, appear semi-nude, and that the job was not so much a walk-on as a crawl-on, on all fours. So I had declined, with a touch of hauteur. I could not truthfully tell my uncles that any better chance was in sight.

I took their letter to the theatre and showed it to Barbara and then to Norman Macdermott. They decided I could be paid three pounds a week, in return for which I would officially work in the afternoons. Officially or not, I always had worked in the afternoons. So I was able to let my uncles off paying me three pounds a week. This meant I had to get along on three pounds, instead of four pounds, but I would manage somehow.

And not long after this I began to have a faint but glorious hope I might get a really good part, or rather, two parts. *You Never Can Tell* and Galsworthy's *The Pigeon* were being cast, to be played both at the Everyman and at a Festival in Zurich. In order to save a fare to Zurich the same actress was to play Dolly in *You Never Can Tell* and Anne in *The Pigeon*. I had been wanting to play Dolly since I was around ten years old and considered myself perfect casting. Anne needed one of Galsworthy's fair, frank, typically English girls; not me at all, but I could take Anne in my stride. I suggested myself for both parts—repeatedly. I strongly suspect that I nagged for them.

I doubt if I was taken seriously, at first. But though many girls were interviewed none of them seemed suitable, and Norman Macdermott undoubtedly found my off-stage personality amusing and intelligent. He began to hint there might be a chance for me, if no one better turned up. . . .

Then my dear friend, Nadine March, asked for an interview and I pretty well kissed my chances goodbye as she had played Dolly in the West End and got excellent notices. But it turned out she merely had an eye on work at some future date. I could again feel excitedly hopeful.

I was, however, more excited about something else. Some weeks earlier I had at last made up my mind that I was going to have a fully consummated affair. Apart from sheer inclination, plus curiosity, I had come to feel it was positively my duty to achieve this before I turned twenty-six.

I now find myself facing a difficulty. I cannot leave out an episode that was of utmost importance in my life and I certainly feel free to write anything I like about myself, but I cannot feel equally free when writing about an ex-lover—not even after fifty years, not even if the man involved may be dead. Wives (in this case several) may survive, children, grandchildren. I should dislike it if any man wrote an account of an affair he had with my grandmother (than which, few things are less likely). So, though I refuse to be inhibited about facts, I will preserve discretion about identity. In the unfinished novel, *As It Happened*, in which I had described my first meeting with the man, I had called him 'Arlington'. That name will do as well as any other, particularly as it has no resemblance to his real name.

Arlington was in his early thirties, a man of great personal charm and many gifts, who ought to have made an enormous success of his life. He was, in my opinion, eventually self-defeated by faults of character, but he did achieve considerable success before these caught up with him. I was aware of them from our first meeting and if some of them caused me extreme suffering it was entirely my own fault. He never pretended to want anything but the most casual affair—which was probably why I kept on refusing to have one.

But gradually the situation had changed. Since that evening when I had returned to the Club feeling 'soiled' and asked Gwen Ffrangcon-Davies to sing 'Searching for Lambs', Arlington and I had met many times and become genuine friends. He had once told me that he didn't believe men and women could simply be good friends except, sometimes, *after* an affair. But, on his side, he was already disproving this. He did continue to suggest an affair, but I think this was mainly a courtesy; he had cheerfully accepted the fact that there wasn't going to be one. And when I suddenly agreed to one, indeed volunteered, he was both startled and, I think, a little dismayed—not that he admitted this; but he did find reasons for delay. Perhaps he thought the whole thing would blow over.

The main reason for delay was that he didn't want his wife to find out. He combined devotion to her with a determination to be unfaithful just as often as he liked. She resented this strongly, but it seemed to me that one girl more or less couldn't make much difference to her. Arlington's efforts to preserve her peace of mind included a studio where he sometimes retired, ostensibly to work. Though he wasn't a painter he did have various artistic interests but, in my view, that beautiful studio was simply a meeting place. It could be reached very quickly by me, on the Hampstead Tube; otherwise I couldn't have combined my goings-on with Arlington with my long hours at the Everyman theatre.

So there I was, in early March, 1922, just waiting until Arlington felt we could safely spend a night in his studio; for I was dead set on a whole night. I couldn't feel that a snatched daylight meeting would be at all right for such a distinguished first occasion. During these weeks I should much have liked to talk to some friend about my plans, but Arlington had managed to sell me the idea that it was much more sophisticated, exciting and, above all, *fair* to preserve absolute discretion. Fair, that is, to men whose beloved wives are not one bit sophisticated about the behaviour of their husbands with other women.

Had I known I was going to get those two parts at the Everyman, it is possible I should have gone on saying 'No' to Arlington, particularly as I did not believe myself to be in love with him. Some of his attitude to affairs had rubbed off on me and I saw myself as light-hearted, *mondaine*, possibly a masked figure at a Venetian dance, almost a *femme galante*. Incidentally, I don't seem to have been troubled by any feeling of guilt towards my Canadian, even though those large photographs continued to stare at his dear little pal. One reason for this callousness may have been that the registered letters were less frequent and gaps between them were no longer explained; Canada seemed to have been free of floods, broken bridges, etc.

But I did sometimes get cables such as, 'Anxious for news of you. Please cable fully.' I usually complied with his request, though even the skimpiest cable cost money.

Early in April I was informed that a night could be spent at the studio without endangering the Arlington marriage, provided extreme discretion was preserved. I must arrive alone, on foot, make sure no one saw me enter the garden which led to the studio; it was the ground floor of a fully occupied house, but had a separate entrance. No one in the house must be aware of an overnight visitor. I accepted all this as part of the cloak-and-dagger nature of the intrigue, which was much to my liking.

It had been arranged I should see Arlington for a few minutes on the afternoon of the night, to be given the key of the studio; I was to arrive there ahead of him. At this afternoon meeting, he astonished me by saying he was far from sure we ought to go through with the affair. His reason for this, he explained very kindly (perhaps with a hint of nobility), was that he was old-fashioned enough to believe that a man who made love to a virgin ought really to feel responsible for her for ever. I assured him that no such idea had ever entered my head. He continued to raise grave objections and I finally said I didn't wish to be seduced by anyone who made a favour of it. He then said he didn't want to make love to anyone who considered it seduction, and I said, 'Well, if you can think of a better word . . .' He found he couldn't and then relaxed and even laughed.

I think the scruples were genuine, and evidence of affection rather than disinclination. But in my view it was much, much too late for scruples. I grabbed the studio key and hastened back to the Everyman office. I had already got Barbara's permission to leave early that evening, in order to go to a party; she would look after my bookstall in the second interval.

After the first interval, I hurried to the Club, had a bath in my favourite top-floor bathroom (misguidedly; there wasn't enough hot water to fill the huge old porcelain bath), then I dressed as for a party, but in a dress short enough to be hidden by the Faikosch coat. I did not want to look conspicuous in the morning. (I had told various Club friends I was going to a studio party—not a bad name for it, really—which might last all night. I painted a gay and entirely fictitious picture of Hampstead parties with guests sleeping on sofas and the floor.) I took my nightdress, yellow chiffon with green ribbons, wrapped up in the Chinese silk shawl I had inherited from my mother; this would do duty as a dressing-gown. Before leaving the room I threw one last look at those two large photographs. I felt apologetic towards them, but it wasn't enough to take the edge off my happiness.

I got a taxi and with reckless extravagance asked the driver to take me, first, round the Outer Circle of Regent's Park which, for years, I had been much attached to. I particularly remember the frieze of classical figures high on Cambridge Terrace, lit by moonlight. My final destination was a not-too-distant suburban Tube station. From there I was to walk (making sure I wasn't followed); I was thankful it wasn't raining.

It was a very deserted suburb; I don't remember seeing one soul along its quiet streets. I felt the click of my high heels was a trifle indiscreet and began walking on tip-toe when I was within sight of the garden gate, which opened silently (oiled?). I looked up at the house above the studio; no face peered at me between the curtains. With infinite caution I crept along the narrow passage leading to the back garden and approached the studio door. Would the key be difficult? Possibly Arlington had feared it might be, because he had left the door open. He had also left the lights on and the gas-fire burning. It was faintly, even pleasantly, sinister coming into that deserted and *prepared* room.

The light came from several amber-shaded table lamps which were just sitting on the floor—a new idea to me. There was a large divan piled with cushions on a platform, also a model's throne on which stood a gilded wooden chair which looked unwelcoming to sitters. I remember no normal chairs and, in the end, I sat on a cushion on the floor, in front of the gold-painted gas-stove. I had been there before, but never alone and I had not previously quite taken the room in. Really, there was very little in it, but I found the snow-white walls, golden lighting and jade green cushions and curtains very beautiful. I even thought the white unstained deal floor attractive. Nothing here resembled any interior I had ever known.

Sitting there gazing at that decorative gas-stove (never before had I admired one), I felt extremely happy. I remember thinking that no one who felt so happy could possibly be doing anything wrong. This, I thought, is what I was made for. I believe countless women, in similar circumstances, have thought the same thing. I wonder how many of them, later, reconsidered that opinion.

I was fully aware the experience might be painful. It wasn't; at worst, it was uncomfortable. My trouble was that I found it dull—and this in spite of great kindness, patience and expertise on Arlington's part. I quite understood I could not expect physical satisfaction on this occasion. What worried me was that I felt little or no emotion. As at my Confirmation, in St Paul's Cathedral, there simply was no Holy Ghost whatever. And though I believed that physical satisfaction might be available later, I was pretty damn sure there never would be any Holy Ghost. I took myself to be, sexually, an atheist.

Probably all this was due to the fact that I still didn't consider myself in love. Certainly I was, as yet, one of the women who find the courtyard more interesting than the castle, both mentally and physically.

Anyway, after a very, very long time (I was asked if I realised what an achievement this was) it became time to sleep. And I soon decided how much I disliked sharing a bed. I lay awake for hours. And when I did eventually sleep I dreamt I was a small child lying beside my mother, and woke up to remember this dream with far more emotion than the loss of virginity had brought me.

It was, for some reason, essential we should vacate the studio very early, so presumably an alarm clock was set. But no doubt it was hoped one of us would wake early enough to stop it going off. I certainly don't recall it committed the indiscretion of ringing. What I do remember, vividly, is waking in daylight and seeing that Arlington's face was pale green. Good God, could he have died in the night? I then realised that, if he had, I had too, as my hands were the same green. The early sun was shining on us through jade green silk curtains.

We dressed in silence, though a perfectly friendly one. The silence was merely due to discretion; I was told that, after Arlington left, I was to wait a good ten minutes and then leave without closing the door, in case the click of the latch alerted some nameless watcher.

I used the ten minutes to make an intensive search for a lavatory. Obviously there was no entrance to one in the studio, but there was a kind of store-room next door which, on the previous evening, I had explored only cursorily. Perhaps I should find something there. It now seems to me incredible that in the nineteen-twenties—or at any period for that matter—a woman of twenty-five, who has just spent a night with a man, could not simply say to him, 'Where is your lavatory—and if you haven't got one, what is one supposed to do?' But I, it seemed, couldn't. My lavatory taboo was far stronger than my sexual taboo, probably because it derived from my childhood, whereas no sexual taboo had then been inculcated, the word sex never having been so much as mentioned to me.

There was no promising door opening out of the store-room and I remembered gloomily that Arlington, before leaving, had merely dressed. Perhaps he had visited some outdoor lavatory. I lifted a corner of the window curtains and looked at the overgrown garden. How grateful I would be for even some ivy-clad Victorian privy! But I couldn't go hunting for one, not if I mustn't draw attention to myself even by closing the studio door. I would simply have to 'manage'. I was good at 'managing', but it was now over ten hours since I had left the Club.

Arlington had thought of arranging for a taxi to wait for me some distance away, but had abandoned this kindly idea as being unwise. (Why? Leading to scandal, even to blackmail?) But the Tube station was not very far. I gave one last look round the room, then tip-toed out. No sign of life in the quiet Victorian street. No sign of life in any of the quiet Victorian streets. And no sign of any Tube station.

Doubtless I had somewhere turned in the wrong direction,

due to lack of concentration and never having a good sense
of direction. Soon I was lost in a maze of small residential
streets. But eventually I turned into a wider one, which I felt
sure led towards London. Early though it was, I could now hope
to be overtaken by a bus or, with any luck, find a public
lavatory. It was some time before I realised I wasn't on a bus
route. As for that lavatory, it had become a lavatory *lointain*.
If only there was someone I could ask! (Not a man, of course;
that taboo was still operating.) As by now it must have been
nearly eight o'clock, the emptiness of those suburban streets
seems to me extraordinary. Many years later I saw a film in
which the whole of London had been evacuated because of
some expected menace and I was instantly reminded of the
atmosphere of my nightmare early morning walk. But in the
film there were deserted pets. I never saw so much as a cat
or a dog.

But, after plodding on for what must have been nearly an
hour, I at last reached streets that were normally populated.
And there were buses, but they were all full and raced past
me. However, I suddenly knew where I was: not far from
Tottenham Court Road. From there I could get a bus back
to the Club . . . only I found that I didn't want to. As it was
now after nine, I should arrive just as members were hurrying
down to breakfast. I didn't fancy that at all. Surely in Tottenham Court Road there must be some café that opened early,
some glorious refuge that could offer a now near-demented
woman a ladies' room?

There was, but only just; the doors were still locked when I,
seeing someone sweeping inside, tapped on them. Blessings on
the girl who let me in. Yes, there was a ladies' room. I rushed
to it through an avenue of chairs piled on tables. By the time
I returned to the shop the chairs were on the floor again and
I could, Heaven be praised, sit down and order a cup of coffee.

During my walk I had thought of little beyond putting down
one foot after the other. Now I began to think about life. I had
studied my face in the glass in the ladies' room. Did it look
any different? Did I feel any different? Surely I must? I was
pondering this when an odd incident happened. A very small

dwarf, a real midget, entered the café. It was on a corner and had glass along its side wall as well as at the front. The dwarf sat down at a table by the side wall and gave his order. Almost at once another dwarf, equally tiny, came to the outside of the café and tapped on the glass close to where the first dwarf was sitting. He then breathed on the glass and wrote a message with one finger. The letters were quite large, but I couldn't read them because they were back to front as far as I was concerned. But this did not trouble the first dwarf at all. He studied the message, then nodded his head. The outside dwarf wrote again, and again received a nod. Then he, too, nodded, smiled and went away. It would have taken far less time if he had simply entered the café and spoken his message. The whole thing seemed to me a suitably grotesque climax to my nightmare walk.

After leaving the café I went along Tottenham Court Road and came to a woman selling daffodils. They were my favourite flower and I somehow connected them with virginity. Feeling positively defiant, I bought a bunch. At least *they* hadn't changed!

Then I returned to the Club, carrying my nightgown, wrapped in the Chinese silk shawl, in the crook of my left arm. The shape of the bundle must have suggested that I had provided myself with an instant-baby. All I needed was a snowstorm.

XIX

'If Dudu Fails . . .'

What happened next would never be believed in a novel, but happen it did. After I'd had a bath and dressed for work at the theatre I went down to an early lunch. The only other person at the table was a particular friend of mine. I would dearly have liked to confide in her, but my habit of discretion held and I began to invent details about the wild artists' party I had attended. I didn't get far because my friend wanted to talk about herself.

It so happened that, early on the previous evening, she had met Arlington. There was nothing astonishing about this, but I can't explain why without disclosing more than I care to. So let's say she met him at a party. She was aware that I knew him, but had no idea I was particularly interested in him. She now informed me she had found him highly embarrassing; he had, in fact, made a dead set at her both verbally and physically.

(Months later she told me that, while she was talking, my expression changed so much she guessed where I had spent the previous night. But she gave no sign of this. What she did do, a few days later, was to put a large and expensive tin of Sanatogen in my room with a note saying she thought I was working rather hard and needed to take care of myself. She was a girl who had plenty of troubles of her own and could no doubt guess when another girl was in for some.)

I was, of course, both furious and stricken, though mainly stricken. I worked it out that the delightful scene described by my friend had taken place only an hour or so before Arlington arrived at the studio. I tried to believe that my friend had exaggerated. Perhaps there was some explanation. Anyway, I had to find out. I was pretty sure I could find Arlington at his business office. I had never been there uninvited, but today I burst in unannounced. I said to myself, 'But don't make a scene' and instantly made one.

He was furious, both with me and with my friend. How dare women talk? Hadn't they any decency? I reminded him that *I* hadn't talked. And as for my friend, why the hell should she be discreet about attentions she hadn't invited and didn't want? And what was it all about? Had he found her so devastatingly attractive that on a first meeting . . . He then astounded me by saying he hadn't even particularly liked her.

I think he must have felt some genuine affection for me because, by degrees, he explained that, though he found it humiliating to offer excuses, he could not bear to see me so unhappy. The truth was it was his habit to make overtures to practically every attractive woman he met, out of sheer curiosity. He seldom carried matters further, even if his attentions were well received. He simply liked the fun of finding out.

I accepted this explanation because I wanted to. It seemed a bit hard on girls who had granted an option, not to have that option taken up; but in my case it had been. Anyway, by now I was being shown some very welcome affection. Life was bearable again. I hurried away to my work with Barbara Kent.

During the next few days I rationalised this trouble out of existence. He was such an unusual man. One just mustn't mind his attentions to other women, even if they went rather further than he was admitting at the moment. There had always been men who made love to many women—Charles II, Don Juan, Casanova . . . really very attractive characters. I began to see myself as a woman of the world, who understood these things. And I must be *fair*. Arlington had never said he loved me, never implied he was going to be faithful to me, or that we had started a permanent relationship. I must accept all this. (But did I? Did I Hell!)

And then the miracle happened at the theatre. After days during which I had almost given up thinking about them, I was suddenly told I could have those two parts, 'Dolly' in *You Never Can Tell* and 'Anne' in *The Pigeon*. It now amazes me I wasn't even asked to read them; after all, Norman Macdermott had never seen me act. But then he had seen very few people act. He mainly judged by personality and usually judged well. And no girl whose personality seemed more suitable than mine had turned up. Anyway, though there was no suggestion that I was merely being tried for the parts, I probably was; this was indicated by a telegram sent by Shaw, when the cast list was submitted to him. He included the phrase, 'If Dudu fails, try Elizabeth Ponsonby'. I thanked heaven Elizabeth Ponsonby hadn't been mentioned before I got the part.

I knew Galsworthy was to attend an early rehearsal of *The Pigeon*—when, no doubt, he could have objected to me. But he merely told me to cut out a bit of business indicated in the script, which would have necessitated my jumping exuberantly on and off a sofa. He said, 'It wouldn't suit your personality. You must stand squarely on your feet and be a staunch little English girl.' It wasn't how I saw myself, but from then on I did my best to be both square and staunch. The leading woman's part had not yet been cast and, after the rehearsal, there was a discussion about who should play it. Mr Macdermott reported to me with considerable glee that Galsworthy had said: 'Little Miss Smith's very quaint. I think the other girl should be pretty.'

It was found that I should need a new passport in order to go to the Zurich Festival and soon after rehearsals began I was sent to get a photograph taken. It was a mild Spring day and as the photographer was no distance from the theatre I ran out without a hat or coat, feeling wonderfully happy. Not only had I got the parts; I had also spent another night at that exotic studio. What I mainly remember about this is that I arrived to find no lights and no gas-stove burning and, as I dared not stumble about looking for light switches, I sat waiting a long time in chilly pitch darkness. But otherwise things were fairly cheerful and I got home quite easily, once I knew how to reach the Tube station. (But I still didn't discover the lavatory; in fact, I never did.)

I told myself the passport photograph should be the portrait of a happy woman and it certainly came out better than most passport photographs, giving an impression of wide-eyed serenity. This may have been partly due to the fact that I had recently conformed to fashion by plucking my eyebrows. I had been overcome with the desire to late at night and only got one eyebrow done. It was days before I had time to get the other one more or less to match. I doubt if eyebrows ever quite forgive such assaults on them. When I wanted mine to grow again they obliged sufficiently, but never resumed their full luxuriance.

Life continued to be full, in fact too full. After morning and afternoon rehearsals I had to hurry to Barbara to catch up on my office work; and I still coped with the bookstall every evening. This left me no time to learn my parts—not that I worried. I'd hardly ever had to learn a part; I usually picked them up at rehearsals. But this time that didn't seem to be happening, especially with Shaw's 'Dolly'. The first time we rehearsed without books I scarcely knew a word. After that I seized every spare moment for study and began to hold on to the words, but fumbling for them made me give a worse performance than when I'd had the book in my hand. I could tell I wasn't making a good impression; indeed, I wasn't making one on myself.

About this time several members of the cast were pushed out. Discussing this I said to Mr Macdermott, 'There, but for the grace of God, go I.' I said it jokingly, but I was careful to watch his reactions. He only smiled and said, 'Well, you're safe so far.' So I relaxed. Now that I knew my lines I should soon feel easy, confident.

But the confidence still didn't come and, a few days later, Barbara Kent insisted I should leave the bookstall to her and go home early. She said I was obviously tired out and needed sleep. Afterwards I guessed she must have known what was in store for me as she would have been aware that there were a number of people who—from the highest artistic motives—were dead set on getting me turned out of my parts. And I really can't blame them.

I didn't feel sleepy. I felt in need of fresh air. I would walk all the way home, cutting across Regent's Park. I would really look at the spring, try to feel in touch with it, count my blessings, *realise* my happiness . . . It wasn't that I was unhappy, it was just that my brain felt woolly, not quite alive; that was why I was having such trouble in playing the clean-cut Dolly. If only I could get my thoughts clear . . .

And suddenly I did, when I came to some blossoming trees in Regent's Park. I stood there gazing at them and *knew* I was happy, just as happy as the day when I had run out to get the passport photograph taken. My trouble had just been tiredness. I would go back to the Club and sleep. But it was early yet, still daylight. I would walk slowly across the park, enjoying every minute of it.

Well, I hope I did, for I was not to be fully happy again for . . . I was going to write months but, in truth, it was years and quite a number of them. But during them I did learn that it is possible to get along quite tolerably without happiness.

The next morning I got to the theatre early, to see if there was anything I could do for Barbara before rehearsing. She at once sent me up to Mr Macdermott who told me he felt he must take the part of Dolly from me. He said he felt guilty because I had tired myself out by working too hard at the theatre and he ought not to have let me. But there it was. And already he had engaged Nadine March, who was now free. I was, however, to keep the much less important part of Anne in *The Pigeon*.

It was, of course, a cruel blow but, even so, I took it worse than now seems to me reasonable. For two days I could not eat, just drank innumerable cups of coffee, when Barbara coaxed me out with her to some café. I was incapable of doing any office work and must have made it hard for her to do hers, but she remained utterly patient and sympathetic. It would have been better for me if I had had to attend rehearsals of *The Pigeon*, but *You Never Can Tell* was being concentrated on so that Nadine could catch up with the rest of the company. The only good mark I can award myself is that I never for a moment resented Nadine, nor did she show any embarrassment. Indeed, I looked forward—if I could be said to look forward to anything

—to having her in the company. During the next few weeks we became much closer friends.

Perhaps it was because I remained so miserable that my memory has blotted out the rest of the rehearsals. I don't even remember the first night of *The Pigeon* which we played at the Everyman before going to Zurich. Only one incident— at a later performance—comes back to me. Milton Rosmer, that brilliant actor and most endearing man, having failed to bring on-stage a necessary visiting card, turned to me and asked me to get one. I dashed off-stage and into the prompt corner where Henzie Raeburn was 'on the book', ready to prompt. 'Quick', I whispered, 'a visiting card!' Henzie, with what seemed to me maddening cheerfulness, said, 'I don't have a visiting card.' I begged her to give me *something* and her gaze fell on a large Victorian photograph (and what that was doing in the prompt corner I can't imagine). 'How about this?' she said brightly. I snatched it and returned to the stage, where Milton was improvising dialogue. I said, 'You've run out of visiting cards' (he played a man who was always doling them out), 'but you could write your address on the back of your photograph.' He proceeded to do so, after taking a non-existent pencil out of his pocket. Afterwards he complimented me on my sense of the stage. 'There are plenty of girls who would have just gone off and stayed off.'

I got a good notice in one of the two important Sunday papers. I discounted this because I knew the critic was accompanied by a friend of mine. However, she assured me he really had liked me—'Though we both thought you looked terribly thin.'

On the way to Zurich we had a few hours in Paris and some of us rode around in a taxi. I retain only an impression of wide streets at sunset and a feeling of great sadness, not only induced by that lost part. For I already guessed that my love affair was nearing its end; not that it had deserved the word 'love' and the fact that, on my side, it now did was probably the true basis of my sadness.

Of Zurich I vaguely remember a cavernous theatre and no sense of contact with the audience. The *pension* where some of

us stayed—Nadine and I shared a room—comes back more
clearly. There was an upstairs sitting-room with a piano at
which Harold Scott sometimes sat, playing and singing delightfully. I found this comforting. And there was a dusty garden
where one hot afternoon Norman Macdermott broke the further
bad news to me that I couldn't have my bookstall job back
at the Everyman. A friend of Mrs Macdermott's had come from
Yorkshire to replace me, as I thought, temporarily. But it seemed
she had looked on the work as permanent and could not now be
ousted. And anyway, wasn't it better for me to return to my
profession of acting? It didn't seem as if there would be any
parts for me at the Everyman, just for the moment . . .

I saw all this, but I also saw I should be minus the three
pounds a week I had been counting on. And I hadn't saved a
penny; usually after five months' work I should have saved
enough to last some time. Also I had come to love my work in
the office, discussion about casting new productions, the whole
feeling of *belonging* to the Everyman. I had really been happier
than in any acting job. But there was nothing to be done about
it. I must just write to my uncles for help, and quickly, because
I should have little more than my week's salary for *The Pigeon*,
seven pounds, in hand—some of which got spent on the journey
home, when Nadine and I stayed a night in Paris. We shared
a room high up in some old hotel, and talked till the small
hours. Nadine was enchanted to find I was no longer the completely respectable young woman she had taken me to be.

Back in London, I had no official reason to go to the Everyman again, but I did go once to take a present, bought in Paris,
for Barbara Kent and to leave one for Mrs Macdermott—
whom I still liked very much, even if her friend had swiped
my job. I sat in the office wistfully picking up theatre gossip.
During the company's visit to Zurich, Mrs Patrick Campbell
had been playing at the Everyman in *Hedda Gabler*. My only
meeting with her (if one can call it that) had been some weeks
earlier when she had shot out of Mr Macdermott's office, in a
raging temper, just after I began to climb the stairs. I decided
to reach the half-landing and then stand back to let her pass,
but such was her speed that I hadn't got so far before she was

swooping down on me. If I had not flattened myself against
the wall, she would certainly have knocked me backwards down
the stairs.

During the run of *Hedda Gabler* it had been Henzie
Raeburn's job to take Mrs Pat home in a taxi every night. On
one of these occasions Henzie had burst into a tirade about her
own exhausted state—'Everyone who works with you is utterly
worn out, while you, you're as fresh as a daisy.' Mrs. Pat had
then clasped Henzie warmly, saying: 'Wonderful girl! You must
come and live with me.'

Barbara assured me that I must visit her often and must come
to all the productions. Dear Barbara! She told me once she liked
me greatly and liked many of my ideas, but was afraid they
might lead me into sin. I felt it might be a good thing if she
could be led into a bit of sin herself, and John Goss did once
say to me he would very much like to seduce her, but he added
that he wouldn't—'Because it would make her unhappy.' I
doubt if many talented seducers show so much consideration.

Which brings me to my next meeting with Arlington when he
hardly surprised me by saying we must not, for the moment,
see any more of each other. His given reason for this was that
he was having a particularly difficult time over his marriage—
'And when a ship is in danger of sinking, sometimes even the
lifeboats must be thrown overboard.' (News to me.) Perhaps I
should have been flattered to be compared with a lifeboat;
even a lifebelt would have over-estimated my value to him.
Anyway, there were other reasons including, to my knowledge,
at least one other girl. But I think the most important reason of
all was that, having become quite fond of me, he was unhappy
at making me unhappy and didn't want to be reminded of it.
By giving in to him, I had not only robbed him of a delightful
occupation, but also put myself on his conscience. We eventually became quite good friends and he several times tried to
re-start the affair, on one of these occasions sending me two
dozen bunches of daffodils. But beyond making me wonder
what the hell I was to do with them in a bed-sitting room
measuring ten foot by ten, in which I only had two vases, they
had no effect.

I wish I could have foreseen my future hard-boiled state (hard-boiled to him, that is) after our last meeting at the studio. Having lost the theatre and now having lost him, I was down and out. And I was about to be downer and outer, for I was to receive the one faintly grim letter any of my uncles ever wrote to me. In response to my request for a renewal of my allowance, Uncle Harold wrote to say that, beyond one month, it could not continue. Business was now really bad. Also they resented the fact that I had sent them so little news of me; it appeared that I had only written twice in six months. Of course I could come home if I wished, and get some work in Manchester. Meanwhile, here was a cheque for one more month's money . . .

The lack of letters was mainly due to lack of time, but also to the fact that I felt guilty—to the family only—because I had been having an affair. Had I returned to them about to have a baby, they would have done all they could to help me, but what would have struck them as very casual goings-on would have shocked them, particularly my aunt; my uncles would have been far more worried by the way I was messing up my life. I was distressed that I had upset them and I quite understood they couldn't go on with the allowance—as I hastened to tell Uncle Harold. What I did not tell him was that his letter had made me feel I would rather starve than go home.

I didn't really expect to starve, but my situation was far more serious than it would be nowadays. There was no kind of unemployment pay for actors and actresses and no temporary jobs that could be picked up easily. One couldn't, for instance, put in some highly-paid hours at domestic work; there were far more domestic workers than there were jobs for them and, anyway, the pay was minimal. (Even nine years later when, in 1931, I first employed a maid of my own, twenty-five shillings a week was considered good pay for a full-time maid who *lived out*.) I had no kind of secretarial training, no training for anything but the stage. Still, I had to face the fact that, unless I could get a stage job within a month, I must get some other type of work. In a shop? I doubted this and, anyway, the pay would not be much better than for domestic work. But I scanned advertisements and wrote in for anything that sounded remotely possible, without so much as getting an answer.

And then I was offered another tour of *French Leave*. I didn't fancy spending four or five months playing that screaming old Frenchwoman again and, as this was to be a less important tour, the salary would now be only four pounds a week, but I could live on that and even save a little (though living on tour was now more expensive than it had been). And the fact that I had got work so soon helped to revive my wilted self-confidence, particularly as none of my friends had jobs. (But what most of them did have were incomes or allowances.)

Out of the blue I then received a cable from my Canadian, from whom I had not heard one word for several months. As usual, he asked me to cable news of myself, but broke new ground by suggesting I should come over and join him in Toronto. This time he got no expensive answering cable; I was finding it hard to make my money last until I got my first salary, also I wanted to do some thinking before I replied. I was no longer in love with him, but I found so much comfort in the thought he might still care for me that I wondered if I might one day revert to caring for him. Ought I to tell him I'd had an affair? Well, of course I would if we went on writing to each other, but when I remembered all the gaps between letters and that nothing was happening about his divorce, I wondered if he thought of his dear little pal as merely a dear little pen-pal, and that only occasionally. I finally hit on a plan which I thought would bring his 'intentions' out into the open. I wrote asking if the invitation to join him meant his divorce was at last underway, and I made it plain I was now very, very hard-up and would be getting no more help from my family. I deliberately made it the kind of letter to which there could be but one acceptable reply: an instant offer of financial help or, at least, an explanation why none could be offered. My guess was that I should get no answer to this letter and I guessed right. (But over seven years later that time-waster of my youth had another bout of cable-sending.)

Just before I went on tour I paid a farewell visit to the Everyman. Norman Macdermott was obviously relieved I now had work and began making suggestions for how I was to enjoy the tour. He said that in every provincial town there was always something of interest to be found; he mentioned various museums, a restaurant in Birmingham where there was some good modern panelling, and he particularly advised me to look at the upper storeys of buildings; there might be a hideous modern shop-front on the ground floor but Georgian or Tudor architecture up above. I have made use of this advice ever since. It was typical of the man who gave it to me; he had a talent for being interested in almost anything and stimulating the interest of others. I was to remain friendly with him and his wife for many years, even after they separated, and they both of them did me various services. One way and another, in spite of my failure as an actress, my time at the little Hampstead Everyman was of the utmost importance to my life.

XX

In My End Was My Beginning

Early on that second tour of *French Leave* I developed an absolute lust for crying. I usually did this in bed at night so that my face would have time to recover before I went to the theatre. But if on my morning walk I came across a really good crying-place, such as a wood, I would cry there—though never on a matinée day. I seem to have been able to turn the tap on to order, but not off.

Probably the main reason for this excessive crying was that I had given up pouring out my troubles into any form of journal; nor was I letting off steam in poetry but I had, back in April, composed one poem. It was never written down but I recall the last lines: 'And if the summer brings regrets and autumn ends the spell, I shall have had the springtime and so—all's well.' This was prophetic as regards facts, but not as regards feelings. By the autumn of 1922 all was far from well. I was bloody miserable.

Nevertheless, I managed to start writing a play, after working up to this by reading books on the craft of playwriting: William Archer's *Playmaking*, a truly admirable book, and the American Professor Baker's *Dramatic Technique*, a mammoth book which impressed me rather less. I suppose Boots' Library provided these books; I couldn't have afforded to buy them.

The play was called *Pirate Ships* (later re-titled *Portrait of the Artist's Wives*). I got half-way through it during the tour, finished it a year later, and during the next few years it was, again and again, almost bought for London production. There was a scene in which a ruthless young actress asks a man to take her away for a weekend which, at that time, was con-

sidered astonishingly daring. However, when it was finally
turned down by a famous American manager who had seemed
almost certain to buy it, his reason was that, taken as a whole,
it was 'not quite salacious enough'.

Depressed though I was all that tour I found several things
to laugh at. There was the landlady who said she would take
me in if I didn't mind sleeping with her husband's leg. This
proved to be an artificial limb which he found uncomfortable
so only wore it on Sundays. She said they had no place for it in
their room, so it stood in one corner of mine and I found I
did mind sleeping with it quite a bit. I used to worry about it
after I put the light out. Then there were rooms where, in the
dead of night, I was awakened by a sepulchral voice calling a
long-drawn-out 'Smith, Smith!' It was some moments before I
remembered that the landlady, too, was called Smith and her
husband was an engine driver. A knocker-up was calling him
through the letter box.

An incident that now strikes me as funny certainly didn't
then. One night I woke to find I was being assaulted by a
bed-bug, the only insect of which I have a horror. Having got
up and put it out of the window (no killer I, even of bugs), I
went back to bed and treated myself to a double-dose of crying.
Lover lost, my career in ruins, my family turned against me,
old age rushing at me (well, I *was* looking old) and now this
last degradation. I finally soothed myself by quoting Francis
Thompson:

> But (when so sad thou canst not sadder)
> Cry;—and upon thy so sore loss
> Shall shine the traffic of Jacob's ladder
> Pitched betwixt Heaven and Charing Cross.

I doubt if anyone, before or since, has claimed such weighty
compensation for a bug-bite.

One last memory of the tour and, to me, a deadly serious
one. Arriving at my rooms in Hastings, late on Sunday evening, I was told by the landlady that she had upstairs a woman
who had had to remain from the previous week as she was

expected to have a miscarriage. Her husband, the musical director, had gone on with the company. The landlady said she might have to ask me to go for the doctor, later that night. Of course I said I was willing and, on the landlady's suggestion, I went upstairs to talk to the woman.

She was in a raging temper. She said, 'Don't you ever get married. See what it leads to,' and then started a bitter tirade against men in general and her husband in particular. (The landlady doubted if he *was* her husband.) I was, anyway, relieved to discover she didn't want the baby so its loss wasn't going to distress her.

After doing my best to cheer her up I unpacked, had my supper and sat reading. It must have been nearly midnight when the landlady asked me to go for the doctor. He lived in the Old Town and, in spite of the landlady's directions, I had difficulty in finding my way, particularly as the narrow streets were lit only by a capricious moon. It was quite a long walk, but I don't remember meeting one person or seeing one lit window. I soon felt as if I'd gone back a couple of hundred years.

At last I found the doctor's house, rang, knocked, but got no answer. I was wondering what on earth I could do when an upper window opened and the doctor put his head out. He wasn't pleased but, after considerable persuasion, he agreed to accompany me and on the way back he became quite pleasant. I discovered that, in this case, 'miscarriage' was going to mean a six-months' child which would be born alive, but would soon die. I asked if it couldn't be put in an incubator. The doctor said there was no incubator available in Hastings, and practically pooh-poohed the idea of trying to save the child.

It was born very soon after we got back, to the accompaniment of terrifying screams from the mother—though the landlady afterwards told me there was unusually little reason for screaming. The baby was then put into a shoebox and showed to me very shortly after its birth. It was much larger than I had expected and much more lively. It seemed to me outrageous that this perfectly formed little creature was going to be allowed to die. Couldn't the mother feed it? The landlady said not;

anyway, the mother didn't want to have anything to do with it—'You see, dear, the poor mite's not wanted.' Couldn't *we* feed it in some way? The landlady said, Yes, the doctor (who had now gone) had told her she could give it a teaspoonful of milk every hour or so and she would do this, all through the night. I offered to help, but she said it would be pointless. She felt she must sit up with the mother and she might as well feed the baby, though she was pretty sure it wouldn't take the milk. It was going to *die*, and that was that.

I had never—and never have—longed to have a child; indeed I consider myself curiously lacking in maternal instincts (all the more curious as I like writing both for and about children). And any feelings I had about that premature baby were entirely on its behalf, not on my own. I could not bear to think it was going to get no chance of life. Lying awake I wondered if I could not, in the morning, telephone until I found a hospital with an incubator, then take the baby there in a taxi. And if it lived, could I adopt it? I was quite sure I couldn't, but surely someone else would? The great thing was to keep it *alive*, to give it a chance of life.

It was still living next morning but only just, and the land-lady assured me that my plan was out of the question. No doubt she was right; I could hardly have driven around Sussex with a dying baby in a shoebox. Anyway, it died before I could do anything at all. Nowadays, I imagine, things would be very different. Presumably the mother would be taken to a hospital, not left on the hands of a landlady (who behaved throughout in the most saint-like way). And surely the baby would be given some chance?

The incident heightened my capacity for feeling to such an extent that my own troubles became, for me, both more poignant and less important. By which I suppose I mean that I could both suffer and condemn myself for suffering. And even to this day I find my attitude to abortion is conditioned by that Hastings baby; and though I tell myself that no woman should be condemned to have a child she doesn't want, and though I can with all my heart cry, 'Long live the Pill', I also find myself adding, almost surreptitiously, 'And long live the embryo.'

During the last weeks of the tour we played in London suburbs so I was able to live at the Club, but I did not any longer feel I could afford a room; seeing an unemployed period ahead of me, I took a windowless cubicle at eleven shillings a week. However, almost at once I heard that I could go back to the Everyman for a Christmas series of matinées of *Brer Rabbit*. I could play one of four girls—glorified walk-ons—and there was a chance I could have an important part if the composer of the music, Martin Shaw, would pass my singing voice. I was given a score and I then engaged the Club Practice Room so that I could work on it.

Much of the music was delightful, but the song I had to learn seemed to me excessively mournful for a children's play and the words were as sad as the music, being concerned with someone whose heart had been a-weeping way down in Galilee. I quickly realised that, with my quite untrained voice, I could only wail my way drearily through that song. I consulted Gwen Ffrangcon-Davies who was back at the Club while making an enormous success in *The Immortal Hour* at the Regent Theatre, and she offered to give me a singing lesson. Again I engaged the Practice Room.

Gwen's first complaint was that I barely opened my mouth. But when I opened it wide I could not articulate the words clearly. I was also found guilty of something positively criminal called *portamento*. And the more Gwen tried to help and the more I tried to do as I was told, the worse was the noise I made. We finally decided I had better sing in the way that came naturally to me and put our trust in Christian Science. Gwen was a very good Christian Scientist and I a very vague one. She assured me that to God all things were possible and there were cases where people had been able to accomplish feats that seemed physically impossible. Thus I might find myself able to a-weep way down in Galilee in a manner acceptable to Martin Shaw.

Actually it was Mrs Shaw I had to sing to, as her husband was away. I went to their house on a cold December morning, taking a letter of introduction from Norman Macdermott. Mrs Shaw received me most kindly and was a most helpful accom-

panist. But she said that, though she was sure from my personality
I would make a great success of the acted part of the role, my
voice was not quite 'vocal' enough for the singing. I never heard
a more tactful word.

She then asked me if I would like some coffee. I was about
to decline politely when it occurred to me that, if I stayed on,
she just might change her mind about the part. So I accepted.
She blew down a speaking tube and the coffee was sent up on
a dumb-waiter. Over forty years later I put this incident into
my novel, *The Town in Bloom*, though in changed circumstances. It was as if for all those years I had been waiting for
the chance to pay tribute to that kindly gesture.

I wasn't particularly disappointed. I knew I couldn't sing
the song and I should have made another failure. As things
were, as one of the four girls, I much enjoyed the production.
Nadine March played Brer Rabbit quite enchantingly and C.
Hayden Coffin, once an Edwardian matinée idol, sang Mr
Kildy. He found the music and the whole production puzzling
and he was greatly distressed when, one afternoon, his ancient
straw hat fell off and was pounced on by Nadine and torn to
pieces. This was completely in character for Brer Rabbit and
gave the cast and the audience much delight, but it also deprived
poor Mr Coffin of a hat which turned out to be his valued old
friend.

At the last performance, when with most of the cast I was
on-stage while Hayden Coffin sang one of Martin Shaw's most
beautiful songs, I saw high up in the back wall of the auditorium
a little oblong patch of light. I instantly knew what it was. Up
in Norman Macdermott's office there was a very small door
which could be opened to provide a spy-hole into the theatre.
I had been shown it on my first evening visit and had found it
fascinating. It was open now, though the line of sight was such
that I could not see who was looking through. After a few
minutes the little door closed and I found myself feeling it
was closing against me. I had never ceased to miss the
front-of-the-house life at the Everyman, the office work, chatting
to bookstall customers in the foyer with its pervading smell of
good coffee. Like Mrs Martin Shaw's kind coffee, that foyer

coffee got into *The Town in Bloom* as did, more importantly, the spy-hole.

It later occurred to me that, as well as symbolically shutting me out of the Everyman Theatre, the spy-hole's closing marked the end of my stage career.

Jobless again, my financial position was now deadly. I had known it was going to be and, in an effort to keep some ready money in hand, I had let my Club bill go unpaid for three weeks. Apart from adding half-a-crown for every unpaid week, the management was reasonable about waiting to be paid, but a tough managerial period was starting and, early in January, the nice young woman who did the accounts warned me that, though she had so far not disclosed I was seven pounds in arrears, she would shortly have to do so and I should then be asked to leave. Her advice was to get out before this happened, in which case the Club would wait patiently. I had already thought of this and had my eye on a nearby furnished room over a bakery. It was fairly large, with two good windows and, though dearer than my cubicle, it had various advantages, including a gas-fire and a gas-ring. I should be able to cook all my food which would mean a vast saving. And it was a *room*, where I could sleep in peace and think my own thoughts.

I worked things out: by leaving my Club bill unpaid I could probably last out in this room for a month. So I moved in early in January.

I soon found that being over a bakery made for warmth, a great blessing in winter. There was one wall so warm that underclothes hung on a line strung against it dried in record time. And after a long, sad, wet day the smell of baking bread could be very comforting. I had been worried in case there were black beetles, having heard there usually were in bakeries. The landlady agreed that this was true: 'There are always beetles in bakeries. But ours *never* come upstairs.' They never did.

My new home was known to the Gang as 'Smith Villa' and much interest was taken in it. Someone was always giving me something to improve it. Madge Compton brought books from the Poetry Bookshop and new Rhyme Sheets. We couldn't decide if they made the awful wall paper look better or worse, but at least they took one's mind off it. A Club member who wasn't even in the Gang arrived when I was out, borrowed vases from the baker's shop and filled them with flowers. She also left a note saying she would do this every week for a month. Perhaps the kindest thing of all was that, almost every evening, Gang members and others stood on the pavement below my windows and serenaded me, inviting me out to dinner. I would lean down and explain that I was just going to boil an egg, but I always ended by going with them and they rarely let me pay for my own meal.

Of course I called on various agents, but they seldom bothered to see me, just sent out a message that they remembered me and would be in touch if anything turned up. Perhaps they remembered me too well. After a few days, I stayed at home in Smith Villa and tried to work at writing. I meant to finish *Pirate Ships*, but suddenly got the idea for a one-act play which could be done at the Club—as it eventually was. But I had barely finished it—in less than a week—when the whole course of my life changed.

My artist friend, Evelyn Herring, had just refused a job to run a small picture gallery at the famous bedding and furniture shop, Heal and Son, in Tottenham Court Road. She had felt she could not tie herself to a permanent job, working from nine till six. Could I? If so, she would suggest me. I certainly didn't fancy the job, especially as the pay would only be three pounds a week, but perhaps as a stop-gap . . . I let her make an appointment for me to see Ambrose Heal. I knew he was one of the original Everyman Theatre backers, and one night when I was in the office I had heard that he and Nigel Playfair were in the theatre. This made me feel I would quite like to see him, whether or not I wanted the job and, more important, whether or not I could get it.

What should I wear for the appointment? My pale grey suit and coat made by Mr Faikosch two years earlier had faded and been dyed black; but it was a good, solid black and they didn't look dyed. The moleskin on the stole of the suit had now been replaced by thick emerald wool fringe, I had an emerald knitted jumper and a black cap heavily embroidered in emerald wool. I somehow felt this was a good outfit for a visit to Heal's—and how right I was; I was practically indistinguishable from a wool-embroidered Heal's cushion.

It was a sunny afternoon when I set out, mild for January. I remember thinking, as I entered the shop, how different this was from an appointment with any theatrical manager: the shining expanse of parquet, the stately, white-haired receptionist who escorted me upstairs. There I was shown into the office that opened on to the material department.

Had I looked through that door five years earlier? *Had* I seen the red-haired man at the desk? I have never been *quite* sure. Possibly that sense of *déjà vu* was simply due to instant liking.

Ambrose Heal was then about fifty. One noticed first his rather fluffy hair which was nearer gold than red, though he was invariably described as a red-haired man. He had the pink, slightly freckled skin that goes with such hair, a long nose (described by him as a 'collector's nose'), rather small, heavily-lidded eyes which were apt to look down that nose, and an indeterminate mouth. His voice was unusually quiet (though unusually audible on telephones) and gave the impression of conscious superiority. I have heard similar superior voices on television, from civil servants or actors playing civil servants.

He was not, of course, to be 'Sir Ambrose' until some ten years later. For the moment he was Mr Heal, more often referred to as A.H.

Having settled me in a chair facing the three arched, Italianate windows (his office was in an old part of the shop) he began by skating around the job. Did Miss Herring—such a pretty creature, he had very much liked her—really think I was suited to it? I said she did and told him I had run the Everyman bookstall. He soon elicited the fact that I had done this while waiting for a chance to act. He then said, 'Yes, I quite see. And now you need a job just to tide you over for a while, don't you?' He said it most sympathetically, as if he would be delighted to provide such a job, but I wasn't fooled. I quickly replied that I was on the look out for a permanent job. He said, 'Ah . . .' in what I can best describe as a sapient voice, and then began outlining the job for me.

I should have to take charge of the Little Gallery, selling—and eventually buying—various types of pictures, mainly prints, coloured lithographs, wood-cuts—I did know what a wood-cut was?

I said, 'Well, not *exactly*—but I know what an etching is.'

He said that was splendid except that Heal's didn't handle etchings. 'Still, we could teach you what a wood-cut is—not that, as yet, I'm considering your application very seriously. However . . .'

I would also be in charge of decorative books, various fancy goods and, most important at Christmas, toys. I said I would love selling toys. He pointed out that there was rather more to it than that, including stock-keeping . . .

Gradually I noticed the conversation was settling into a pattern. If I showed eagerness for the job, he retreated, said it really didn't seem as if I had the necessary qualifications; whereas if I expressed doubts of myself, he assured me they could be overcome. Thus, when we were discussing the making out of bills for customers, I said I wasn't good at arithmetic and he instantly countered with, 'Well, I could instruct the cashier to check your addition for you.' One cannot, after over half a century, recall many details of a conversation but I can, most vividly, recall the general weather of it and it was certainly set fair—both in and outside the office, for a spectacular sunset was beginning beyond the roofs of Tottenham Court Road. I was often to see such a one through those three arched, Italianate windows.

Finally, he said he would show me round the Little Gallery—and then slid back into doubt. Might I not dash away if Mr Norman Macdermott asked me to play Lady Macbeth? I said I would be extremely bad casting. He laughed, but added that he was serious. 'It would take us at least six months to train you to do this job. Would you promise to remain at least a year—that is, if I and my fellow directors decide to employ you, and I still can't hold out much hope.' A whole year? Well, it would

only be like a very long tour and what he asked was perfectly
fair. I promised.

We walked up a short flight of stairs to the China Department. I would officially be under the China Buyer until I knew
enough to be in sole charge of the Little Gallery. Then we
passed through a deserted showroom filled with unpolished oak
furniture and at last reached the gallery, which was really a
wide bridge between the new shop and the old. It was lit only
by a long skylight and seemed to me, in the already fading
light, more than a little melancholy. The walls were hung with
large and small pictures and there were tables on which decorative books were displayed—and one survivor from Christmas, a
highly polished white wooden duck. Mr Heal ran his hand over
it while remarking, 'Amusing creature,' then pointed out various
pictures, 'That yellow thing, *The Mustard Field*, I'm told is our
best seller.' He went back to the showroom and looked around.
'Well, Miss Swinney must have gone to tea.' If so, she wasn't
missing any customers; not a soul was in sight.

Mr Heal then led the way back through the Little Gallery
into the old shop where a much larger gallery, filled with bedroom suites, ran round the walls. One could lean over the
balustrade and look down past a lower floor to the ground
floor. Above was a glass roof now grey with twilight. Mr Heal
said the lights ought to be on and, as if in obedience, they
suddenly came on. They were all housed in opaque glass globes
hung from the roof. (I came to think of that gallery as 'The
Gallery of Many Moons.') Mr Heal then went to a house telephone on a wall and, after some complicated dialling and
several boss-shots, proceeded to put through something he
described as a 'Round Call'. 'Four buzzes will always locate me.
One buzz calls all salesmen. And there are a different number
of buzzes for different directors, managers, etc. It's quite simple.'
Simple? In all my years at Heal's I never got on good terms
with that house telephone.

At last someone answered. Mr Heal, his voice now a highly
audible whisper, said, 'Ah, Hamilton! I have an applicant here
for the Little Gallery. Would you come up and take a look at
her?'

We were soon joined by a tall, almost painfully thin man: 'One of my fellow directors, Mr Hamilton Smith.' The name rang a bell. Had not a Club member, the singer Alma Goatley, married him? I blithely asked if this was so and he agreed that it was, but somehow managed to convey that I was being a trifle familiar. However, he was perfectly pleasant. Mr Heal assured him that I had practically none of the qualifications needed for the job, that engaging me was only the barest possibility . . . He was still continuing in this strain when he courteously showed me out of the shop. But I was ninety per cent certain the job would be offered to me, as it was. I received the offer two days later.

It was handwritten, in Ambrose Heal's small, neat, upright hand, which suggested print-script but was surprisingly illegible. I would be paid thirteen pounds a month plus one per cent commission on my personal sales (the commission came as a pleasant surprise though I'd no idea what it would amount to). If I would kindly confirm that I accepted the offer. I could then report for work at nine o'clock on the first of February.

I read that letter with the very essence of mixed feelings. It represented a small victory, but also the acceptance of a much larger defeat—the end of my lifetime hope to succeed as an actress. However, I must go through with it now and I only had a few days in which to get ready. It dawned on me that, working from nine till six—and nine till one on Saturdays— I should never have any time at all for personal shopping. How, in such circumstances, did one clothe oneself? How, indeed, did one *live*?

I broke the news to the Gang, who were highly congratulatory—though only on pain of death would any of them have accepted such a job. They became hilarious when I told them I would be 'under the China Buyer'; indeed, the China Buyer now became a Gang joke just as my Sergeant-Major had been. Anyway, a year would soon pass. And I should have my evenings free.

Gwen Ffrangcon-Davies insisted on lending me ten pounds. Out of this I paid my Club bill of seven pounds and had enough over for some shoes, stockings and a hat. My uncles, pleased with me for accepting the job, sent me ten pounds with which I repaid Gwen, and could thus start work fully solvent; though I was none too sure I could remain so on only three pounds a week. Perhaps that commission would help out.

Soon after seven on the morning of February 1st, 1923, I was as usual awakened by the merry voices of men throwing loaves into a van. Their talk could be astonishing, as when I heard one of them remark with heavy humour: 'So *he* said to *her*, what have you gone and been and done? You've got me with child.' I have never ceased to wonder how this unlikely event came about. As a rule I went to sleep again after this dawn chorus, but not today. I was too afraid of being late at Heal's.

I had my bath. (I shared the bathroom with other lodgers whom I never saw. Once I rashly tried to give that bath a thorough cleaning, but found I was bringing off not only dirt but all the paint. There was, however, a good supply of hot water from a perfectly civil geyser.) Then I dressed with care. I had gathered I could wear what I liked and I had seen no assistant in conventional black, still I felt I ought to be quietly dressed. I had on a pale grey flannel dress, tight-bodiced, full-skirted and with a white, pleated, cape-like frill which fell low over my shoulders. The effect was distinctly demure. (Months later, the stately white-haired receptionist, who became my good friend, told me: 'When I saw that frill I said, "Yes, very nice—but she won't keep *that* standard up".')

I got my breakfast and took my time over it. I was at the beginning of a regime of enjoying small pleasures, such as my bath, reading over breakfast, the walk to work. I had decided I must always walk, cross-country—or rather cross-back-streets; otherwise I would have to walk to a bus and then from it, with hardly any saving of leg-work, and the risk that all buses would be full. I came to love that morning walk, though it could be none too pleasant in wet weather. It took me twenty minutes, but that morning I allowed half an hour.

Arrived outside Heal's I wondered where the staff entrance was. Would I have to clock-in, whatever clocking-in was? Then

I saw that a large number of men and women were going into the shop through the front entrance. It was too early for customers; besides, customers wouldn't walk in that brisk, businesslike manner. I watched for a moment, then crossed the road and went towards the glass doors.

Had a flash of prophecy warned me of how long, once through those doors, I should remain at Heal's, I believe I would have turned tail and rushed back to Smith Villa, prepared to risk starvation. This would have been a pity, for all the most important events of my life, all the success that has ever come my way and all the genuine love (excluding family love, which I then took for granted and can now never be sufficiently grateful for) came as the direct result of the years I spent at Heal's.